The India: An Analytical Glance

The India:
An Analytical Glance

Edited by

Dr. G. VISVANATHAN
Professor, Department of Education,
Annamalai University, Tamil Nadu

and

Dr.S.K.PANNEER SELVAM
Assistant Professor, Department of Education
Bharathidasan University, Tamil Nadu

RANDOM

RANDOM PUBLICATIONS
NEW DELHI (INDIA)

The India: An Analytical Glance

ISBN 978-93-5111-316-4

Published in 2014 in India by
RANDOM PUBLICATIONS
4376-A/4B, Gali Murari Lal, Ansari Road
NewDelhi-110 002
Phone : +9111-43580356, 011-23289044
E-mail : sales@randompublications.com
info@randompublications.com

Reprinted 2026

Type Setting by : Shah Computer Graphics, Delhi-110094

Contents

1

Introduction

India is fast learning that corruption is one of the major impediments to effective development. The greater openness that democracy has brought since 1947, offers new opportunities to deal with the problem of corruption in the context of the country's new constitutional values. But it also brings into sharper focus the constraints posed by corruption, past and present, for development.

History of India, an Overview

The people of India have had a continuous civilization since 2500 B.C., when the inhabitants of the Indus River valley developed an urban culture based on commerce and sustained by agricultural trade. This civilization declined around 1500 B.C., probably due to ecological changes.

During the second millennium B.C., pastoral, Aryan-speaking tribes migrated from the northwest into the subcontinent. As they settled in the middle Ganges River valley, they adapted to antecedent cultures.

The political map of ancient and medieval India was made up of myriad kingdoms with fluctuating boundaries. In the 4th and 5th centuries A.D., Northern India was unified under the Gupta Dynasty. During this period, known as India's Golden Age, Hindu culture and political administration reached new heights.

Islam spread across the Indian subcontinent over a period of 500 years. In the 10th and 11th centuries, Turks and Afghans invaded India and established sultanates in Delhi. In the early 16th century, descendants of Genghis Khan swept across the Khyber Pass and established the Mughal (Mogul) Dynasty, which lasted for 200 years. From the 11th to the 15th centuries, southern India was dominated by Hindu Chola and Vijayanagar Dynasties. During this time, the two systems—the prevailing Hindu and Muslim—mingled, leaving lasting cultural influences on each other.

The first British outpost in South Asia was established in 1619 at Surat on the Northwestern coast. Later in the century, the East India Company opened permanent trading stations at Madras, Bombay, and Calcutta, each under the protection of native rulers.

The British expanded their influence from these footholds until, by the 1850s, they controlled most of present-day India, Pakistan, and Bangladesh. In 1857, a rebellion in North India led by mutinous Indian soldiers caused the British Parliament to transfer all political power from the East India Company to the Crown. Great Britain began administering most of India directly while controlling the rest through treaties with local rulers.

In the late 1800s, the first steps were taken toward self-government in British India with the appointment of Indian councilors to advise the British viceroy and the establishment of provincial councils with Indian members; the British subsequently widened participation in legislative councils. Beginning in 1920, Indian leader Mohandas K. Gandhi transformed the Indian National Congress political party into a mass movement to campaign against British colonial rule. The party used both parliamentary and nonviolent resistance and non-cooperation to achieve independence.

On August 15, 1947, India became a dominion within the Commonwealth, with Jawaharlal Nehru as Prime Minister. Enmity between Hindus and Muslims led the British to partition British India, creating East and West Pakistan, where there were Muslim majorities.

India became a republic within the Commonwealth after promulgating its constitution on January 26, 1950.

After independence, the Congress Party, the party of Mahatma Gandhi and Jawaharlal Nehru, ruled India under the influence first of Nehru and then his daughter and grandson, with the exception of two brief periods in the 1970s and 1980s.

Prime Minister Nehru governed India until his death in 1964. He was succeeded by Lal Bahadur Shastri, who also died in office. In 1966, power passed to Nehru's daughter, Indira Gandhi, Prime Minister from 1966 to 1977. In 1975, beset with deepening political and economic problems, Mrs. Gandhi declared a state of emergency and suspended many civil liberties. Seeking a mandate at the polls for her policies, she called for elections in 1977, only to be defeated by Moraji Desai, who headed the Janata Party, an amalgam of five opposition parties.

In 1979, Desai's Government crumbled. Charan Singh formed an interim government, which was followed by Mrs. Gandhi's return to power in January 1980. On October 31, 1984, Mrs. Gandhi was assassinated, and her son, Rajiv, was chosen by the Congress (I)—for "Indira"—Party to take her place. His government was brought down in 1989 by allegations of corruption and was followed by V.P. Singh and then Chandra Shekhar.

In the 1989 elections, although Rajiv Gandhi and Congress won more seats in the 1989 elections than any other single party; he was unable to form a government with a clear majority. The Janata Dal, a union of opposition parties, was able to form a government with the help of the Hindu-nationalist Bharatiya Janata Party (BJP) on the right and the communists on the left. This loose coalition collapsed in November 1990, and the government was controlled for a short period by a breakaway Janata Dal group supported by Congress (I), with Chandra Shekhar as Prime Minister. That alliance also collapsed, resulting in national elections in June 1991.

On May 27, 1991, while campaigning in Tamil Nadu on behalf of Congress (I), Rajiv Gandhi was assassinated, apparently by Tamil extremists from Sri Lanka. In the elections, Congress (I) won 213 parliamentary seats and put together a coalition, returning to power under the leadership of P.V. Narasimha Rao. This Congress-led government, which served a full 5-year term, initiated a gradual process of economic liberalization and reform, which has opened the Indian economy to global trade and investment. India's domestic politics also took new shape, as traditional alignments by caste, creed, and ethnicity gave way to a plethora of small, regionally based political parties.

The final months of the Rao-led government in the spring of 1996 were marred by several major political corruption scandals, which contributed to the worst electoral performance by the Congress Party in its history. The Hindu-nationalist Bharatiya Janata Party (BJP) emerged from the May 1996 national elections as the single-largest party in the Lok Sabha but without enough strength to prove a majority on the floor of that Parliament. Under Prime Minister Atal Bihari Vajpayee, the BJP coalition lasted in power 13 days. With all political parties wishing to avoid another round of elections, a 14-party coalition led by the Janata Dal emerged to form a government known as the United Front, under the former Chief Minister of Karnataka, H.D. Deve Gowda. His government lasted less than a year, as the leader of the Congress Party withdrew his support in March 1997. Inder Kumar Gujral replaced Deve Gowda as the consensus choice for Prime Minister of a 16-party United Front coalition.

In November 1997, the Congress Party in India again withdrew support for the United Front. New elections in February 1998 brought the BJP the largest number of seats in Parliament—182—but fell far short of a majority. On March 20, 1998, the President inaugurated a BJP-led coalition government with Vajpayee again serving as Prime Minister. On May 11 and 13, 1998, this government conducted a series of underground nuclear tests forcing U.S. President Clinton to impose economic sanctions on India pursuant to the 1994 Nuclear Proliferation Prevention Act.

In April 1999, the BJP-led coalition government fell apart, leading to fresh elections in September. The National Democratic Alliance-a new coalition led by the BJP-gained a majority to form the government with Vajpayee as Prime Minister in October 1999. Now Sri Manmohan Singh is a Prime Minister of India. The Government was formed in 2004. This is called as UPA (United Progressive Alliance). The

Chairperson of UPA is Mss. Sonia Gandhi. Under her direction the UPA has formed government again in the year 2009. Dr. Manmohan Singh has elected as Prime Minister of India.

Corruption - Introduction

Corruption is a universal phenomenon. It is not something new either. Corruption in one form or another existed since time immemorial. A review of penal codes utilized in various ancient civilizations clearly demonstrate that bribery was a serious problem among the Jews, the Chinese, the Japanese, the Greeks, the Romans as well as the Aztees of the New World (Thakur, 1979:7). In ancient India large-scale corruption dominated public life (Thakur, 1979:12). From this one can assume the nature and scale in the increase of corruption from medieval to the present time in the countries of the Indian sub-continent. One of the greatest evils of medieval administration in India was the extortion of perquisites and presents (Sarkar, 1935:83). Corruption was evident during the British rule in India. There was almost regular and systematic corruption involving almost all officials at different levels in the political and administrative hierarchy. There was an underlying belief among officials of "making hay while the sun of British Raj shone" (Dwivedi and Bhargava, 1967:7).

Corruption - Synonyms, Related Words and Antonyms

(A) Noun

1. Corruption - lack of integrity or honesty (especially susceptibility to bribery); use of a position of trust for dishonest gain corruptness.

Infection - moral corruption or contamination; "ambitious men are led astray by an infection that is almost unavoidable".

Venality - prostitution of talents or offices or services for reward.

Dishonesty - the quality of being dishonest.

Jobbery - corruptness among public officials.

2. Corruption - in a state of progressive putrefaction, Putrescence, rottenness, Putrefaction, rot - decay usually accompanied by an offensive odor

3. Corruption - decay of matter (as by rot or oxidation)

Decay - the process of gradually becoming inferior

4. Corruption - moral perversion; impairment of virtue and moral principles; "the luxury and corruption among the upper classes"; "moral degeneracy followed intellectual degeneration"; "its brothels; its opium parlors; its depravity".

Depravity, degeneracy Immorality - the quality of not being in accord with standards of right or good conduct; "the immorality of basing the defense of the West on the threat of mutual assured destruction".

5. Corruption - destroying someone's (or some group's) honesty or loyalty; undermining moral integrity; "corruption of a minor"; "the big city's subversion of rural innocence". Subversion, Degradation, debasement - changing to a lower state (a less respected state).

6. Corruption - inducement (as of a public official) by improper means (as bribery) to violate duty (as by committing a felony); "he was held on charges of corruption and racketeering".

7. Degrading, immoral acts or habits: bestiality, depravity, flagitiousness, immorality, perversion, turpitude, vice, villainy, wickedness.

8. Departure from what is legally, ethically, and morally correct: corruptness, dishonesty, improbity.

9. A term that offends against established usage standards: barbarism, solecism, vulgarism.

B) Corruption - Meanings

Meaning 1: lack of integrity or honesty (especially susceptibility to bribery); use of a position of trust for dishonest gain

Synonym: corruptness

Meaning 2: in a state of progressive putrefaction

Synonyms: putrescence, rottenness

Meaning 3: decay of matter (as by rot or oxidation)

Meaning 4: moral perversion; impairment of virtue and moral principles; its opium parlors; its depravity

Synonyms: degeneracy, depravity

Meaning 5: destroying someone's (or some group's) honesty or loyalty; undermining moral integrity

Synonym: subversion.

Present Concern with Corruption

"If corruption has been an age-old phenomenon, deep-rooted evil and an universal malady afflicting each and every society in one form or another at one time or another" (Padhay 1986:1), then why there is so much concern at the present time with corruption. The reasons are obvious.

"Corruption at the highest levels distorts competition so denying the public access to the competitive marketplace. It induces wrong decisions resulting in: wrong projects, wrong prices, wrong contractors, substandard delivery to recoup overpricing, promotes corruption at lower levels and eroded public confidence in leaders. At lower levels, petty corruptions are damaging because they add to transaction costs, exclude those who cannot pay, foster contempt for public servants amongst public and erode capacity for revenue collection" (Pope, 1996:23).

There are still other reasons as to why now corruption is receiving serious attention. First, "there is a widespread perception that the level and pervasiveness of corruption is not only much greater but may well be increasing" (Harris-White, and White 1996:1). Harris-White and White state that both political and administrative corruption is doggedly entrenched in Sub-Saharan Africa and South Asia and very much part of newly-industrialized countries (NICs) of South East Asia, has touched the very highest levels of political office in many Latin American countries and has quickly reached alarming proportions in the post-communist transitional countries including the former Soviet Union and China (1996:1). Second, developments in the 1980s and 1990s against the backdrop of increasing economic liberalization, third wave of democratization and floating of good governance agenda have heightened expectations that an effective and root-and-branch cure of corruption may be found (Harris-White and White, 1996:2). Third, the coming into prominence of such concepts as decentralization, accountability and transparency, human rights, rule of law and sustainable development have considerably influenced efforts to minimize political and administrative corruption in many countries.

Corruption of Corruption

Defining corruption is also important in the context of global efforts to reduce its influence in public life. But that is not an easy task. Corruption is a social, legal, economic and political concept enmeshed in ambiguity and consequently encouraging controversy. The ambiguity and controversy result from the fact that a number of competing approaches to understanding corruption is available.

Naturally, definitions of corruption focus on one of several aspects of the phenomenon. Various approaches to corruption can be placed into five groups. These are public-interest-centered, market-centered, public-office-centered, public-opinion-centered and legalistic.

Proponents of the public-interest-centered approach believe that corruption is in some way injurious to or destructive of public interest (Rogow and Laswell, 1970:54).

Market-centered enthusiasts suggest that norms governing public office have shifted from a mandatory pricing model to a free-market model, thereby considerably changing the nature of corruption (Tilman, 1970:62-64).

Public-office-centered protagonists stress the fact that misuse by incumbents of public office for private gain is corruption (Theobald, 1990:2).

Those who believe in public-opinion-centered definitions of corruption emphasize the perspectives of public opinion about the conduct of politicians, government and probity of public servants (Leys, 1970:31-37).

Others have suggested looking at corruption purely in terms of legal criteria in view of the problems inherent in determining rules and norms which govern public interest, behaviour and authority (Scott, 1972).

The five approaches, as discussed above, have concentrated on the nature of corruption. Though the approaches throw some light they do not clarify the meaning of corruption to any satisfaction.

Now there are four divergent views on the definition of corruption. The definitions have come from moralists, functionalists and social constructionist realists.

The moralists view "corruption as an immoral and unethical phenomenon that contains a set of moral aberrations from moral standards of society, causing loss of respect for and confidence in duly constituted authority" (Gould, 1991:468).

One of the well-known proponents of this view, Nye, portrays corruption as "a behaviour that deviates from the formal duties of a public role (elective or appointive) because of private-regarding (personal, close family, private clique) wealth or status gains, or violates rules against the exercise of certain types of private-regarding influence" (Nye, 1997:417). But this way of defining corruption suffers from a number of limitations. It tends to individualize a societal phenomenon and attempts to dichotomize as to what is good and what is bad. In the process societal contexts are ignored and the gap between formal norms and the underlying practice-girded norms are not analysed (Caiden and Caiden, 1977).

The functionalists usually look at corruption in terms of the actual function that it plays in socio-economic development. Claims are made by functionalists that corruption flourishes as a substitute for the market system; offers an acceptable alternative to violence; increases public participation in public policy (Leff, 1979; Gould, 1980). Some functionalists believe that political and bureaucratic leaders may see a national interest in actively pursuing or tolerating a certain degree of administrative corruption (Klitgaard, 1988). The major criticisms against functionalists are that they ignore the political significance of deviance and lack any consideration of power, interest and social structure in their analyses and at the same time the whole question of the origins of corruption is not considered (Lo, 1993:3).

The two comparatively recent perspectives, i.e., social censure and social construction reality, view corruption radically differently from the other two approaches, i.e. moralists and functionalists. Both the approaches tend to look at corruption from a broad societal perspective. The proponents of social censure believe that in understanding corruption one should take into consideration the capacity of the state to produce a particular form of social relations and shift the theoretical emphasis to the interplay of law, ideologies and political economy (Lo, 1993:5). On the other hand, social construction reality views corruption as problematic and the actors involved can be studied by relating them to contextual information on their social positions, interests and stakes in the system as well as on the political, economic and social conditions within which they function (Pavorala, 1996:25).

In view of the multitude of approaches and views on corruption it is not easy to agree on a unanimous definition of the term. Two definitions of corruption can prove handy.

The shorter definition of corruption includes "abuse of authority, bribery, favouritism, extortion, fraud, patronage, theft, deceit, malfeasance and illegality" (Caiden, 1991a).

The broader definition of corruption refers to "use of one's official position for personal and group gain and that includes unethical actions like bribery, nepotism, patronage, conflict of interest, divided loyalty, influence-peddling, moonlighting, misuse or stealing of government property, selling of favours, receiving kickbacks, embezzlement, fraud, extortion, misappropriation, under- or over-invoicing, court tempering, phony travel and administrative documents and use of regulation as bureaucratic capital (AAPAM, 1991). In conformity with these two definitions of corruption the following definitions of political corruption and administrative corruption are adopted here.

Political corruption is "the behaviour of (elected) public officials which diverges from the formal components - the duties and powers, rights and obligations - of a public role to seek private gain" (Kramer, 1997).

Administrative corruption is defined as "the institutionalized personal abuse of public resources by civil servants" (Gould, 1991). In both cases public officials (elected and appointive) can convert public office into private gain in many ways.

A) Important Definitions of Corruption

o Inducement (as of a public official) by improper to violate duty (as by coming a felony) he was held on charges of corruption and racketeering.

- o Destroying someone's honesty or loyalty, undermining moral integrity "Corruption of minor" the big city's subversion of rural innocence.
- o The misuse of public or private position of direct or indirect personal gain.
- o Influence over another person exercised through channels that are not socially accepted.
- o Corruption is influence over decisions that doesn't pass through the public mechanisms for influence.
- o The practice of unlawful or improper use of influence, power and other means. Political offices have been susceptible to corruption throughout history.

Literature Survey of Corruption

This section contains a review of important facets of corruption from both conceptual and comparative perspective. The discussion has follows logically from what has been presented in the introductory section. Here the focus is on a number of important yet interrelated aspects of corruption. So, there remains a possibility of overlap in the discussions that follow in this section.

Causes of Corruption

Corruption is a phenomenon that takes place due to the presence of a number of factors. An understanding of such factors requires, among other things, a kind of general framework for a clearer understanding of the causes of corruption, especially from a broader perspective.

Genesis of corruption can be explained by looking at three levels - international, national and individual institutional levels (Goudie and Strange, 1997). Competitiveness of international markets provides multinational companies of various sizes with an incentive to offer bribes to gain an advantage over competitors. At the national level basic development strategy of any government moulds opportunities and incentives for corruption. At the same level three relationships - between the government and the civil service, between the government and the judiciary and between the government and the civil society - also affect the nature and discussions of corruption. Three areas of government activity - customs administration, business regulation and management of foreign aid - act as sources of corruption at the level of individual institutions.

Corruption also results from the presence of a number of factors. These include: rapid economic and social change, strong kinship and ethnic ties, new institutions, overlapping and sometimes conflicting views about what is proper public behaviour, governmental monopoly over economic activities, political softness, widespread poverty and socio-economic inequalities, ignorance, lack of knowledge about individual entitlements, communal bonds, ambivalence towards legitimacy of governmental organizations, asymmetric relationship favouring those in control of state power, economic shortages in which public officials assume extraordinary control over scarce goods and services, greed, patronage and systematic maladministration (Gould and Amar-Reyes, 1985; United Nations, 1990). Most of the above-mentioned factors contributing to corruption can be categorized into "six-fold typology". This typology contains ideological, external, economic, political, socio-cultural and technological variables (Caiden, 1991a).

Some of the major reasons as to why people "collude in different ways, rationalize corrupt practices and tolerate corruption in a large scale" are because of the presence of number of factors. These are: governments act as monopolies in many respects, discretion that government and its monopolistic public agencies enjoy in their decision making and allocate roles, lack of effective accountability in government except in the nominal sense of presenting annual audited accounts and reports to parliament or answering questions in the parliament, citizens have limited information about the rules of the game and the standards of service they can expect from public agencies, and exposure of the average citizen to corruption in the public sector tends to be episodic (Paul, 1997a:1350-1351).

Forms of Corruption

Corruption takes many forms. These forms are: acceptance of money and other rewards for awarding contracts, violation of procedures to advance personal interests, kickbacks from developmental programmes or multi-national corporations, pay-offs for legislative support, diversion of public resources for private use, overlooking illegal activities, intervening in the justice process, nepotism, common theft, overpricing, establishing non-existing projects and tax collection and tax assessment frauds (UN, 1990).

These many varieties of corruption can be categorized further in terms of their nature. Corruption can be foreign-sponsored, institutionalized, outcome of political scandal and administrative malfeasance (Caiden, 1988). In foreign-sponsored corruption the main actors are public officials, politicians, representatives of donor and recipient countries. Bureaucratic elites, politicians, businessmen and middlemen are responsible for political scandal. Corruption becomes institutionalized as a result of the support provided by bureaucratic elites, politicians, businessmen and white-collar workers. In administrative malfeasance petty officials and interested individuals play major role.

Corruption has been differentiated into three types - collusive, coercive and non-conjunctive (Arora, 1993). In collusive corruption the corruptees themselves are willing and active participants in the process and use of corruption as an instrument for inducing wrong action or inaction on the part of authorities, deriving benefit greater than the costs of corruption on their part. Corruption is forced upon the corruptee by those in the position of power and authority in coercive corruption. In non-conjunctive corruption benefits are obtained at someone else's cost and victims are unaware of their victimization. Five major strategies - mystification, distancing, folklore, colonization and pacification - have been used by the beneficiaries to protect, promote and sustain corruption in diverse contexts (Arora, 1993).

Costs of Corruption

Corruption is not cost-neutral. There have been claims that not everything is bad about corruption. Its effects can be positive too. Corruption, among other things, assists in capital formation; fosters entrepreneurial abilities, allows business interest to penetrate bureaucracy and permits the logic of market to insinuate itself into transactions from which public controls exclude it (Theobald, 1990). But overwhelming evidence in recent decades suggests that the impact of corruption has been and continues to be negative on all fronts. Corruption has a negative, deleterious and divesting influence on investment and economic growth, administrative performance and efficiency and political development. Continuance of corruption in a country leads to economic malaise and squandering of public resources, lowers governmental performance, adversely affects general morale in the public service, jeopardizes administrative reform efforts and accountability measures, and perpetuates social and economic inequalities (UN, 1990). Corruption reinforces political instability and underdevelopment (Ouma, 1991). In short, corruption impedes economic growth, stifles entrepreneurialism, misuses scarce national resources, weakens administrative capacity, contributes to serious political decay and undermines stability, democracy and national integration (Theobald, 1990).

Checking Corruption

Checking corruption is no easy task. Still no one denies the need to check corruption effectively. It may not be possible to eradicate corruption completely but then vigorous and determined actions will go a long way to minimize it. The measures suggested are too many and defy any easy characterization. To contain and minimize corruption a number of measures have been recommended. These include: driving out corruption by means of usually one-off purges or campaigns, setting up of anti-corruption boards, commissions and the like, campaign for moral regeneration or moral re-armament, strengthening of checks on abuse of power and the enhancement of accountability of the powerful as well as public officials, ensuring transparency and openness in governmental activities, develop positive social attitudes, enforcing a code of public ethics, supporting the role of media, improving educational procedures (Theobald, 1990; UN, 1990).

To reduce corruption drastically, a number of fundamental changes must be brought about. These include: reducing the opportunities for corrupt transactions by cutting back the state's activities; emergence of new centres of power outside the bureaucracy; development of competitive party politics; ascendance of universalistic norms; effectuation of far-reaching administrative reform measures affecting policy, institutional and process levels;

strengthening of preventive structures and tightening of prosecuting techniques (Theobald, 1990; UN, 1990).

What is important about checking corruption is that to be successful one must take into consideration both short-term and long-term views combating corruption.

Experiences of Countries

The experiences of a number of countries pertaining to corruption are reviewed in this sub-section. Cross-country survey covers nature, scope, type of corruption as well as the measures taken to curb corruption and outcome of such efforts. But it needs to be stated that not all aspects of corruption have been covered in the countries concerned due mostly to the non-availability of information.

In the Philippines the network of corruption in the public sector is rather extensive and covers petty fixers, workers at lower levels of the organizational hierarchy to mid-level officials taking undue advantage of their positions, and extending to the elite whose profit from corruption transactions with government runs into millions of pesos but whose powerful positions render them almost untouchable by the law enforcement agencies (Alfiler, 1979). Six types of corruption in the public sector of the Philippines have been identified (Carino and Guzman, 1979). These are: tong, lagay or arreglo, retainer, favor, individualized and systematic corruption. Anti-graft and investigatory agencies appointed by a number of Philippine Presidents failed to effectively check corruption due to organizational instability, frequent changes in leadership, political pressure in employee recruitment, public apathy and strained relations with other branches and agencies of the government (Alfiler, 1979).

In Uganda corruption is the outcome of self-aggrandizement, of unrealistically low remuneration for public servants and a closed political system (Ouma, 1991). Corruption has resulted in the loss of badly needed revenue and skilled manpower, distorted priorities of public policy and shifted scarce resources away from the public interest (Ouma, 1991). Naturally, distrust among different segment of the society has increased and despondency of the people-at-large has been exacerbated.

In Ghana the way corruption has been institutionalized in the government is fascinating. In one ministry bribe money is divided in the following manner: 50% to the minister, 20% to the junior ministers, 10% to go-between, 10% to the secretary of the political party in power and the rest to an open cash fund kept by the minister for expenses like paying informers within the ministry, providing gifts to individual visitors and maintaining attractive women around the office (Vine, 1975). The causes for such widespread political corruption are: traditional contexts and effects of colonialism; the new men who inherited political leadership after independence; and bureaucratic transition from a colonial to an indigenous administrative system. Political corruption took its toll in the form of waste of resources, instability and reduction in the capacity of government (Vine, 1975).

It is now commonly agreed that corruption has vitiated India's public life like a cancer spreading over a human body. All sectors, be they administrative or political or economic, have come under the ever-increasing onslaught of corruption. There are many reasons as to why this has happened. Political actors of all shades including ministers, legislators, office-bearers of political parties, and other political office-holders are involved in corruption (Padhay, 1986). Members of the public bureaucracy are no less corrupt. Measures taken to combat corruption like setting up of inquiry commissions have failed. These commissions' findings have not been taken seriously by successive governments and consequently their recommendations have gathered dust. At the same time, some of the commissions were created with a *mala-fide* and political intent. Corruption control is possible only with the adoption and implementation of four national agenda. They are: reforming the political process, restructuring and reorienting the government machinery, empowering the citizens and creating sustained public pressure for change (Guhan and Paul, 1997). Under each a number of appropriate and timely recommendations are made to cleanse the widespread corruption that exists in India at all levels touching almost each and every governmental institution and their functionaries.

Singapore and Hong Kong are two countries whose success in effectively tackling corruption in the public service is well-known.

When the People's Action Party (PAP) came to power in June 1959 it found a colonial corrupt bureaucracy in place. The PAP, which is still in power, realized something had to be done to minimize corruption in the Singapore Civil Service (SCS). Over a period of time the PAP government introduced a number of measures to curb corruption.

The then existing Prevention of Corruption Ordinance was amended and replaced with the Prevention of Corruption Act (POCA) to curb opportunities for corruption and to increase the penalty for corrupt behaviour (Quah, 1995:148). At the same time additional powers were given to the Corrupt Practices Investigation Bureau by POCA. It is obvious that Singapore's anti-corruption strategy has been effective because it is designed to remove two major causes of corruption - the incentives and opportunities (Quah, 1989).

Corruption in Hong Kong public service had been well-entrenched. Public officials were known to make money utilizing their positions. But the situation changed drastically with the arrival of a new Governor, Sir Murray MacLehose, in 1973. He estabilished an Independent Commission Against Corruption (ICAC). The ICAC under the leadership of a distinguished former public official was given a wide array of powers. The ICAC had the power to arrest people on suspicion, search and seize without a warrant, require information, freeze assets and property and prevent people from leaving the colony (Caiden, 1991b:249). The Commission was assisted in its operations by five advisory committees on Corruption, Operations Review, Prevention, Community Relations and Complaints, drawn from cross-section of the population and reported directly to the Governor (Caiden, 1991b:249). The ICAC was organized into three areas: (a) an operations department to investigate, arrest and help prosecute suspects; (b) a corruption prevention department to restructure government organizations to reduce opportunities for corruption; and (c) a community relations department to change people's attitudes toward corruption (Caiden, 1991b:249).

Political and Administrative Corruption

Corruption has a deep root in the society in this part of the world. A chapter in Kautilya's Arthasastra titled "Detection of what is embezzled by government servants out of state revenue" is so vivid and detail that it resembles largely any meticulously prepared official report of today on modes of corruption and how to control such corruption. Kautilya writing many centuries ago identified forty types of embezzlement committed by public servants (Padhay, 1986). In ancient India corruption was prevalent in administration, judiciary and trade. As indicated earlier corruption in one form or another became an integral part of politico-administrative systems during the Khilji and Tuglaq dynasties. The situation did not change during the rule of Mughals and the British. Many politicians were charged with corruption and debarred from politics after the promulgation of the first martial law in Pakistan in 1958. Many civil servants, some belonging to the elite Civil Service of Pakistan (CSP), were dismissed from their services on corruption changes.

It has been argued by some that Bangladesh society is a highly complex network involving reciprocal favours and obligations, and that as a result payoff is the lifeblood of the country (Maloney, 1986:173). Payoff benefits include money, jobs, luxury gifts, building supplies, overseas travel and the payment of foreign tuition bills, foreign medical bills, overseas hotel and restaurant bills and personal liabilities (Kochanek, 1993:258). The symptoms of patron-client relationship are further reflected by the practice of some businessmen to maintain rest houses and high-class exclusive hostesses to entertain important foreign guests and big bosses (Siddiqui, et al. 1990). Many of these big bosses are no doubt top-ranking politicians and senior civil servants.

Political Corruption

Using position while in power to grant undue favour and benefit to one's relatives, friends and key supporters is a hall-mark of politics in Bangladesh. All the effective rulers have been accused of either direct or indirect involvement in large-scale corruption. During the rule of Sheikh Mujibur Rahman (Mujib) that lasted little over three-and-a-half years (1972-1975) corruption became a major issue in public discussion. Mujib's tendency to grant political and financial benefit to his close relatives and associates is well-known. Awami League (AL) activists received jobs in nationalized industries, grew rich as smugglers, appropriated Pakistani houses and sold off government permits and licenses to the highest bidders (Kochanek, 1993). Sheikh Abu Naser, Mujib's only brother, and four sisters were believed to have benefited excessively from their ties of kinship with Mujib (Franda, 1982). Some of the nouveaux-riches created through the distribution of patronage by the Mujib government were ring leaders of smuggling operations (Maniruzzaman, 1982). Election-related corruption was prominent during Mujib's rule.

Though General Ziaur Rahman (Zia) was not personally involved in corruption, he is credited with institutionalizing corrupt activities (Franda, 1982). It must be said that he instituted legal actions or sacked some ministers on corruption charges, but these people were calling for decentralization in the internal working of his party, i.e. Bangladesh Nationalist Party (BNP). Local units of BNP became pockets of corruption. Zia's failed initiative of Sawnirvar Gram Sarker as the model of "grassroots democracy" was built on loyalty to his party and patronage distribution. During his time corruption and misuse of power resulted in the wastage of almost 40% of the total resources earmarked for development (Kochanek, 1993). Under Zia presidential, parliamentary and local level elections were to some extent manipulated in favour of his party (Khan and Zafrullah, 1979; Khan 1989a).

General Hossain Mohammad Ershad's (Ershad) government established record levels of venality (Blair, et al., 1992). Ershad's government was primarily based on calculated and selective patronage distribution to a favoured few. In fact, under Ershad corruption prevailed in each and every sector of national life and the forms of corruption included petty corruption, project corruption and programmatic corruption (Kochanek, 1993). Ershad holds the record of totally distroying the credibility of the electoral system of the country. Like Mujib and Zia before him he considered the Election Commission as a normal administrative unit to be used and misused to serve his personal, coterie and party interests. The control of the Election Commission was ensured through the appointment of weak and pliable persons as Chief Election Commissioner and Election Commissioners. Introduction of the upazila system in 1982 not only legitimized and strengthened his rule but at the same time contributed immensely to the spread of corruption to the grassroots and in the process vitiated local development and adversely affected local participation. Politics of patronage and corruption became the order of the day in the delivery of local services. An overwhelming majority (93%) of the respondents in a survey conducted in 1991 and 1992 in two upzilas in the districts of Kurigram and Mymensingh held the view that corruption had increased significantly since the introduction of the upazila system (Siddiquee, 1997). Most respondents in the same survey felt that the upazila council was the nerve centre of corruption, nepotism and patronage networks (Siddiquee, 1997).

The study based on survey indicated how upazila councils in study areas extended their patronage networks by: distributing various construction tenders and work orders to their relatives, friends and political allies; leasing out hats, bazars and jalmahals to their chosen parties; issuing these same people with licenses and permits and selecting the members of their own lobby for various project committees (Siddiquee 1997). During Ershad's time the politics-business nexus in the arena of corruption became rather prominent. He is known to have received a fixed percentage on any deal involving any amount of money. This contributed to the emergence of a class of fabulously rich people without much effort on their part and who had little understanding of business ethics or norms and adversely affected those who wanted to pursue business in the traditional manner. These new rich people also became prominent in politics as members of parliament and cabinet and eventually some of them became leader of different chambers and other bodies, thereby cementing a close link between politics and business premised on corruption and patronage. One of the outcomes of such a development has been increasing criminalization of politics. Individuals with proven track records as criminals became an indispensable party in this unholy alliance between Ershad and his promotees in business. It needs to be added that both Mujib and Zia were instrumental in making individuals with obscure background millionaires. But the difference between Ershad and Mujib and Zia is that the former transgressed all norms, bent rules and broken regulations in order to excessively profit from all state business transactions while the latter operated within limits of civility.

Administrative Corruption

Corruption has been and continues to be an integral part of culture. The level of corruption varies depending on how influential a position the particular civil servant holds (Khan, 1997). The civil servants have by and large become accustomed to live a life style far beyond their legal income (Zafarullah, 1987). The citizens have accepted the stark reality that nothing moves without adequately satisfying the concerned civil servant (Khan, 1997).

An opinion survey conducted in 1992 of household heads in Dhaka City found that 68.25% of respondents paid bribes to concerned officials to get services (Aminuzzaman, 1996). The findings of the survey indicated that members of law enforcing agencies, customs and income tax departments were involved in administrative corruption (Aminuzzaman, 1996). Another finding of the survey reaffirmed the commonly held belief that the higher the level of bureaucracy the lower the frequency but higher the amount of bribe; and the lower the level of bureaucracy the higher the frequency but less the amount of bribe (Aminuzzaman, 1996).

The Bangladesh Unnayan Parishad (BUP) only recently conducted an opinion survey of 2197 individuals selected randomly from sixty districts. This survey indicated that 95% of respondents felt that the police department was most corrupt while 82% opined that the secretariat (where most ministries/divisions are located) and the judicial system were most corrupt. In the corruption indicator the customs department came second with 91% of respondents considering its officials extremely corrupt. The officials of the Taxation Department were placed in third position as 90% of the respondents felt they were extremely corrupt (BUP, 1997).

Both the surveys reaffirm the ever-widening horizon of administrative corruption. Another survey of people's opinions at two upazilas in Northern Bangladesh indicated that the then upazila structure was not only controlled by centrally-debuted civil servants posted there but they were involved in misappropriating public funds for their own use (Rahman, 1994). Villagers had to bribe civil servants on a routine basis either to bypass certain access encounters or to speed up the process of service delivery (Rahman, 1994). The surveys as part of three case studies indicated that civil servants' control over massive financial resources without proper accountability and the self-seeking nature of civil servants were major contributing factors to the growth and sustenance of administrative corruption at the local level (Rahman, 1994).

Now one may ask the question as to why such large-scale administrative corruption exists. The reasons for such corruption can be summed up (Khan, 1997). First, civil servants involved in corrupt practices in most cases do not lose their jobs. Very rarely they are dismissed from service on charges pertaining to corruption. Still more rarely they are sent to prison for misusing public funds. They have never been compelled to return to the state their ill-gotten wealth. Second, people have a tendency not only to tolerate corruption but to show admiration to those civil servants who make a fortune through dubious means. The underlying assumption is that it does not matter how one has acquired wealth as long as he has done so. Third, it is easier for a citizen to get quick service because he has already paid the civil servant rather than wait for his turn. Fourth, there is now social acceptance of corruption by public officials. Fifth, barring occasional public procurements, the representatives of the people, i.e. politicians in power, are unwilling to take effective measures to curb corrupt practices in public dealings.

Nature, Forms and Consequences of Corruption

Corruption is all-pervasive in Bangladesh. Though corruption has been a part of our politico-administrative heritage, there is little denying the fact that after independence the tentacles of corruption have engulfed the entire society. So strong and sustained is the influence of corruption that most people have come to accept it as a fait accompli. Not only do citizens have accepted it as a part of their daily life experience but more frighteningly they feel themselves powerless to address the phenomenon at any level (Lewis, 1996). The reason for such helplessness is to the presence of corruption in almost all levels of government (World Bank, 1996). The changeover from an authoritarian to a democratic system of government in the 1990s has not had any effect on the nature and dimnensions of corruption. Information obtained from the Finance Division of the Ministry of Finance show that over a period of twenty-two years, i.e. between 1971 and 1993, taka 18,000 crore were lost in the public sector due to misappropriation of public funds and theft (Alam, 1996). But this huge amount of money, which is substantial for a resource-poor and aid-dependent country, is only the tip of the iceberg if one takes into consideration all cases of corruption that have been reported by the Bureau of Anti-Corruption over the same period (Khan, 1997).

A government Task Force Report identified a few years back a number of areas where corruption was likely to manifest itself. These areas include: procurement of goods and services including award of contracts by the government; administration of taxes and prevention of smuggling, disposal, sale and allotment of government property are including disinvestment of industries and other commercial units; administration of loans by public financial institutions, outright embezzlement of government fund and all kinds of shop-floor malpractices (Ahmed, 1992).

It is usually known that almost all kinds of corruption perpetuate in politics and administration in Bangladesh. The most common form of corruption is pecuniary bribes (Taslim, 1994). Other forms of corruption are: abuse of authority, nepotism, favoritism, fraud, patronage, theft and deceit. In many cases forms of corruptions are intertwined with their consequences.

As one scholar noted:

"Petty corruption takes many forms. Payments are required simply to obtain an application form or a signature, to secure a copy of an approved sanction, to ensure proper services and billing from telephone, natural gas, electric power and water employees.

Project corruption permeates both public and private sector contracting. A substantial commission must be paid to secure large public sector contracts in Bangladesh.

Programmatic corruption involves Food for Work and relief programmes" (Kochanek, 1993:259,263).

The consequences of these three forms of corruption included among others: high losses suffered by public-sector utilities; forcing donor countries and agencies to hire lobbyists to clear their projects by bribing officials at different levels and failure of Food for Work and relief programmes to reach their targets due to massive theft and huge misuse of resources (Kochanek, 1993).

Other baneful consequences of corruption on the economy include: siphoning away a large chunk of public resources which could have been productively employed somewhere in the economy; undermining of productivity, efficiency and effectiveness of the government; diminishes efficient mobilization of resources and management of development activities; gains through corruption used either in conspicuous consumption or transferred to foreign bank accounts; generates allocative inefficiency by permitting the least efficient contractor or most costly supplier with the highest ability to bribe; bribes and payoffs instead of expediting decisions and facilitating movement of files encourages civil servants to hold back all papers until some payment is made to them; money gained from bribes becomes a part of the expected income; and over-invoicing and under-invoicing of imports and exports and smuggling increases lead to distortion in investment decisions and to capital flight (Ahmed, 1992). Some other equally damaging consequences of corruption are: undermines public confidence in government; engenders wrong economic choices and constrains government's ability to implement policies; makes the poor pay the price; and threatens government's strategy of private-sector-oriented growth (World Bank 1996a: 66).

A recent report of the United Nations Development Programme (UNDP) titled "Corruption and Good Governance" found that bureaucratic corruption and inefficiency are taking a heavy toll on the Bangladesh economy, causing hundreds of millions of dollars' worth of loss in terms of unrealised investment and income (Mustafa, 1997). The report pointed out: "If Bangladesh were to improve the integrity and efficiency of its bureaucracy, its investment would rise by more than five percentage points and its yearly GDP rate would rise by over half a percentage point" (Mustafa, 1997).

Eradicating Corruption

Eradication of corruption should be the nation's number-one priority in view of the ever-increasing horizon of political and administrative corruption and its baneful multifarious effects on the society-at-large. It needs to be understood by all that eradication of corruption is only possible if strong political commitment exists. Without strong political commitment, bureaucratic reorientation and a vibrant and effective civil society, checking corruption turns into a very difficult almost impossible task. In the context of Bangladesh only radical and fundamental policy measures initiated and strongly backed by a committed political leadership and supported and implemented by a reoriented bureaucracy and watched and monitored by an organized and vocal civil society can control corruption.

Given the presence of three crucial variables - committed political leadership, reoriented bureaucracy and an organized and vocal civil society - other policy measures need to be adopted to effectively contain as well as control corruption. What is proposed below are a number of long-term and short-term policy measures placed in wider socio-political and economic contexts to control corruption.

The public sector employs over a million people in 35 ministries, 50 divisions, 221 departments, 139 directorates and autonomous bodies and 153 state enterprises (World Bank 1996b:57). It may also be added that since independence the number of ministries, departments and public servants has doubled (Khan, 1997). In the context of present reality there is little rationale for maintaining a huge public-sector edifice which contributes to corruption in public dealings. There is now justification for right-sizing the government. Right-sizing of government will, among other things, will discourage creation and maintenance of redundant agencies and units and restrain doling out of public-service jobs as political favours.

Public-sector accountability is weak, fuzzy and tenuous at best. This has resulted in the inability to enforce financial contracts, stop theft in public enterprises and hold officials accountable for improper or delayed judgment (World Bank, 1996). Number of actions need to taken simultaneously to institutionalize and strengthen accountability to effectively counter corruption. First, a bi-partisan parliamentary task force be established to bolster the standing committees, instituting the practice of questioning ministers and providing members of parliament with adequate office and research facilities and setting up of an office of Ombudsman (World Bank, 1996a:viii). A parliamentary secretariat should be established outside the sphere of civil service and manned by competent personnel recruited separately and controlled by the speaker of the parliament (Khan, 1997). Second, the office of the Comptroller and Auditor General (CAG) must be reorganized and strengthened by enhancing the capacity of the CAG (World Bank, 1996). Third, the standards of performance of ministries/divisions and their attached agencies should be made known to the citizens (Rahman, et al., 1993:52). Fourth, complaint procedures should be in place in government agencies for wider use of citizens (Khan, 1997). Fifth, monitoring procedures need to be tightened so that the concerned civil servant knows the extent of compliance by his subordinates to relevant orders and directives as well as services provided to citizens. Sixth, units are established in each ministry and division to develop and apply performance criteria and measures and to develop internal performance audit (UNDP, 1993:106).

Transparency in public-sector decision making is totally absent. This absence, in turn, contributes to corruption. Civil servants by and large value secrecy and are totally unwilling to share information about decisions with citizens. Openness and transparency are alien concepts in public bureaucracy in Bangladesh (Khan, 1997). A number of actions have been recommended to ensure transparency and thereby considerably empower citizens and consequently contain corruption (World Bank, 1996). First, the Official Secrets Act of 1923 and Government Service Conduct Rules of 1979 should be suitably modified. Second, a task-force on public-sector transparency should be estabilished with membership from different professional and occupational groups to suggest measures to enhance transparency. Third, necessary steps should be taken to make all contract evaluation reports public, thereby enabling all bidders to see how evaluations are made. Still other steps should be taken to ensure transparency and reduce corruption (Khan, 1997). Fourth, earning and tax payments of all public officials - elected as well as appointed - should be published each year to enable the people to learn about the assets of public officials. Fifth, interested citizens must be allowed access to relevant files and documents. For this happen the number of files marked secret and top secret should be drastically reduced. Sixth, civil servants long accustomed to transact public business under the veil of secrecy should be appropriately trained and indoctrinated to bring about necessary changes in their attitudes and work habits.

A number of specific policy measures have been recommended to control corruption in politics and administration (World Bank, 1996a: xii; Rahman, et al., 1993:97 and Khan, 1997). First, a high-powered task force to be established consisting of public officials, parliamentarians and leading citizens to review all relevant issues pertaining to corruption and to suggest a comprehensive eradication programme. Second, an autonomous standing committee to be formed with judges, senior public officials and leading citizens to oversee the activities of the Bureau of Anti-Corruption (BAC) as well as authorize investigation in ministries, corporations and other agencies by a statutory appointed and protected public prosecutor. Third, salary and benefits of civil servants need to be at par with their counterparts in the private sector. Fourth, provision of severe punishment including long stays in jails and confiscation of assets and properties to be instituted for civil servants involved in corruption. Other measures have also been suggested to counter political and administrative corruption (Paul, 1997:288-304). Fifth, a code of conduct should be adopted by the parliament to provide guidelines for the conduct of elected representatives and to take appropriate steps when departures from accepted norms are detected. Sixth, elected representatives must be compensated suitably to enable them to devote their attention only to public welfare and service. Seventh, enactment of a law to regulate the functioning of political parties is needed. This law would require political parties to hold regular organizational elections at different levels; maintain prompt and systematic accounts and submit audited accounts to either the Election Commission or the Comptroller and Auditor General; and comply with income tax regulations and guidelines. Eighth, election expenditure needs to be reduced and closely monitored by a designated body. Ninth, deregulation and debureaucratisation, bounded discretion in decision making, realignment of the government's audit and intelligence are to be encouraged to control corruption. Tenth, existence of free media so that they can investigate and expose corrupt practices. Eleventh, voluntary agencies and religious groups as well as other components of civil society can play significant role in constraining corruption in public deal in.

Nayar's Contributions

1. Undoubtedly the problem of corruption is a cancer for many countries in the world including ours.
2. We all more or less agree to the fact that while politicians/ bureaucrats/officers initiate corruption, we all support corruption in some way or other. Whether it paying bribe to House Tax/Income Tax/Sales Tax/Excise officers to reduce our tax liabilities or paying bribe to the traffic police to avoid a simple Rs. 100 challan for a mistake you just committed.
3. Complexity of laws is very much responsible for advancing corruption. Much has been talked about making the laws simple, but as the politicians and bureaucrats would be the most effected class that never seems to happen.
4. Our politicians are very poor. And have crossed all the boundaries of dignity and respect to earn money. Most of them are involved in huge scams and acts of corruption; no one seems to put a full stop. All the reports conveying that only 10% of the funds reach the public are never discussed in any of the houses of parliament. I think those manager are better who exploit employees for the ultimate gain of the company. Our politicians, in last 50 years, have never thought about the country and development. Look at the way other countries have grown and where are we. Sounds good when we hear economy growing at 8%, but, shamefully, we still are at the bottom end of the development list. Those countries of Africa and South America, which we talk as tribal countries, are far ahead of India in terms of per capita income. Still the leaders concentrate on accumulating personal wealth for the term they are in power.
5. Good people either never come in politics or have to get corrupted to reach the top. I think this is one area where we all can work. No point just talking about corruption lets fight it out.
6. You go to any other country and observe the same Indians; they would be following all the regulations and rules dedicatedly and religiously. Why not in your own country. Because we know we can get away by laws/police/courts by paying bribes. Ask any lawyer/judge and you would know

anything is possible by paying bribes. I don't think I need to comment on policemen.

One of our school teachers used to say that you just need three Cs to achieve anything Courage, Conviction and Confidence and three D's - Determination, Dedication and Discipline. It is good to talk about it like I have done above, but the real crux of the matter is to act in the direction of curing the cancer. It's not only about corruption; it's about the way of living. All aspects of life, if you have to stop at the stop line while driving, what encourages us to cross the same by 5 feet and then stop - no corruption involved here, but surely something to do with how you want to lead your life. Sandeep Kulkarni truly said that we are all not satisfied by what we have - I would add to that - that we all want to get more by wrong means thinking that we are smarter than others.

Thoughts of Investigator

Now, I would like to put forward some of my thoughts on the subject:

1. The root cause of corruption appears to be "Ever growing needs of a common man". To put in other words, "No one is satisfied with whatever he/she has got"; and with the advent of new and newer technologies, I do not think the greed is going to end anywhere. May be, I would call 'corruption' is a by-product of 'evolution'.
2. To eradicate (or even to reduce) the evil, firstly, I was trying to figure out the problem area i.e. whether bribing someone to do something, which he/she would not have done other-wise, is the problem after all. To be true, I am still groping in the dark.
3. I believe, there are millions who would not be able to make ends meet, if corruption ceased to exist. For many, there is no choice but to go for it and most of the programmer's of World Bank (and like agencies) are targeted towards increasing the standard of life of those people.
4. Acts of corruption done by a person to sustain his/her life cannot be treated a par with Corrupt practices at high places.
5. To reduce the menace of corruption, we may priories our target areas, based on some criterion which should not only include

monetary aspect, but also its effect in the society. For example- Police, Judiciary, Legislature, Corporate etc. Bureaucrats may take lead in this regard, as they have ample power and areas under their jurisdiction to implement clean and transparent governance standards.

6. Completion amongst corporate is another area, which leads to corruption. There, the root cause is not "bare sustenance" but profits, prestige, brand value etc. Thanks to some big corporate, better standards corporate governance have at least started in our economy. I hope others will take a cue from them and follow the policy of "Be good do good".
7. World Bank sources say that the cost of corruption is around $ 1 Trillion. I hope, it is the amount which goes into circulation without being accounted/audited/taxed etc. (Black Money). But after all, that money is also public money and is being circulated amongst them, and put for their use. Even if it would have been accounted/ taxed, it was supposed to be utilized for socio-economic development of the public.

   Take for example if a person/corporate has X amount of black money, he will try to derive most profit out of it. Many of the real estate purchases involve flow of black money, and the real estate so formed give profits as well as asset for its owner.

   The underlying point is that if a person/corporate executes all his liabilities towards the government by way of taxes etc. his money is not put for efficient use. Rather, he can use that more efficiently. I believe, the inference is that the management of public money is not being done properly (that puts a question mark on faith of a person/ corporate in government).
8. Hence, it is more or less up to public representatives, bureaucrats and how they manage public money that the level of corruption in an economy is dependent upon. We need more and more competitive & sincere people at the topmost level.

Lastly, I would further like to say that apart from making contributions in this forum, if we could impress/ push for better governance in some form, it would be more practical approach, and who can be a better person than yourself to lead such a thing.

Conclusion

Corruption is a complex multi-faceted social phenomenon with innumerable manifestations. It takes place as an outcome of deficiencies in the existing public administration apparatuses and systems as well as cultural, economic, political and social factors.

Differences of opinion still exist as to the meaning of the term corruption. This is primarily because individuals look at corruption from their own vantage points influenced by surrounding environment. But what is heartening is that in recent years corruption is viewed from a much broader perspective rather than looking at it from moral and functional angles only.

The causes of corruption are as varied as the phenomenon itself. Corruption results from the presence of a number of factors. Typologies have been offered to make a sense out of so many contributory factors.

There are many forms of corruption. To understand the dynamics of so many types of corruption attempts have been made to classify different forms of corruption into broad categories. What transpires from such a categorization is that corruption can be sponsored by outsiders, resultant of political scandal, institutionalized and administrative malfeasance.

The cost of corruption has been enormous in terms of a country's socio-political and economic advancement. What has been conclusively demonstrated is that corruption has negative consequences on economic growth, administrative efficiency and political development.

Checking corruption is a crying need of today's world. At the same time, it is understood that total eradication of corruption is not possible. But that does not mean in any way that corruption cannot be effectively contained. A number of recommendations have been offered as how to check corruption in a decisive manner. But what has been realized is that in order to drastically reduce corruption fundamental changes must be brought about without any delay or hesitation.

Experiences of the Philippines, Uganda, Ghana and India have clearly indicated that corruption networks are extensive and cover within their realms public servants of all types. What is more alarming is that a rather cozy nexus exists among public servants and politicians in power to share the booties of corruption. Almost all efforts to contain corruption in these countries have been unsuccessful. On the other hand, experiences of Hong Kong and Singapore demonstrate in no uncertain terms that given political will and the institution of appropriate anti-corruption mechanisms incidence of corruption can be drastically contained.

The root of corruption in Bangladesh runs deep in history. The existence of a patron-client relationship reinforces corrupt practices in all spheres of public dealing. Almost all political regimes in Bangladesh have been corrupt. Only the nature and extent of corruption varied depending on the nature of the regime, its key leader and his popular power base.

Corruption in the public service is extensive and all-pervasive. Corruption in the political arena has emboldened public servants to become unabashedly corrupt and not bother about it at all.

The prevalence of systematic corruption in Bangladesh society can be explained due to a number of factors. Lack of political will, lack of organized movement by civil society for a change in the status quo, and presence of a change-resistant institutional bureaucracy, lack of ethics in public life, absence of independence of judiciary and media, have all contributed in varying degrees to the continuance of large-scale and systematic corruption in all spheres of Bangladeshi society.

2

Review Of Literature

Review of related literature is an important prerequisite to actual planning and then the execution of any research work. Familiarity with the literature in any problem helps the investigator to discover what is already known, what others have attempted to fine out, what methods can be promoting and disappointing and what problems remain to be solved. The review of related literature enriches the investigator and directs him to go deep in the investigation.

The study of related literature helps in acquiring information about the study done in the field, protects against unnecessary duplication, guides in carrying out the investigation successfully and makes him families with the steps. The existing researches that are directly or indirectly related to present study may be conveniently classified under these broad categories.

Due to rich tradition of philosophical thought, a substantial research must be done in philosophical thought of education. But researchers have not sufficiently focused their attention on value oriented education and philosophical thought of education. Even those studies on value oriented education carried out in India have been isolated, fragmentary and do not contribute much qualitatively to arrive at meaningful and comprehensive conclusions. Here an attempt was made to study the attitudes of engineering students towards value oriented education. The literature to the present problem is described under sub-heads of

- o Studies related to Meaning, Definition and Current situation of Corruption.
- o Studies related to Women role in Good Governing.
- o Studies related to Women role in fighting against Corruption.
- o Studies related to Education-Corruption.
- o Studies related to Commissions and Committees towards Corruption.
- o Studies related to Teachers and Parents role towards Corruption.
- o Studies related to Survey towards Corruption.
- o Studies related to Causes of Corruption.
- o Studies related to Corruption Rally.

Studies Related to Meaning, Definition and Current Situation of Corruption

CORRUPTION

1. Dishonest or illegal behaviour, especially of people in authority.
2. The act or effects of making somebody change from moral to immoral standards of behaviour.
3. The form of a word or phrase that has become changed forms its original form in some way.

Definition: An act done with intent to give some advantage inconsistent with official duty and the fights of others. It includes bribery; but is more comprehensive, because an act may be corruptly done, through the advantages to be derived from it be not offered by another.

Sometimes corruption is understood as something against law, such as, a contract by which the borrower agreed to pay the lender usurious interest. It is said, in such case that it was corruptly agreed.

1. **Word reference.com:** Lack of integrity or honesty (especially susceptibility to bribery) use of a position of trust for dishonest gain.

Global Corruption Report: Global Corruption Report focuses on the need for greater access to information in the struggle against corruption.

Transparency International: Transparency international is the leading global non-governmental organization devoted to combating corruption. Its mission is to create change towards a world free of corruption.

December 9 2004 An International Anti-Corruption day.

CURRENT SITUATION

- o The integrity of the state's authority is very important to people.
- o The population is dissatisfied with the irresponsible use of state authority and their representatives who have permitted corruption to prosper.
- o Non-Governmental Organization (NGOs) and media are focusing attention on the problem of corruption.
- o The political parties support the development of an anti-corruption policy.
- o Sufficient information is available to build a successful anti-corruption bureau has been created to play a central role in preventing and combating corruption.
- o Legislation is being enacted but its implementation is often delayed.
- o International organizations insist on the prevention and combating of corruption and offer assistance.
- o Therefore the people and the government must demonstrate a true, common, natural will to prevent and fight corruption.

Studies Related to Women Role in Good Governance

Women Justify Reservation Policy in Panchayats

Bharat Dogra portrays Indian women leaders in local governments.

In 1993 one of the most important step for the empowerment of women and increasing their participation in decision making was taken by reserving 33% seats for women in panchayat raj institutions.

This paved the way for election of around one million at the village, block and district level. By now most states with a few exceptions like Bihar have completed at least one five year term. What has been the experience of around 7 to 8 lakh women during their first tenure? What lessons can be learnt for the future from this experience?

Given the Chance, They Excel

It is easy to point out numerous examples of women who have worked entirely according to what they were told by their husbands or other male members of their families. In some cases elected women remained at home while their husbands attended the panchayat meetings and carried out official transactions on their behalf. Some of the elected women were approached by men only when their signatures (or thumb impressions) were needed.

All this is true to a substantial extent, but this is not the whole picture. In our male dominated society it is easy to hear jokes about the subservient role of several elected women, and some fierce arguments based on that reservation for women has failed. Nothing could be further from the truth. In order to realize the greater potential created by these reservations, we should look at several other examples in which women got an opportunity to play an independent role. In such situations time and again, we see them making remarkable achievements for development of their village and quite often resisting the presence of vested interests with a lot of grit and determination.

They Bring New Perspectives

The yearnings of several women to assert their independence and make a significant contribution to the welfare of the people are visible in many such examples. In many cases they have been helped by volunteer organizations and people's movements active in their region. In some cases enlightened family members, including husbands, have also encouraged them to realize their potential of initiating meaningful social change.

From such examples it is quite clear that when the conducive conditions exist for women to play a leading and active role in the decision making of the village, the entire village community benefits.

This increased participation of women is often associated with better utilization of financial resources, increased harmony in village and prioritization of some important but neglected aspects of development such as girls' education and sanitation. Social reform measures such as reduction in alcohol consumption and domestic violence clearly get more prominence when women come to the forefront in rural communities.

Corruption has been one of the main problems of panchayat raj institutions. Interviews in several villages confirm that when women representatives function in an independent way, possibilities for corruption are lesser. Even if a pradhan or sarpanch is honest, there is the other threat that government officials refuse to release money and do not cooperate in other ways unless a certain commission is paid to them. There have been numerous examples of women sarpanchs resisting these demands of officials. In fact one hears of such resistance from women more frequently than from men. This opposition to the demand for commission has been strongly voiced by several women pradhans at their open meetings and training programmes.

Specific cases

Pushpa Rana, pradhan of Arakfarm panchayat in Dehradun district strongly resisted the bribe demands of officials. Although this created a lot of delays and other problems, she finally had her way. Sojar Bai of Ramtek panchayat [district Harda in Madhya Pradesh] went one step further and got the corrupt official [who demanded a cut from her] suspended from his job.

As for the careful use of scarce funds, Alka Chauhan provided a lesson to government engineers. A support wall that had been built in her village Nalapani [district Dehradun] at a cost of Rs. 42,000 had collapsed. A junior government engineer estimated that it will cost Rs.45, 000 to rebuild the wall. But Alka Chauhan mobilised the villagers to build the wall at a cost of only Rs.23, 500 and the money saved in this way could be spent on other development work.

When Suraiya Begum became the chairperson of Sultanpur Chilkana Nagar panchayat, it was saddled with debts and even some of her supporters feared that new development work may be hindered by the need to first clear old debts. But she managed the situation in such a way that by the time she completed her first five year tenure, a record number of development works worth Rs.80 lakhs had been completed.

More women leaders

As Rehana, a social worker of Sultanpur says, "Women are known to use money very carefully at home and somehow manage the family budget even when income is low. Women show the same abilities when they manage the village funds." Her colleague Shaheen adds, "When men are in-charge of development works, they indulge in a lot of wasteful spending in inaugurations and completion ceremonies. Women know how to be frugal and concentrate on the real work." Women representatives have shown the capacity to increase the panchayat income to make the development work more self-reliant. Many elected women have been closely involved with the promotion of self-help groups in villages. Urmila Yadav, sarpanch from Kosli village [Haryana] first took a step to clear encroachments on panchayat land and then built some shops on it. The rent from these shops can provide a regular income to the panchayat.

Women are generally known to have a greater capacity for resolving disputes. When she was the chairperson Suraiya Begum's door always remained open for many victims domestic violence. She helped to resolve many disputes. Pushpa Rana prevailed upon villagers to first settle all disputes locally and go to the police only if village level efforts failed. The result was that the money people had to spend on paying bribes to the police and middlemen was saved.

Many elected women representatives have made an effort to reduce liquor consumption and to remove liquor vends. In Ghazidipur village of Saharanpur district, a panchayat member Kamia confronted the pradhan who supported the location of liquor vend in the village and successfully mobilised village women for the removal of this liquor vend. Veena Sajwan, who was elected block pradhan of Bhilangana block (Tehri Garhwal district) at the young age of only 23 says, "I have taken up anti-liquor issue as the most important issue to mobilise women. When I had the opportunity to meet the

Chief Minister, I immediately reminded him of his promise to curb the liquor menace." All over Uttaranchal state this has been an important issue for elected women and they raised it vociferously at a recent 'Open Forum' meeting in Almora.

Battling the Male Empire

It is hoped that greater participation of women will result in better implementation of water, sanitation, girl's education, women's health and maternity. Chandravati Singh made a detailed survey of where exactly hand pumps were needed in her panchayat. This led to maximising benefits from the limited budget at her disposal for drinking water schemes. Some women elected members have prioritised toilets for ladies at bus stops, a clear need which had been ignored earlier by men pradhans.

In Sirmaul panchayat of Indore district, the sarpanch Kiran Kanchal not only set up a maternity home but also set up a committee to run it on a viable basis without raising the service charges too high for villagers. Madhu Semval [Nathuvala panchayat, Dehradun district] helped to check the spread of a cholera epidemic. Natho Begum [pradhan of Enfield gram panchayat, Dehradun district] was so devoted to promoting the education of girls that she donated her own land for this purpose, even though she herself belongs to a poor family.

Some women have overcome heavy odds to accomplish very commendable work in panchayats. Sudha Patel [sarpanch of Changa village, Anand district of Gujarat] is blind, but her work with the help of a friend has won widespread praise. Rajjo, a Dalit woman is completely illiterate and comes from a very poor family. However her work in Sultanpur Chilkana as deputy chairman was so good that almost the entire village adores her.

Some women have resisted efforts of vested interests to harass and dislodge them with a lot of courage and firmness. So many efforts were made to dislodge Ramali Behn from Ahmedabad zila panchayat by powerful vested interests, but she survived them all by her transparent way of functioning and by establishing direct relationship with people. When efforts were made to implicate Savita Behn Bharat Singh Pasaya [sarpanch of Pandra, Dohod district, Gujarat] and her family members in false allegations, she proved her innocence before a large gathering of villagers and officials.

All round progress

When women succeed in overcoming heavy odds to achieve good results in panchayats and also face vested interests with courage, it has an exemplary impact on a large number of other women. They also want to come forward to participate more actively in village affairs and contribute to the welfare of the community. Apart from this, it is also quite evident from the examples given above that the more active role of women in village often contributes to the welfare of the entire community and several important areas which were neglected earlier, now get prioritised. Thus it is in the interests of not just women but the entire village community to encourage the further empowerment of women in village affairs. The 33% reservation for women in panchayat raj institutions is an important part of this empowerment of women. To further strengthen the effort of elected women representatives, the government should provide greater security to women from the anger of powerful vested interests who try to harm and harass them in various ways. Voluntary organisations should also play a crucial role in helping and training elected women representatives.

Studies Related to Women Role in Fighting Against Corruption

Addis Ababa, July 01, 2003 (WIC) State Minister of Finance and Economic Cooperation, Dr. Mulu Ketsela said Women's active involvement in the fight against corruption was crucial.

Speaking at an awareness raising workshop organized for women representing all the regional states under the theme "women's role in the anti-corruption struggle", Dr. Mulu Ketsela said because women represent the most vulnerable half of the society, the enhancement of their participation in combating corruption would have a tremendous impact on the overall program underway across the nation.

Due to various cultural and social factors posed against them, women are the prime victims of poverty Dr. Mulu said adding that corruption has compounded the challenges to their lives.

She said studies have repeatedly disclosed that females are more responsible and are more adherent to ethical standards in their positions than are men, and their participation in fighting this social malpractice is therefore essential.

Dr. Mulu added that women's natural and social responsibility in raising children and building a society will make easier the effort to create ethical and corruption-free society in the country.

She therefore, underscored the importance of scaling up the awareness level of women about the impacts of corruption and the need for ethics so that they can play their share in alleviating the problem.

Public Relations Counselor with the Commission Birhanu Asseffa said on the occasion that the Commission has realized from the outset that without the empowerment of women the anti-corruption program launched in the country would not be successful.

The workshop was therefore organized with the view of making them aware of the prevailing problem of corruption in the country and the means of tackling it, Birhanu said.

Participants are expected to replicate the knowledge they have obtained among their respective organizations, he said. Taking part in the two-day workshop are 60 participants representing Community Based Organizations (CBOs) in all regional States non-governmental organizations working on women and children, and civic societies.

Studies Related to Education-Corruption

Corruption in all of its many forms has become a central issue in higher education worldwide. Rapid expansion, fueled by growing demand for access; dramatic increase in private higher education providers; the marketization of many aspects of higher education; and the financial problems faced by institutions and teaching and administrative staff have all contributed to a variety of corrupt practices. Academic corruption can be found in all countries but is especially prevalent in countries facing severe economic hardships and resultant pressure on their higher education systems, in systems with little external supervision and inadequate quality assurance mechanisms, and in countries in which there is a good deal of societal corruption.

Because of its tradition of probity and reliance on objective and meritocratic values, the problem of corruption is especially important for higher education. Academic institutions and the professoriate claim a special status in all societies—the right to academic freedom and individual and institutional autonomy and a high social prestige. Universities, after all, are responsible for educating the next generation of leaders, conducting scholarly research, and providing objective social analysis. As the national competitiveness in the global economy comes to increasingly depend on the quality of knowledge generated within and on the quality of education provided by a country's higher education institutions, the costs of academic corruption become considerable.

The dictionary definition of corruption will suffice for academe: "impairment of integrity, virtue, or moral principle; inducement to wrong by improper or unlawful means." Corruption in higher education can occur at both institutional and systemic levels and influences university examinations, the conferring of academic credentials, the procurement of goods and services, academic and administrative staff recruitment and promotion, budget allocation and utilization, property management, and the licensing and accreditation of institutions. Instances of academic corruption may involve bribery, facilitation of cheating and impersonation, the establishment of diploma mills, forgery and falsification of examination results, degrees and credentials, patronage, cronyism, and professional misconduct among teachers.

The primary goal of the Higher Education Corruption Monitor is to shed light on corrupt practices of all kinds in different countries, provide resources on current research on corruption in higher education, and serve as a forum for information exchange. The Monitor will collect and, in some cases, summarize news reports, documents, legal testimony, university reports, conference materials, research articles, and other kinds of documentation, and make the data available through a dedicated website. The Monitor will also collect information on policies and initiatives of international agencies and on various measures and reforms undertaken in different countries to address the challenges of corruption in higher education. The Monitor will link its website with websites of other institutions and agencies interested in the topic and with other on-line resources on corruption in order to avoid duplication and at the same time provide maximum attention to the issue. From time to time, the Monitor may issue reports on specific themes relating to corruption in higher education. The Monitor will not seek to verify each item placed on its website but will make every effort to choose reputable reports. The website will be part of the Center for International Higher Education's widely used website. The Monitor will be coordinated by Natia Janashia, graduate assistant in the Center for Higher Education (e-mail: janashia@bc.edu) a complete whole, connecting them by notes and explanations, where these were necessary; not putting the history in his own words or presenting it from his own standpoint as a modern historian would do, but piecing together the sections of the sources which referred to the same events, and thus preserving not only the history, but the very words in which it had reached him, for all coming generations. In this writer's work we have the Pentateuch of the OT Scriptures.

Geddes MacGregor has afforded, inter alia, another type of corruption in his esteemed book 'The Bible in the Making'. It would be pertinent to give an excerpt from it as well. For all the care that scribes often devoted to their task, a great many errors inevitably crept in. Deviations occur even among the most reliable of the ancient Greek manuscripts.

Before the invention of printing, the difficulty of reproducing the Bible did not consist solely in the labour of copying by hand. Parchment was scarce, so that contractions were very freely used. Sometimes a valuable manuscript, such as the Codex Ephraim, a fifth-century Bible now in the Bibliophile National, Paris, was treated so that, the writings have been erased by scraping and pumicing, the pages might be used over again for making another book. The lower writing was not usually quite obliterated, however, though it was extremely difficult to decipher it until chemical means were found to revive what had been rubbed out. Such a book, with one set of writing superimposed upon another, is called a palimpsest [stress added]. Again, MSS were often corrected by later copyist who scraped out with a knife what seemed to them incorrect, and modern scholars know that in many cases it was the corrector, not the MS, that was at fault. Sometimes a note would be made in the margin which a subsequent copyist would take to be part of the text. The hazards of inaccuracy in copying out the Bible by hand in the circumstances that prevailed in those days were so great that it is indeed astonishing that a text has been preserved which, despite technical problems it presents to the learned, may be taken as generally not straying very far from the sense of the original.

Point-wise recapitulation summaries have been afforded for some of the early parts of this article. They cover almost all of the important points. Thereafter, it was not deemed necessary. It was also not considered proper to quote more authorities. All the important themes have been elucidated. Moreover, almost all of the real and unbiased authorities unanimously endorse these themes. It can safely be concluded on the basis of the above evidence that the text of the OT of the Bible, verbatim et literatim, cannot be taken as free from corruption and alteration. However, the real message can be collected from it, using the critical and analytical apparatus. It may be noted that these types of corruption crept into the text of the Bible in spite of all the humanly possible care that had been sincerely afforded by the early scholars of the Bible. Geddes MacGregor has noted some measures taken towards the faultless transmission of the Bible texts. He notes... With the fall of the Temple at Jerusalem in that year [A.D. 70], the ritual worship with its animal sacrifices was at end, and the dispersed Jews had nothing to take with them on their wanderings but their Bibles. To the copying out of these they devoted immense care. The regulations for making a copy of the Scriptures are set forth in the Talmud (the great post-Biblical collection of Jewish law and legend) and show how scrupulously careful the scribes had to be. The scroll of the Law for use in a synagogue had to be fastened, for instance, with strings made from the skin of 'clean' animals. The length of each column was prescribed: not more than sixty or fewer than forty-eight lines were permitted. Lines had to be drawn before the writing was done, and if a scribe inadvertently wrote more than three words without first lining his copy, the whole thing was rendered worthless. He had to see that the space of a thread lay between each two consecutive letters that he wrote, and he was not allowed to write even a single letter from memory, without first looking at the approved text from which he was making the copy. He had to see that he never began the sacred name of God with a pen newly dipped in ink, lest he spatter this. The ink had to be black, made exactly according to a carefully delineated prescription. Throughout the whole of his work, the scribe was required to sit in full Jewish dress, and he was forbidden to speak to anyone, even a king. Any copies that did not entirely conform to the exacting standard had to be destroyed. What chiefly accounts for the absence of early Hebrew MSS, however, is the fact that as soon as any scroll became worn out it had to be put in a special room called Geniza, adjoining the synagogue, the contents of which room were periodically cleared out and destroyed. The Jews had no interest in preserving tattered old copies of the Scriptures for the sake of their antiquity: what they wanted were accurate copies, and so long as accuracy of current copies was censured by the rigid regulations, old ones could be discarded.

It can thus be safely concluded that the text of the OT had to suffer many a type of setback due to a number of reasons as detailed above. As such all possible analytical and critical measures should be adopted to ascertain the validity and intent of its text. But, at the same time, withal its shortcomings, it has preserved a lot of theological, historical, and prophetic substance in it and is not to be discarded outright.

Studies Related to Commissions and Committees towards Corruption

National anticorruption agencies, which could be a vital force in preventing corruption, are frequently so politicized that they are ineffective. In this article, two officials of Transparency International discuss how anticorruption agencies can become key players in the war against bribery.

Most development institutions today are promoting good governance in an effort to ensure the success of the projects they are helping to finance. Their focus is on curbing corruption among government officials—the abuse of public office for private gain. But the challenges of preventing and curbing corruption are, if anything, becoming more complex. Transparency International's experiences and those of its national chapters leave little doubt that the rising number of anticorruption initiatives being developed are running up against a massive wall of corrupt practices.

Transparency International's Corruption Perception Index and Bribe Payers Index show that bribe taking in many developing and transition countries is extensive, primarily because of low public sector salaries, senior public officials' and politicians' de facto immunity from prosecution, and greed. Meanwhile, transnational corporations' propensity to pay bribes is considerable. To be effective, ant bribery initiatives must recognize and confront these realities.

Although national anticorruption agencies can be critical in preventing corruption before it becomes rampant, not only are they difficult to set up but they often fail to achieve their goals once they have been established. They may be so beholden to their political masters that they dare not investigate even the most corrupt government officials; they may lack the power to prosecute; and they may be poorly staffed.

One key to success in building effective anticorruption agencies rests in the willingness of the proponents of good governance to share their experiences and to work together to develop greater knowledge of best practices. Our experience suggests that international organizations can make a major contribution on this front, but only if they work in partnership with national authorities and civil society, which, in turn, need to embrace business, academia, and a broad range of nongovernmental organizations. This can happen only when the organizations themselves approach the challenge with a fresh and open mind.

If major anticorruption initiatives are to be firmly anchored, there need to be distinct national government agencies dedicated to curbing corruption. These agencies must command public respect and be credible, transparent, and fearless. They must be subject to review by a free press and by civil society—indeed, they must be accountable to the public. But they must also be given considerable political independence so that they cannot be removed at the whim of enraged political elite.

A prime challenge in many countries is to mobilize the necessary political will to establish such agencies. The World Bank, the IMF, and bilateral aid agencies may call upon governments to establish anticorruption agencies as components of good governance programs and may even make loans conditional on the establishment of such agencies. But these agencies are not likely to succeed unless they are strong enough and politically independent enough to win the public's respect. Reforms therefore need to be firmly grounded within a particular country and not imposed from the outside.

New public procurement approaches

Anticorruption agencies need to focus on public procurement, which gives rise to some of the most egregious abuses. A recent survey in leading emerging market countries that was commissioned by Transparency International and carried out by Gallup International found that public works and construction are widely perceived to be the sectors most riddled by corruption, followed by the defense sector. On a scale of 0 to 10, with 10 being corruption free, the perceived level of corruption in public works and construction was 1.5, while defense scored a miserable 2.

Recently, Transparency International started to work with the government of Nigeria to devise ways of tackling corruption in public procurement. Drawing on the experience of New York City, where efforts to drive organized crime out of the school-construction industry have been successful, a working group established by the Nigerian government determined that bidders should be required to disclose all commissions by affidavit and on oath and that the names of all agencies involved in procurement proceedings should be published. Further, contracts should state that a substantial percentage of the purchase price will be forfeited to the government as liquidated damages should there be any breach. By focusing on changing the way contracts are written, the government was able to avoid the legislative battles that would have occurred had it tried to get new procurement rules passed by parliament, while ensuring that the new requirements were clearly stated in bidding documents.

Transparency International

Transparency International, founded in 1993, is a not-for-profit, nongovernmental organization dedicated to curbing corruption. Its headquarters are in Berlin. National chapters of Transparency International exist, or are being developed, in more than 70 countries. The organization works to strengthen civil society leadership and to forge coalitions—led by civil society and embracing business, government, and academia—in efforts to curb corruption. Transparency International has participated actively in building international support for the Organization for Economic Cooperation and Development's Anti-Corruption Convention, which came into force in February 1999, and other legislative actions to criminalize the payment of bribes. At the same time, Transparency International works to stimulate the development and expansion of anticorruption programs by national governments and international organizations and to build a base of knowledge and best practices that can be widely used in these efforts. Transparency International's research and its national integrity source book, working papers, and overall information base can be found on its website, http://www.transparency.org/.

Hong Kong SAR as a model

Nigeria has a long way to go, but it can be encouraged by examples of effective approaches in other countries. National anticorruption agencies, for example, can go far beyond merely identifying and prosecuting corrupt officials, vital as this is. They can also assist in creating an environment in which large public works proceed without corruption. They can operate in ways that command the respect of contractors and contribute to the building of a business environment that is imbued with integrity. Although these aspirations sound utopian, they can be realized, as Hong Kong SAR has demonstrated.

Michael Wiehen and Peter Rooke, members of Transparency International's Board of Directors, recently examined the procurement processes involved in developing Hong Kong SAR's Airport Core Program (ACP), which included construction of the Hong Kong airport, as well as of high-speed rail and road connections, a major suspension bridge, and a cross-harbor tunnel. The total capital cost of the ACP exceeded HK$160 billion (US$20.6 billion at the current exchange rate of US$1 = HK$7.75), making it one of the largest infrastructure projects ever undertaken anywhere in the world. The ACP was virtually free of corruption, owing to several factors:

- Hong Kong SAR's clear, strict Prevention of Bribery Ordinance and strong Independent Commission Against Corruption

(ICAC), which has impressive legal powers and a staff of about 1,350 professionals;

- o clear rules and effective control mechanisms for selecting and procuring consultant and construction services and equipment supplies, supervising and monitoring the implementation of contracts, enforcing the accountability of government staff as well as of consultants and contractors, and resolving disputes;
- o the establishment, for ACP purposes, of special institutions such as the New Airport Projects Coordinating Office (since dissolved), which had a dispute-resolution team that stepped in whenever problems occurred, and the Engineering and Associated Consultant Selection Board, which is also involved in non-ACP projects; and
- o a favorable working environment, including appropriate salaries for civil servants, a high degree of professionalism and pride among the officials, and a relatively small society in which businessmen caught offering bribes or otherwise trying to manipulate the processes find it difficult to obtain other business, making corruption a high-risk activity.

The ICAC has been pivotal to the success of transparent public procurement in Hong Kong SAR. Its work is carried out by three departments. The Operations Department carries out the investigation and prosecution of offenses; the Corruption Prevention Department examines the practices and procedures of government departments and public bodies and makes recommendations on how opportunities for corruption can be eliminated or reduced; and the Community Relations Department is responsible for educating the general public about the evils of corruption, instilling positive values in Hong Kong's youth—starting as early as kindergarten—providing advice to business organizations on drawing up codes of conduct, and harnessing support for the ICAC.

Other successful anticorruption agencies are found in Australia, Botswana, Malawi, Singapore, and South Africa (under the post-apartheid government). However, most countries are just starting to think about setting up anticorruption agencies, so there is an urgent need to establish clear guidelines of best practice.

Guidelines

The starting point should be identifying the core role of anticorruption agencies. Given that prevention is always better than prosecution, a small investigative and monitoring unit with appropriate authority and political independence may be much better placed than other government agencies to ensure that effective preventive steps are identified and taken.

Research by Transparency International suggests that to operate successfully, an anticorruption agency must have the following:

- o Political support not only from a country's president but also from a broad array of national political leadership.
- o The political and operational independence needed to investigate the highest levels of government (some agencies that have failed—for example, those in Tanzania and Zambia—are housed within the president's office and therefore have scant opportunity to tackle corruption involving the national political leadership);.
- o Access to documentation and the power to question witnesses; and
- o Leadership with great integrity.

Further, credibility and effectiveness depend on the exemplary behavior of the anticorruption agency itself. It must act, and be seen to act, in conformity with international human rights norms. It must operate under the law and be accountable to the courts.

A test for a government establishing an anticorruption agency is whether it would find the agency's actions acceptable if it were the political opposition rather than the party in power. An enduring formula, which seems fair and workable to everyone, whether in or out of government, needs to be found. This requires, for example, that the agency have significant powers of investigation, prosecution, and deterrence, independent of political parties and government leaders. Accountability is critical to the agency's success, as are checks on its power and the method used for selecting its leadership. Anticorruption agencies will fail if they can be subjected to political direction and used as a weapon to attack critics of the government. Safeguards have to exist as well as to ensure the agency does not itself become a source for extortion and corruption.

Who should run national anticorruption agencies? Certainly not the hand-picked supporters of politicians in power. Such leaders could, at best, be relied upon not to rock the boat; at worst, they could be deployed to intimidate political opponents. Appointment procedures need to address the issue of whether the proposed mechanism sufficiently insulates the process to ensure that persons of integrity are given the leadership and that they are protected from political pressures while they are in office. Approaches widely used to provide security of tenure to high court judges could be applied here.

Checks and balances

In designing an anticorruption agency, one should consider how, in theory, the new agency would act in the worst-case scenario: that is, in response to allegations of major corruption by the nation's president. Lawmakers, after all, need to reflect on the issue of public distrust if the president is seen to be above and beyond the jurisdiction of the anticorruption authority. Establishing an agency with a special provision in its statute that highlights the power to investigate and assist the prosecution of all public officials, irrespective of rank, can strengthen a new agency and send a vital signal that builds public support from the start. A country's leaders need to accept that their successors may not share their standards and that the agency must be empowered to deal with corruption in high places.

To be sure, an anticorruption agency typically cannot prosecute presidents in office because they usually have immunity under the country's constitution. Impeachment proceedings are generally a matter for a national legislature. Accordingly, the framework of an anticorruption agency can be fashioned to enable the agency to provide reports to the leadership of the legislature, if there are reasonable grounds to believe that the president has committed an offense and if there is prima facie evidence admissible in a court of law. Similarly, the relationship between an anticorruption agency and the office of public prosecutions is critical. Agencies must be seen to have real impact leading to prosecutions and convictions. Otherwise, as has happened in several countries, they will be widely viewed as a farce. A country must have legislation that ensures the political independence not only of the anticorruption agency but also of the judiciary and the public prosecutors.

Ensuring accountability is probably the most difficult issue related to building successful anticorruption agencies. Some authorities, such as Hong Kong SAR's ICAC, have established arrangements that ensure public participation in policy formulation and oversight. By providing for such an arrangement (which could take the form of a committee chaired by the minister of justice), the anticorruption framework would encourage transparency. In Hong Kong SAR, a file that has been opened cannot be closed without the consent of the external oversight committee, which includes representatives of civil society and the private sector. This protects against corruption inside the agency.

Reaching beyond formal processes, a successful agency needs to have a charter that provides for the involvement of a wide range of people and interests in the formulation of prevention policies and their execution. In this way, various stakeholders become involved in the prevention process, and their own institutions—in both government and the private sector—can be mobilized in support of the agency's efforts. The agency's work has to be seen as meaningful, which requires that the agency be as open as possible with the press and that it publish frequent reports on its activities.

Should a new law be retroactive?

Anticorruption agencies are established to solve problems that are widely recognized. They come into being to confront, in all cases, years of corruption. Should they be focused only on the future, or should they also look to the past and investigate previous public officeholders and others who are perceived to have benefited at the public's expense? There is no certain answer, but it is evident that if a new anticorruption agency delves too deeply into past corruption it may become so overwhelmed by outstanding investigations inherited from the police that it is wholly unable to focus on the present. The legislation establishing the Hong Kong ICAC overcame the problem by stating that the commission should not, with a few exceptions; deal with matters prior to its January 1, 1977 establishment.

Conclusion

While an effective national anticorruption agency that enjoys the public's trust and that is respected by business is difficult to establish and maintain, it is all too easy to undermine. Ultimately, an anticorruption agency will be deemed successful if a nation's citizens see major public works contracts completed on time, according to plan, and with enough transparency to convince even the most skeptical observer that bribery has not been a factor. As a corruption-free, transparent project, Hong Kong's ACP has enhanced the stature of the ICAC. By contrast, Jamaica's independent contractor general's repeated reports to parliament on abuses in public procurement seem to have been consistently ignored by those on both sides of the political spectrum, undermining the credibility of Jamaica's efforts at reform.

Transparency International is convinced that greater in-depth knowledge of the successes and failures of national anticorruption agencies can be valuable. This conviction derives from the recognition that internationally coordinated efforts to curb corruption are still in their infancy and that, to ensure action and rapid results, lessons learned and best practices must be disseminated as broadly as possible.

This is not merely an academic issue. When Nigeria's President Coliseum Obasanjo was elected in the spring of 1999, he turned to many international organizations, including Transparency International, for assistance in curbing corruption, inviting detailed suggestions on how to build a new anticorruption sensitivity in the government and the institutions to support it. He has taken the advice offered and put many ideas into practice that are now being tested.

The better the advice that can be given to new leaders across the globe who are determined to confront corruption, the greater will be the chances of scoring real successes. The demand for expertise is formidable; the level of real knowledge remains at a premium. Only by pooling research and experience between public sector organizations, at the national and multilateral levels, and civil society, business, and academia can best practices be widely determined and disseminated. Building effective anticorruption agencies is one priority area where progress is being made.

Corruption is difficult to prosecute because it is shrouded in a cloud of secrecy, protected by the very same individuals we consider victims of this crime. This is precisely because most of those who partake on this practice do not see themselves as "victims" nor "accomplices," but rather as business partners closing a "profitable" deal. While they perceive this habit as producing a win-win situation, they do not realize the hidden costs that are borne by society as a whole.

Creating a corruption-free government cannot be done if its citizens are also corrupt. Therefore, fighting corruption must be done by securing a partnership with the people and make them understand that everyone loses when they participate in corrupt practices. By raising their level of awareness about the ills of corruption and the extent of damage that it does to the community, the people themselves will act to eliminate this practice once and for all. Public education must focus on making people realize that everybody has a stake in fighting corruption.

Corruption and Commissions

In an effort to propagate the idea of zero tolerance for corruption, the Central Vigilance Commission (CVC) in India has begun to share with citizens a large amount of information related to corruption. The CVC website has published the names of officers from the elite administrative and revenue services against whom investigations have been ordered or penalties imposed for corruption. Newsweek magazine carried an article about this effort, calling it E-shame.

Application Context

In the Transparency International rankings for 1999, India was placed 73rd among the 99 countries rated. Corruption flourishes in India because it is perceived to be a low risk, high profit business. In service delivery, there is lack of transparency in rules and procedures, and significant delays in operations or functioning. The lack of transparency provides an opportunity for public servants to mislead citizens who have to transact business with them, and extract bribes.

Certainly, the size of India's parallel economy (or black market), estimated at 40% of GDP, provides fertile ground for corruption to flourish. Equally important, the corrupt face little deterrent. There are enormous delays in the prosecution of cases in courts. What is worse, the conviction rate is hardly 6% in criminal cases.

There is a perception that corruption begins at the top, but senior bureaucrats are never investigated or punished. The main investigating agency – the Central Bureau of Investigation (CBI) – has little credibility in the eyes of the public.

The Central Vigilance Commission was set up in 1964 as a Government agency. Vigilance Commissions and institutions called Lok Ayukta have also been set up and in some states. These institutions are generally headed by retired public servants or High Court judges. Their effectiveness has been mixed.

A New Approach

In 1998, based on the directive of the Supreme Court, the Government converted the Central Vigilance Commission into a statutory body through an executive order. (A bill to formalize the statutory existence of the commission was under consideration of the select committee of the Indian parliament in 2001.) The newly independent commission has taken several initiatives, particularly in recommending the use of IT by banks and other public institutions to bring in transparency.

One of the initiatives was the creation of a website; and one of the first actions (January 2000) was to publish the names of senior officers who were charged with violating conduct rules. The CVC website contains the following sections/features through which the CVC communicates with the public:

1. The commission informs the public about its role, responsibility, and strategies to combat corruption. This is an effort keep the agenda of fighting corruption alive in the public mind.
2. The commissioner communicates directly with the public through messages and speeches to bolster confidence in the institution.
3. Instructions for how any citizen can lodge a complaint against corruption, without fear of disclosure or reprisal.

4. Central Vigilance Officer's List: each organization is expected to nominate a senior officer to whom an employee can take a complaint on corruption.
5. Statistical reporting of the achievements of the Commission (Annual Report).
6. Details of convictions of public servants by the courts are also presented, along with Information on officers from the All India Services against whom an enquiry has been initiated or a penalty imposed. This section also highlights the performance of various departments responsible for conducting investigations.

Although the public at large often knows who is a corrupt public servant; there has been no systematic method by which this information could be brought to the notice of either the CBI or the Income Tax department. A new feature of the CVC site will now increase the risk element for the corrupt whose ill-gotten wealth is stashed away in the form of black money, foreign accounts, benami bank accounts (wealth hidden under false names), jewelry and other valuables, benami property, etc. Members of public can now report information against a public servant about possession of black money or assets, which are believed to be disproportionate to his known sources of income. The Commission would scrutinize the information so received, and if the information is considered sufficient for carrying out detailed investigations, the CBI or the Income Tax authorities would be advised accordingly.

The Commission clearly states that it does not entertain anonymous or pseudonymous complaints. However, the identity of the complainant can be protected if he/she so desires. Section 182 of the Indian Penal Code makes it a criminal offence for a person to report about a public servant any information which he knows or believes to be false.

The CBI and the Income Tax Department have schemes under which informants are rewarded for the information they provide. The informants who provide information under CVC notification also will be eligible for such rewards.

Implementation Challenges

The display of names of the senior officials of the Government of India – including IAS and IPS officers – on the CVC website in January 2000 caused a mild furor in the media. According to the CVC, the publication of these names was intended to meet a long-standing demand of the media for information about senior officials facing corruption charges and inquires. (The general perception of the public was that this kind of negative publicity appeared only against mid-level or junior officials.) Over 90 percent of those polled by the Hindustan Times welcomed the action. However, some newspapers decried the publication of the list in their editorials. Many citizens would conclude that a person is corrupt if their name appears on the website. But, in fact, only an inquiry had been ordered, which might ultimately exonerate the person.

One of the IAS Associations passed a resolution against the CVC stating that publication of a name on the site could bias the process of departmental inquiry/action. Under the law, no defamation has been caused by publicizing the names of the charged officers; yet the general perception seemed to be that the CVC website exposed a kind of a rogue's gallery.

In response to these criticisms the CVC argued that all it had done was to extend to the departmental inquiries a practice that is as old as the Indian Penal Code in criminal cases. Under criminal law, when a person is accused he is legally innocent until proven guilty; but the name of the accused enters the public domain.

Benefits and Costs

Some of those whose names have appeared on the CVC website occupied sensitive positions in government. It is a common principle in government that if a person is facing a vigilance inquiry, he should not be placed in a sensitive post. However, this practice was not being followed in India. That is one reason why corruption has flourished in the system. The CVC site brought this issue to the fore.

Another positive outcome from the site is that several people whose names appeared complained that they had never even been served with a charge sheet. Lengthy delays in the conduct of a departmental inquiry help corruption to flourish. Delay provides a cover of respectability for the guilty. Worse, perhaps, is that if departmental inquires are delayed, an innocent person may become a victim of mindless departmental procedure. His career may be ruined due to delays in getting his name cleared. The CVC now sends a monthly reminder to all departmental authorities so that the disposal of the cases may be expedited. The CVC aims to have all departmental inquires completed within six months.

The question may be raised whether in a country like India, with a low computer density; a website like the CVC's can be an effective anticorruption tool. By September 2001 only 150,000 hits had been registered on the site. Fortunately, India has a free and vibrant press. Both print media and the radio have been able to transmit the content of CVC website throughout the country. Thus, the site has had a much bigger impact than what could be expected based on India's computer density alone.

Key Lessons

Although a large volume of information is available on the CVC website, only certain specifics were picked up by the media. The publication of the names of high-placed members of government attracted significant media attention. However, when sensitive information is shared, the media must also have the ability to analyze and draw conclusions. The media will need to be educated (and educate themselves) in order to perform such a role effectively.

The CVC experiment may embolden other agencies like public banks to publish the names of willful defaulters. The Governor of the Reserve Bank of India has announced that the Reserve Bank is examining this issue. Similarly, there were reports that the Department of Company Affairs was thinking of publishing the names of its defaulters.

Despite the fact that Indian society has become insensitive and cynical about corruption, the website seemed to cause some stirring of conscience. Officers whose names were published were indeed shamed. In an article, the CVC commissioner noted that some of these officers came and cried before him saying that their children were asking why their names were on the website. A poll by the

Economic Times, a leading business paper of India, reported that 83 percent of respondents believed that publishing the names of charged officers on the CVC website will have a deterrent effect.

Other websites run by Indian NGOs have begun to focus on corruption. For example, Tehalka.com exposed a major bribery scandal in the defense department by publishing a secretly filmed video clip on its website. Overall, Web publishing has emerged as an interesting new instrument to promote greater transparency and improved governance.

Case study author: Subhash Bhatnagar

Information used to develop the case: This case has been developed from a presentation by the Central Vigilance Commissioner in the India States Forum 2000, held in New Delhi, 23-25 November 2000, and from newspaper reports on CVC website.

Studies Related to Teachers and Parents Role towards Corruption

Educating the people can be done using many avenues—the formal education system, religious communities, mass media, or direct face-to-face contact. In India, schools are the targets of an NGO's initiatives to promote moral and ethical education, whose curriculum includes good citizenship and democracy. In Cambodia, a group called "Transparency Task Force" has been formed, composing educators and anti-corruption pundits, which is developing a wide-ranging, counter-corruption curriculum, which will be adopted by the Ministry of Education in its formal educational program. It is based on putting forward traditional moral and ethical values that are advanced by Cambodian folk tales and Buddhist teachings.

In Australia, on the other hand, corruption education has mainly focused on training and educating civil servants and anticorruption practitioners. In 1998, the Australian National University introduced a course on Corruption and Anti-Corruption as part of its Masters Degree in Development Administration. By using its own anti-corruption agency as an example, the ANU course trains its students on identifying where corruption starts and develop strategies to reduce or eliminate corruption entirely.

The content and approach of each curriculum developed in these countries differ precisely because they are personalized to fit the culture and environment of its audience.

In Hong Kong, their anti-corruption agency has a different strategy. It educates its citizens through direct contact by setting up local offices across the region, with extended office hours and a round-the-clock hotline for complaints and reports of corruption in the community. It has also undertaken a massive publicity campaign using posters, advertisements and dramatizations of prosecuted cases in order to educate the people and at the same time, encourage them to report incidents of corruption. Coupled with harsh punitive measures and a "zero tolerance" policy from the government, it is one of the most successful models of an anticorruption agency in the world.

The Philippine experience in similar undertakings has not been quite as successful, despite a long running policy against corruption at the highest level of government. The policy of using mass media as a tool to campaign for ethical behavior from civil servants has not been consistent with each change in the administration. The lack of sustainability of anti-corruption strategies is exemplified by the fact that after the Marcos regime, each succeeding president has had a different anti-corruption agency, run by political appointees, which uses the media to create hype about its investigations about cronies of the previous administration.

We might have better success in combating corruption if an anticorruption module is embedded within the curriculum of both primary and secondary schools. A strong civics background will greatly help in developing a law-abiding and responsible citizenry. Values education can also be tapped as a conduit to inculcate principles of honesty and transparency such that the opportunity to educate spreads from the school to the church, and eventually to every single household. As the typical Filipino family is closely knit, an ideal starting point for educating the youth about corruption should be at home.

Combating corruption will be truly successful if every citizen can be mobilized to act against it. In order to do so, the mass public should be educated on the evils of corruption. By explaining clearly and explicitly how ordinary citizens are personally disadvantaged by corruption in society, the public will learn that it is commonsensical to steer away from graft and corruption, and be intolerant of those who continue to practice it.

Corruption – Teacher Role

Certainly in the traditional Indian context, the teachers and the parents transmitted values. The teacher was interestingly called acharya, a word that is based on the root achar, or conduct. Thus the transmission of values was by personal example and conduct of the teacher, not by "moral science" lessons. Values were embedded in the role models of daily life.

The other form of transmittal of values is via stories and exemplars. Stories that were told by grandparents and parents during childhood also have a positive role in the creation of values. Finally, the example set by parents as well as those portrayed as "successful" role models to emulate is certainly also important. In the contemporary world, mass media is a very powerful force in the creation of samskara. In a responsible society, mass media would recognize this role rather than view its role solely as "anything goes" entertainment, blindly aping western mores or measuring its success in purely materialistic terms. But this is ultimately a matter of awakening to responsibility, not ham-handed government censorship.

So, once the systematic problems are tackled, we will be at the level of the "developed" world in terms of corruption. As we mentioned earlier, the developed world is certainly no exemplar as far as morality goes. To go beyond this, one comes back to the messages of the rishis on inner transformation. This inner transformation is ultimately what can enable us to go beyond greed, avarice and a consumerism that obsessively seeks satisfaction outside oneself to move towards "santosh", a santosh that is ultimately the basis for the elimination of all corruption.

Studies Related to Surveys towards Corruption

Changing in India: Survey

NEW DELHI, PTI

Bofors to Telgi and telecom to stock, corruption and scams have always been an inalienable part of India. But believe it or not, greasing the palms at the urban public services level is on a decline, according to a new report, indicating that corruption has moved from the mere middlemen outside the government offices level to more sophisticated areas.

While, public services like regional transport offices, railways and municipal corporations are still plagued with the middlemen menace, other areas like hospitals, civil supplies, urban development, electricity and water supplies have shown a remarkable turnaround, thanks to the newfound e-governance mantra, the report released by the Centre for Media Studies says.

Contrary to the popular perception that corruption is rampant, the survey which covered five major cities - Delhi, Hyderabad, Kolkata, Chennai and Mumbai - reveal that corruption in our public services has come down drastically or moved to more lucrative areas of operation, N Bhaskar Rao, CMS Chairman, says.

"An interesting fact that the survey found out was corruption has come down drastically at the middlemen level. It is not high as is often believed and the reasons for this can be attributed to the large-scale computerization of services, reforms initiated by the vigilance departments and the rise in awareness among the consumers," Mr Rao says.

According to the survey, which covered eight major public utility services, corruption has shown a declining trend. Around 28 per cent of citizens who participated in the survey admitted that they have dealt through middlemen, which is a sharp decline from 48 per cent in 2000. Another 30 per cent admitted giving bribe, which was as high as 51 per cent in 2000.

Interestingly, the hi-tech city of Hyderabad, where the e-seva centers are popular and widespread, the presence of middlemen and corruption has declined to 27 per cent from a whopping 63 per cent in 2000. While Kolkata and Chennai records dwindling corruption rates, 19 and 18 per cent compared to 51 and 38 per cent in 2000 respectively, Mumbai remained static and the national capital Delhi showed a spurt in corruption from 40 to 49 per cent, it says.

The survey, which questioned 4500 users in these five cities, covered utility services like electricity, municipal corporation, urban development, transport, civil supplies, hospitals, water supply and railways and went into specific services like metering, billing, issue of driving license, railway ticket reservation, registration of land, and documentation. All the departments surveyed had recorded a decline in corruption levels. While Municipal Corporation and transport offices still topped the list corruption levels in railways and hospitals remained virtually unchanged, the survey reveals.

But, despite the dip in corruption levels in these five cities, experts and officials are skeptical and have struck a cautious note as they feel corruption has disguised itself and has moved to more sophisticated areas. Corruption has shifted to more dangerous areas as softer areas are no longer available and the Telgi (stamp scam) and Dubey cases are pointers in this direction, Chief Vigilance Commissioner, P Shankar opines.

Studies Related to Causes of Corruption

Why is India Poor? Classifying the Reasons

Before picking up individual issues on why India is poor, I'd like to classify the issues that came out of the comments. The classification is not going to be perfect, but it allows me to club the issues into manageable morsels. BTW, these are in no particular order.

- o Corruption
- o Lack of education
- o Democracy (including universal adult franchise)
- o Over population
- o Poor Governance and Development Policies (includes resource miss- utilization, top heavy federalism, poor development, poor plan implementation, Nehruvian socialism, not enough emphasis on cities, monarchies in politics, equality "fetish", agriculture un-reformed, bureaucracy / red tape, opaque and uneven taxes)
- o Lack of a strong middle class
- o Culture (Lots of points get clubbed here. Acceptance / appeasement of poverty, "we hate being rich," laziness, service

mentality, social and religious factors, family values, caste systems, feudalism, treating women badly, Indians are happy as they are, "monsoon complacency")

- o Colonialism
- o Lack of economic freedom (including lack of micro finance institutions,
- o War
- o Weather (Does living in the tropics make you poorer?)

If there is something I've missed out, or newer points that someone just thought of, please let me know. If you want to add a new point or change the classification, give me compelling reasons to do so.

Studies Related to Corruption Rally

Once again it's time for us to fight for our freedom. This time it is against the corruption. By listening to the corruption news every day, is your blood boiling to do something for your country? So why don't you join the largest national rally ever conducted before to generate awareness and swipe-off the corruption in India.

On behalf of IndiaEyeWitness.com we want to inspire students and teachers. At the same time teachers can also collect valuable solutions to get rid of the corruption and bring up a list of best possible solutions and mail it to our honorable President, Prime Minster and the state Chief Minister. If possible send it to news media groups for public awareness. We are gathering some slogans and pamphlets, which you may use them in the rally.

STUDENTS ROLE IN THIS RALLY

As everyone knows, "Students have the power to rewrite the history". We want you to be the initiative and be the leaders to start this rally. As a student you have the right to fight for a corruption free future. Read all the slogans provided in the website and choose the best slogan and write them on the barricades and holding boards. Print pamphlets with your suggestions to clean the corruption and distribute them during the rally. For instance, tell your parents that you don't want to grow with the money earned in a corruption deal. Ask your neighbours not to take the bribes.

TEACHERS ROLE IN THIS RALLY

Take the initiative. Motivate your students. Guide them throughout the rally process and be the leader of the rally. We request all the teachers to participate in this revolution and help them in making a peaceful rally represented by your institution. Give your ideas and collect valuable suggestions from the students in the class and create a list of best possible solutions to fight corruption. Help them in preparing the banners with slogans. Show your students a bright and corruption free future.

NRI'S ROLE IN THIS RALLY

What can an NRI do? Directly or indirectly you can participate and make this rally a great success. Since IndiaEyeWitness.Com is a no-income website, we request you to take the initiative. Sponsor an advertisement in local newspaper so that it will reach every corner of the country. Talk to your friends and families in India and let them know about this rally. Encourage and help them in whatever the form of support you can provide. Give financial support to print the pamphlets and banners for the rally. Show them what you can do to your homeland, even though you are not living there. Send an email to all your friends to spread the information as quickly as possible. Write a letter or post one of the pamphlets to your school/ College/ University where you did your education to let them know about this rally and encourage them to participate.

Anna Hazare's fight against corruption

Kisan Baburao Hazare is popularly known as Anna Hazare. He is an Indian social activist and a prominent leader in the 2011 Indian anti-corruption movement, using nonviolent methods following the teachings of Mahatma Gandhi. Hazare also contributed to the development and structuring of Ralegan Siddhi, a village in Parner taluka of Ahmednagar district, Maharashtra, India. He was awarded the Padma Bhushan—the third-highest civilian award—by the Government of India in 1992 for his efforts in establishing this village as a model for others.

Anna Hazare started an indefinite hunger strike on 5 April 2011 to exert pressure on the Indian government to enact a stringent anticorruption law as envisaged in the Jan Lokpal Bill, for the institution of an ombudsman with the power to deal with corruption in public places. The fast led to nation-wide protests in support of Hazare. The fast ended on 9 April (Friday) 2011, a day after the government accepted Hazare's demands. The government issued a gazette notification on the formation of a joint committee, consisting of government and civil society representatives, to draft the legislation.

Anna has been ranked as the most influential person in Mumbai by a national daily newspaper. He has faced criticism for his authoritarian views on justice, including death as punishment for corrupt public officials and his alleged support for forced vasectomies as a method of family planning.

The instant of victory came on Saturday at 10.30am. Having humbled a government and captured the imagination of a nation, the frail 73-year-old broke his fast by first offering sips of water to women who had fasted with him. Anna Hazare then had a glass of juice.

The Gandhian leader's marathon ended on the fifth morning of his protest with a large crowd of supporters breaking into loud cheers even as hundreds more poured in at Jantar Mantar, ground zero of the campaign to ensure civil society's participation in drafting the Lokpal Bill.

Hazare held aloft a copy of the official notification constituting a joint committee and said "In this fight against corruption, India has won, not Anna. You have shown we are united. But the fight must continue." He warned he will be back if the law to combat corruption in public life is not passed by August 15.

That lies is in the future. On Saturday morning firecrackers went off and people smeared gulaal on one another, a celebration that will freeze frame a historical moment.

"I will not let this public movement die down. If the government does not pass the bill in Lok Sabha in the monsoon session, I will carry the national flag on my shoulders to protest once again," he said. "Next on my agenda is working for the right to recall," Hazare added.

Hazare pointed out the pitfalls. "I know that there will be further impediments in the implementation of this new bill, which will ensure action against corrupt politicians and bureaucrats and bring in accountability"

His question "Will you support me?" had the crowd roaring in affirmation. "Anna tum sangharsh karo, hum tumhare saath hain," they yelled.

The warning is well taken. It is a declaration of intent as Hazare and thousands who turned out in his support in several cities will know that their struggle for an effective anti-corruption ombudsman might be just beginning. Hard negotiation and parliamentary approval lie ahead.

There are larger implications of the four-day revolution. The swiftness with which the official Goliath succumbed to Hazare's simple but powerful message changed some rules the political class feels are immutable. Arrogance of power met an irresistible force.

With grammar of politics and governance rewritten after effects of civil society getting its foot through the policy door will emerge. Although the Jantar Mantar rumble is not be easy to replicate as the aam aadmi's extraordinary anger gave the protest its dangerous edge, more civil society offensives are certain.

The debate over unelected persons – and unelectable as politicians whisper — wielding power will intensify although the heady April feeling is exhilarating. Somehow, the Gandhi topi-clad man from Maharashtra's heartland seems to have pushed back a weary cynicism over official inaction, offering hope that things can change.

Prime Minister Manmohan Singh in a statement saw "an agreement in our mutual resolve to combat corruption. This is a scourge that confronts all of us. The Government intends to introduce the Lokpal Bill in Parliament during the monsoon session. The fact that civil society and government joined hands to evolve a consensus to move this historic legislation augurs well for our democracy."

Parliament will test the resolve the campaigners but at least this much is certain: India is likely to get a muscular lokpal sooner than later. The bill may be scrutinized by a standing committee and miss a deadline or two. But the people power on display – translated as votes for politicians – will make parties and leaders wary.

The increasing value of good governance will make such models more attractive. If after Bihar, the current round of assembly elections delivers a thumb down to the "corrupt", the message will begin to really sink in.

The Gandhian himself led the crowd to sing patriotic songs like Ragupati Raghav Raja Ram and Vande Mataram. He had nothing to eat for four days, but the energy and enthusiasm seemed to feed him.

During past weeks we saw a leader for the entire nation ...a leader to drive common people's fight against corruption ...Many mentioned him as a true Gandhian ...and even named him as Gandhi of Modern India. Anna Hazare's fast till death to support Jan Lokpal bill against corruption saw the entire nation supporting him. The huge support he got at Jantar Mantar,where Hazare is fasting in New Delhi,was compared to Cairo's Tahrir Square. After a long period India saw a non-violent protest of such extent ,even supported by Young Indians.

Beginning his day-long hunger strike at Rajghat to protest against corruption and the recent police brutality, the 73-year-old-Gandhi devotee Anna Hazare said that if the Lokpal Bill was not passed, he would fast unto death at Jantar Mantar from August 16.

Anna described his movement as the second battle of independence but underlined Gandhi's non-violent path. He said his Wednesday fast was to condemn the police action on Ramdev's supporters at Ramlila ground. Anna likened the police brutality to the British repression of Indians in Jalianwala Bagh on April 13, 1919. He advised his supporters to refrain from violence. "The government is very powerful, if we indulge in violence, it will give the government an excuse to quash the movement," he warned. We hope that India will become corruption free country in the world......

Conclusion

If there is no corruption all peoples in the world live happy. Some steps are necessary to remove corruption in the society. There is nothing in the world impossible.

Principles Governing the Strategy for preventing and combating corruption:

- Adherence to the rule of law.
- Openness and accountability.
- The national will to fight corruption and to co-operate in the attainment.
- A complex approach to the war against corruption.
- Preventing corruption.
- Combating corruption.
- Educating the population.
- The National Program for preventing corruption is prepared on the basis of this strategy.
- The National Program defines priorities, allocates responsibilities and sets deadlines.

3

The Present Study

In the modern India, there has been a revolutionary change in the field of values due to many factors in addition to the influence of western culture industrialization, modernization, urbanization. It is necessary for us to preserve our traditional value. However, a conflict between traditional values is inevitable. It is also necessary to make efforts to present a new sense of values in a clear and complete form. One of the chief tasks of the contemporary Indian society is to bring about a synthesis of the traditional social values and modern social value.

If we give importance to social value then the corruption automatically decreased. There has been much research work in the field of corruption but no work has done on the Attitude of Scholars towards corruption. So the present investigation is intended to probe into this.

Statement of the Problem

The problem taken by the investigator for investigation is "Analytical study of the attitude of scholars towards Corruption.

This investigation is intended to the following questions specifically.

- o Is there any difference in the attitude of the male and female scholars towards corruption?
- o Is there any difference in the attitude of different religion scholars towards corruption?
- o Is there any difference in the attitude of different caste scholars towards corruption?
- o Is there any difference in the attitude of different local scholars towards corruption?

Objectives

The following are the main objectives of the present study.

- o To identify the importance of rules and regulation in the present day situation.
- o To identify the various components which influence corruption?
- o To identify in which department corruption is high.
- o To identify the relationship between corruption and education in scholars.
- o To investigate significance of corruption and with the variables like sex, locality, course of study, religion, caste, mother occupation and father occupation, mother educational qualification, father educational qualification and educational qualification of scholars.
- o To identify the solutions of the problem of corruption.

Basic Assumption

- o Difference to exists between male and female scholars towards corruption.
- o Difference do exists between scholars who came from different local areas towards corruption.
- o Difference do exists between scholars belongs to various religions towards corruption.
- o Difference do exists between scholars belongs to various casts towards corruption.
- o Difference do exists between scholars in relation with whose father educational qualification.

- o Difference do exists between scholars in relation with whose mother educational qualification.
- o Difference do exists between scholars in relation with whose father occupation.
- o Difference do exists between scholars in relation with whose mother occupation.

Need for Study

Now we are living in the modern world. There are so many changes occurring day to day life. But all peoples are not good. Some persons are in poverty. They have no food, shelter and education. This is because of corruption in various fields. All are equal. It is necessary to give primary needs to all persons in the world. It is important to know the causes of corruption and solution for corruption. Values are important for all persons. So I taken this topic it is important to everybody.

Scope of Study

This study is purely prepared to fine "An Analytical Study of the Attitude of Scholars towards Corruption."

This investigation is particularly done to bring out the differences if any among the scholars of sex, course of study, locality, religion, caste, mother occupation, father occupation, educational qualification of father, educational qualification of mother, educational qualification of scholars.

Purpose of Study

The present study aims to investigate the attitudes of the scholars towards corruption. This study specifically attempts to answer the following aspects.

- o Whether there is any difference in the attitudes of male and female scholars towards corruption.
- o Whether there is any difference in the attitudes of M.Phil. and Ph.D. scholars towards corruption.
- o Whether there is any difference in the attitude of scholars who came from different locality towards corruption.

- o Whether there is any difference in the attitude of scholars who belongs to different religions towards corruption.
- o Whether there is any difference in the attitude of scholars who belongs to different castes towards corruption.
- o Whether there is any difference in the attitude of scholars who belongs to different annual income categories.

Method of Investigation

The study is conducted on a sample of 200 scholars (100 male and 100 female scholars)

Limitations of the Study

- o The study is limited only to the scholars of M.Phil. and Ph.D. scholars in the University.
- o The study is limited only in Tirupati city.
- o Student of M.Tech. are not included in this study.
- o Professors, students, other staff members and administrators are not included for the purpose of this study.

Variables

There are seventeen variables in this investigation. But the present investigation is chiefly concerned with sex, course of study, annual income, educational qualification of father, educational qualification mother, educational qualification of scholar, scholarship holder, occupation of mother, occupation of father, religion, caste and native place (locality).

- o **Course of study**

  According to course of study M.Phil. and Ph.D. scholars were taken.
- o **Sex**

  According to sex male and female scholars were taken.
- o **Annual Income**

  According to annual income, Rs. up to 12,000, 12,000-25,000, 25,000-1 lakh and above one loch were included.
- o **Educational qualification father**

  According to educational qualification of father, Illiterate, up to X class, Graduate and Professional were included.

- **Educational qualification of mother**
  According to educational qualification of mother, Illiterate, up to X class, Graduate and Professional were included.
- **Educational qualification of scholar**
  According educational qualification of scholar M. A./M.Com., M.Sc., M/Phil. and Ph.D. were included.
- **Scholarship holder**
  According to scholarship holder yes or no were included.
- **Occupation of father**
  According to occupation of father, Labour, Caste occupation, Below gazetted and Gazetted were included.
- **Occupation of mother**
  According to occupation of mother, Labour/House wife and Employee were included,
- **Religion**
  According to religion Christian, Muslim and Hindu were included.
- **Caste**
  According to caste SC/ST, BC and OC were included.
- **Native place**
  According to native place, Village, Mandal Head Quarters/ Small towns and Municipal town were included.

Hypotheses

1. There would be no significant difference between male and female scholars towards corruption.
2. There would be no significant difference between M.Phil. and Ph.D. scholars towards corruption.
3. There would be no significant difference between scholars under the variable scholarship holder towards corruption.
4. There would be no significant difference between scholars under the variable mother occupation towards corruption.
5. There would be no significant difference among scholars under the variable educational qualification of scholar towards corruption.

6. There would be no significant difference among scholars under the variable annual income towards corruption.
7. There would be no significant difference among scholars under the variable educational qualification of father towards corruption.
8. There would be no significant difference among scholars under the variable educational qualification of mother towards corruption.
9. There would be no significant difference among scholars under the variable occupation of father towards corruption.
10. There would be no significant difference among scholars under the variable religion towards corruption.
11. There would be no significant difference among scholars under the variable caste towards corruption.
12. There would be no significant difference among scholars under the variable native place towards corruption.

Conclusion

The Problem taken by the investigator is very interesting. It is much and should to know about "CORRUPTION". If we destroyed the corruption in the society automatically development takes place in the country. So I request everyone tell about corruption to others.

4

Methods of Investigation

An attitude scale, specially constructed for the purpose of the study was used for collecting the data.

Before describing the method used in the construction of the attitude scale, it may not be out of the place of discuss the meaning of the term 'attitude' and its nature.

Meaning of Attitude

In the dictionary of philosophy and psychology, Baldwin (1905) defined attitude as "readiness for attention or action of a definite sort".

Allport (1929) prefers to treat attitude as a mental and neutral state, a directive or dynamic influence upon the individuals' response to all objects and situations with which it is related. This definition stresses that attitude in a generalized pattern of perception or action which is the result of an integration of various experiences.

From the point of view of Gestalt psychology, a change of attitude involves a definite physiology stress exerted upon a sensory field by processes originated in other parts of the nervous system (Kohler, 1929).

According to BOGARDUS (1931), ATTITUDE IS "tendency to act for or again something in the environment which becomes thereby positive or negative value".

"Attitudes are literally mental postures and guides for conduct to which each new experience is referred before a response is made" (Morgan, 1935).

In the dictionary of psychology, attitude is defined as "the specific mental disposition toward an incoming (or arising) experience, where by that experience is modified or a condition of readiness for a certain type of activity" (Warren. 1934).

According to the dictionary of education (Good, 1945), an attitude is "a state of mental and emotional readiness to react to react to situations, persons, or things in a manner in harmony with these stimuli".

Guilford (1954) defined attitude as a personal disposition common to individuals, but possessed to different degrees, which impulse them to react to objects, situations, or propositions in the way that can be called favourable or unfavourable".

In attitude is a dispositional readiness to respond to certain situations, persons, or objects in a constant manner which has been learned and has become ones' typical mode of response (Freeman, 1964).

English and English (1958) defined attitude as "an enduring learned predisposition to behave in a consistent way towards a consistent way towards a given class of objects".

In the words of Kerechet al.962), the attitude is pro-enduring system of positive or negative evaluations, emotional feelings and process action tendencies with respect to a social object.

All definitions cited above give importance to the degree of 'liking' or 'disliking' towards a psychological object and in line with the above, Thurstone (1946) defined attitude as "the degree of positive or negative affect associated with some psychological object".

Though attitude and opinions are related terms they are not synonymous. Attitude is the inner feeling or belief of a person towards a psychological phenomenon, whereas opinion is what a person says out his attitude towards the phenomenon. Opinion is therefore, a verbal expression of attitude.

Dimensions of Attitudes

In addition to being predisposition's to respond to social objects, attitudes have been said to possess the following general characteristics.

- o Attitudes are based upon evaluative concepts regarding motivated characteristics of the referent object and give rise to behaviour (Anderson and Fishbein, 1965).
- o Attitudes are constructed as verifying in quality and intensity on a continuum from positive through neutral to negative (Krech et al., 1962 and McGroth, 1964).
- o Attitudes are learned rather than being innate or a result of constitutional development and maturation (Sharif and Sharif, 1956; New Comb et al., 1959).
- o Attitudes possess the varying degree of interrelatedness to one another (Krech et al., 1962 and McGrowth, 1964).
- o Attitudes have specific social referents or specific classes there of (Kerech et al., 1962 and McGroth, 1964).
- o Attitudes are relatively stable and enduring (Newcomb et al., 1965 and Sharif, 1956).

Construction of the Attitude Scale

For the purpose of the present investigation, an attitude scale for the problem of "An Analytical Study of Scholars towards Corruption". The attitude scale was used, as the students were educated and intelligent enough to give correct responses without any chance of inhabitation or resistance on their part.

The two popular and useful methods of measuring attitudes indirectly were Thurstone techniques of scale values and Likert's Method of summarized ratings. Likert's method of summed rating was used in this investigation as most of the following advantages:

- o Greater easy preparation.
- o The method is based entirely on empirical data regarding student's responses rather than subjective opinions of judges.

- This method produces more homogenous scales and increases the probability that unitary attitude is being measures.
- Provide more information about the student's attitude.

While constructing the attitude scale, the suggestions given by the experts in the field were considered. The summary of the suggestions were as given below:

- Avoid that statement refers to the past rather than to the present.
- Avoid statements that are factual or capable of being interpreted as factual.
- Avoid statements that may be interpreted in more than one way.
- Avoid statements that are irrelevant to the psychological object under consideration.
- Avoid statements that are believed to cover the entire range of the effective scale of interest.
- Select statements that are believed to cover the entire range of the effective scale of interest.
- Keep the language of the statements simple, clear and direct.
- Statement should be short, rarely executing twenty words.
- Each statement should contain only one complete thought.
- Statement containing universal such as "all", "always" "none" and "never" often those introduce ambiguity and should be avoided.
- Words such as "only", "just", "nearly" and "others" of a singular nature should be used with care and moderation in writing statements.
- Whenever possible statements should be in the form of simple sentences rather than in the form of compound or complex sentences.
- Avoid the use of words that may not be understood by those who are to be given in the complete scale.
- Avoid the use of double negative.

The following main aspects of value oriented education were taken into consideration for the preparation of the individual statements in the attitude scale.

- o Purpose and functions of value oriented education
- o Nature of value oriented education
- o Approaches to value oriented education
- o Inculcation of values
- o Physical aspects of value oriented education

Bearing the above important aspects of test system in mind as a first step in the development of this questionnaire, a number if items (opinions) that are related to value oriented education were collected from the released literature and a large pool of ninety items were prepared. The pool of items, thus collected was refined by observing the criteria lay down by different authors like Likets (1932), Edwards and Kilpatrick (1954) and others.

- o The statements must be clear, precise and straightforward.
- o They should be short and to the point.
- o They must be constructed as expressions of desired behaviour not as statements of fact.
- o Double barred statements should be removed.
- o They must be in a form that the ideas can be accepted or rejected.
- o Both favourable and unfavourable statements should be included.
- o Statements that could be endorsed by everyone or none must be avoided.
- o Positive and negative statements must be arranged randomly throughout the attitude scale so that any space error may be avoided.

Thus refined item pool was presented to the ten experienced male and female teachers who were requested to:

- o Add the statements that might be relevant to the subject
- o Point out redundant statement.
- o Mark ambiguous and double barreled items, if any.
- o Give suggestions for refining the items.

Their suggestions were incorporated and seventy items were selected to be included in the preliminary form. The items were randomized each of the items was arranged on a five point scale with alternatives viz., Strongly Agree (SA), Agree (A), Doubtful (D), Disagree (DA) and Strongly Disagree (SD).

Different Methods of Measuring Attitudes

Attitude can be measured in several ways. Attitudes are revealed in the behaviour of an individual. So they can be measured by direct observation of overt behaviour of the individual this method, needless to point out has all the defects of observation. In addition to the difficult of experimentally creating a stimulated situation where on the behaviour can be observed.

Distinguished techniques like error technique (Hammond, 1848) sentence completion technique (Karr, 1943), story and argument completion techniques (Murray and Margpm. 1945), pictorial techniques (Smith, 1954) can also be used to assess on individuals attitudes. The basis for the use of protective techniques to measure attitude is that attitudes can be inferred by one's unconsciousness responses certain stimuli like photographs, cartoons, etc. This method's to all the disadvantages of projective technique like, difficulty in administration scoring, low inter scores, reliability etc.

The most common method of obtaining an estimate a Person's attitude is through an attitude scale. In this technique, the individual is asked to exams this opinion on several controversial statements about the psychological object under consideration. The logic behind the use of opinion to measure attitude is that they will do about it. To the extent people's actions correlated with the expressed opinion. We can naturally predict the former from the later, any single statement of opinion and any single action, however, will be extremely unreliable from the point of view of measurement. Further, though a Pearson's particular actions cannot be predicted with high degree accuracy, one's position on an attitude from expressed opinion is also subject to some limitations like faking of the response by the individual, where he tends to give socially acceptable responses there by concealing his real attitude. Nevertheless, this could be overcome in several ways like making the questionnaire anonymous, giving concealed statements etc. There are various methods of contracting attitudes scale some of them are:

- o Methods of equal appearing intervals (Thurstone, 1929)
- o Methods of grades dichotomists (Saffir,1937)
- o Methods of summated rating (Likert, (1937)
- o Scalogram analysis (Guttaman, 1944)
- o Scale discrimination technique (Edwards and Kilpatrick, 1948)
- o Unfolding technique (Combs, 1950)
- o Method of unfolding partial rank order (Banta, 1961)
- o Latent structure analysis (Lazarsfield, 1950) and
- o Semantic differential (Osgood et al., 1957)

Among these, the most well known procedures are:

1. ***Thurstone's*** methods of equal appearing intervals
2. ***Likert's*** methods of summated ratings.

An overwhelming majority of scales have been developed by either of these techniques. According to Shaw and Wright (1967), this is probably a result of the greater complexity of the newer procedures.

In this study, Likert's (1932) method of summated ratings is used because it is for easier than Thurston's method, but at the time yields scores very similar measure of attitude obtained by the two method was as high as 0.92 (Edwards and Henry, 1946 and Edwards, 1948).

Development of Instrument Selection of items for Attitude Scale

To select different items for construction of attitude scale number of books and newspapers articles dealing with attitudes of corruption were reviewed and views expressed by different persons were collected in the form of statements. All the opinions thus obtained were pooled for coming-up into conclusion.

All statements thus obtained were pooled and then item pool was gone through by two judges. Sixty three statements were thought most appropriate for the purpose were selected and included in the preliminary form. The statements were translated into Telugu, the regional language of Andhra Pradesh, so that the students who have passed in Telugu medium do not have any difficulty in understanding the statements.

The sixty three statements thus selected were randomized to avoid response, set on the part of respondents. Each statement was arranged on a five-point scale, Strongly Agree (SA), Agree (A), Doubtful (D), Disagree (DA) and Strongly Disagree (SDA).

TABLE: 1 Weightage had given to the five alternatives responses in the scale to measure the Scholars' Attitude towards Corruption

Type of Management	Strongly Agree	Agree	Doubtful	Disagree	Strongly Disagree
Positive	5	4	3	2	1
negative	1	2	3	4	5

In this questionnaire, the negative questions are 7,8,9,12,14,18, 20,24,25,29,31,35,37,43,44,48,49, and 57. Remaining are positive questions.

Items analysis was done, validity and reliability of the tool established as following:

Validity

The validity of a psychological tool can visualize in different connotations. The following types of validity were established

Content Validity

This form of validity is established by evaluating the relevance of the lat items and as a whole. The construction of the present instrument items were collected from a large number of scholars and made all possible items was included. Thus, it can be reasonably assumed that the inventory has content validity.

Item Validity

The discriminative power of each the items was established by carrying out item analysis. Thus each of the items could discriminative between those who have a favourable attitude and those who did not have a favoufable attitude making the instrument valid.

Intrinsic Validity

The intrinsic validity of an instrument is defined by Guilford as the amount of true variance in the obtained scores. This is given by the square root of the reliability. The reliability scale was 0.95. Thus, the intrinsic validity of the instrument was 0.95-0.975.

Reliability

The reliability of the attitude scale was established by split half method by correlating the score obtained on the odd items with those obtained on the even items.

Main Study

Sample

The research is proximal time specific and context specific in nature. It will be very difficult for the investigator to take entire population of students studying in all existing universities. Hence, the investigator decided to take random sample to pursue his research work keeping the various variables like sex, course of study, religion, caste and native etc. Investigator conducted the questionnaire on a random sample of 200 scholars.

TABLE: 2 Sample Distribution according to Variables

S.No.	Variables	Number
1.	Sex	
	Male	100
	Female	100
2.	Course of study	
	M.Phil.	38
	Ph.D.	162
3.	Scholarship holder	
	No	122
	Yes	78
4.	Mother occupation	
	Labour/House wife	191
	Employee	9
5.	Educational qualification of scholar	
	M.A/M.Com.,	59
	M.Sc.,	95
	M.Phil.	20
	B.Ed.,	26
6.	Annual income	
	Up to 12,000 Rupess	104
	12,000-25,000	30
	25,000-1 lakh	42
	Above 1 lakh	24
7.	Educational qualification of father	
	Illiterate	39

	Up to X class	74
	Graduate	54
	Professional	33
8.	Educational qualification of mother	
	Illiterate	91
	Up to X class	81
	Graduate	23
	Professional	5
9.	Occupation of father	
	Labour	33
	Caste occupation	84
	Below gazetted	49
	Gazetted	34
10.	Religion	
	Christian	6
	Muslim	7
	Hindu	189
11	Caste	
	SC/ST	40
	BC	45
	OC	115
12.	Native place	
	Village	97
	Mandal head quarter/small town	38
	Municipal town	65

Administration

The attitude scale was administered to the sample of subject in groups of scholars in the university.

Before distributing the questionnaire, the subjects were informed about the nature and significance of the work. They were informed about the nature and significance of the work.

The attitude scale is self-administering. Nevertheless the instructions where read aloud to the subject while they read themselves as given in the attitude scale.

As there were 63 statements, the score of an individual could vary between 63 and 315 with neutral point 189.

According to Krech et al. (1962), McGrawth (1964), New Comb, Tunner and Converse (1965) attitude may be constructed as varying in quality and intensity on a continuum form positive through neutral to negative. The strength of an attitude is represented by the extremity of the position occupied by it on the continuum, becoming stronger as it goes outward from neutral position. But the neutral point of the attitude continuum possesses a problem with regard to its meaning and interpretation, to which several alternative solutions have been proposed.

First, one may consider the statement that an attitude is neutral is to self-contradictory indication the presence of a response predisposition on the hand and the lack of predisposition on the other. From this point of view, the neutral position on the attitude continuum represents to attitude towards the object in question (Show Wright, 1967).

The interpretation supports the idea of Krech and Crutchfield (1948) that, "Attitude always have either a positive or negative sign if they have now sign. They cannot be called attitudes at all".

The second alternative interpretation suggested by Show and Wright (1967) is that which represents conflict, thereby reflecting an ambivalent attitude the point of balance in the positive, negative, evaluative where ambivalent is used to indicate the existence of two or more attitudes towards the same referent or several referents possessing some degree of similarity of stimulus value and being grouped as a referent class.

A mean score above the neutral point indicates that the scholars with high positive attitude towards corruption. It is needless to point out, that a mean score of say 191 just two point above the neutral point does not indicate positive attitude towards corruption, as the little difference between the mean and neutral point may be due to error variance that is bound to occur in any investigation, more so in educational and psychological research.

Statistical Analysis

The data relating to the attitude score of scholars towards corruption has been summarized in a data sheet for 200 scholars according to departments, sex, religion and native. Appropriate coding was given to facilitate statistical calculations. The data is entered in excel work sheet and the analysis is done by using S.P.S.S. (Statistical Package for Social Science) software.

The mean score between two groups are compared using't' test. The mean score, S.D., mean difference and the 't' value statistics have been reported in the results and significant difference between the mean scores at 0.05, 0.01 levels. The mean score among groups (more than two groups) are compared with 'F' test. The mean score, S.D., mean difference and the 'F' value have been reported in the results and significant difference among the mean scores at 0.05, 0.01 levels.

Conclusion

The selection of method of investigation is very important. The investigator should take care in selection of method of investigation. For my topic "An Analytical Study of Attitude of Scholars towards Corruption" I had taken Five Point Scale.

5

Analysis and Discussions

The results and discussions are analyzed in this chapter for the scores obtained.

Distributions Characteristics of the Attitudinal Scores of Scholars towards Corruption

The present investigation was conducted to study an attitude of scholars towards corruption.

The total attitudinal score of the each individual is calculated and presented in the form of frequency distribution.

TABLE 1 : Frequency Distribution of Attitudinal Score of Total Scholars Towards Corruption

S.No.	CI	MP	F	CF
1.	210-219	214.5	4	4
2.	220-229	224.5	6	10
3.	230-239	234.5	10	20
4.	240-249	244.5	23	43
5.	250-259	254.5	37	80
6.	260-269	264.5	28	108
7.	270-279	274.5	44	152
8.	280-289	284.5	31	183
9.	290-299	294.5	14	197
10.	300-309	304.5	3	200

Mean	= 264.92
Median	= 267.00
Mode	= 272.00
SD	= 19.49
Skewness	= -0.353
Kurtosis	= .298
Q1	= 252.25
Q3	= 279.00
Q.D	= 13.375

From the table it is clear that the mean scores of scholars towards corruption for total sample 200 is 264.92. Since Mean, Median, Mode are not same, the curve not be a normal, the kurtosis obtained is .298 is slightly greater than 0.263. The peak of the curve is platy. In this distribution mean is less than Median. So the skewness is negative. The peak is shifted towards left.

FIG. 1 : Bar Graph showing the Frequency Attitudinal Scores of Total Scholars towards Corruption

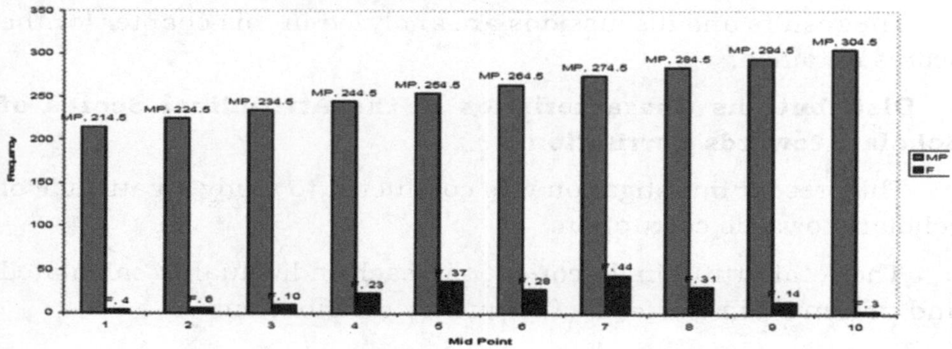

FIG. 2 : Frequency Polygon showing the Frequency Attitudinal Scores of Total Scholars towards Corruption

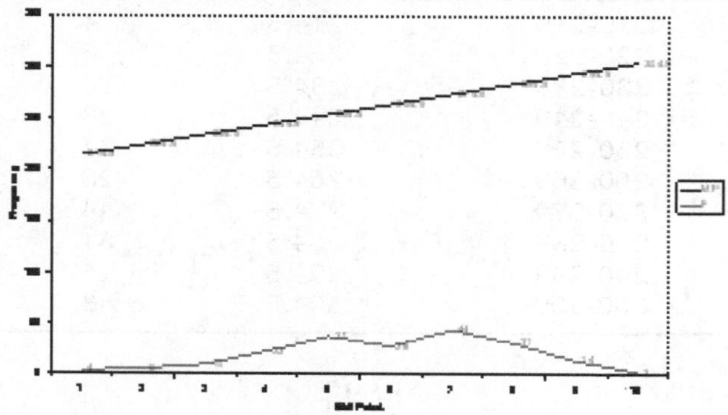

TABLE 2 : Frequency Distribution of Attitudinal Scores of Male Scholars towards Corruption

S.No.	CI	MP	F	CF
1	210-219	214.5	1	1
2	220-229	224.5	4	5
3	230-239	234.5	3	8
4	240-249	244.5	11	19
5	250-259	254.5	24	43
6	260-269	264.5	19	62
7	270-279	274.5	17	89
8	280-289	284.5	13	92
9	290-299	294.5	6	98
10	300-309	304.5	2	100

Mean = 264.00
Median = 264.00
Mode = 255.00
SD = 18.481
Skewness = 0.336
Kurtosis = 0.054
Q1 = 253
Q3 = 278
Q.D = 12.5

From the table it is clear that the mean scores of male scholars towards corruption for total sample 100 is 264.00. Since Mean, Median, Mode are not same, the curve not be a normal, the kurtosis obtained is .336 is greater than 0.263. The peak of the curve is platy.

FIG. 3 : Bar Graph showing the Frequency Attitudinal Scores of Male Scholars towards Corruption

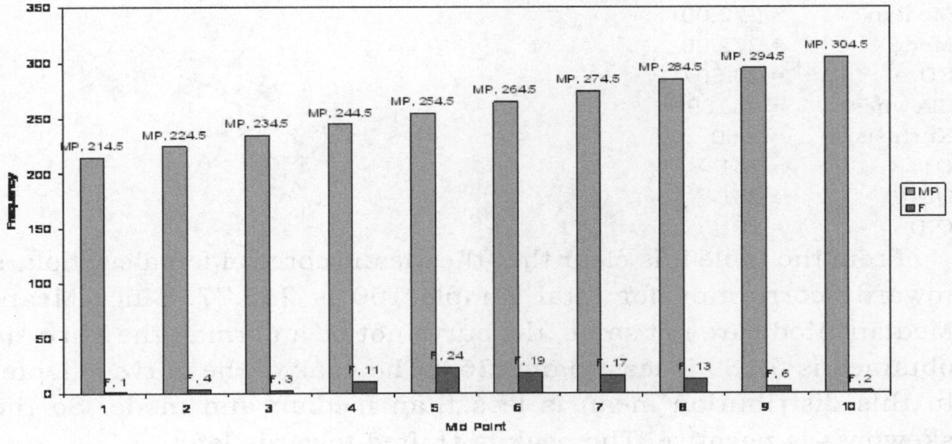

In this distribution mean is equal to median and greater than mode. So the skewness is positive. The peak is shifted towards right.

FIG. 4 : Frequency Polygon showing the Frequency Attitudinal Scores of Male Scholars towards Corruption

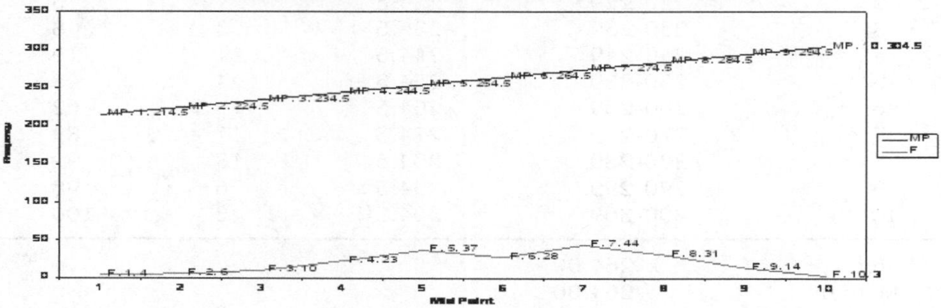

TABLE 3 : Frequency Distribution of Attitudinal Scores of Female Scholars towards Corruption

S.No.	CI	MP	F	CF
1	210-219	214.5	3	3
2	220-229	224.5	2	5
3	230-239	234.5	7	12
4	240-249	244.5	12	24
5	250-259	254.5	13	37
6	260-269	264.5	9	46
7	270-279	274.5	27	73
8	280-289	284.5	18	91
9	290-299	294.5	8	99
10	300-309	304.5	1	100

Mean = 265.77
Median = 272.00
Mode = 272.00
SD = 20.507
Skewness = -0.189
Kurtosis = 0.60
Q1 = 251
Q3 = 281
Q.D = 15

From the table it is clear that the mean scores of female scholars towards corruption for total sample 100 is 265.77. Since Mean, Median, Mode are not same, the curve not be a normal, the kurtosis obtained is 0.189 is less than 0.263. The peak of the curve is lepto. In this distribution mean is less than median and mode. So the skewness is negative. The peak is shifted towards left.

FIG. 5 : Bar Graph Showing Frequency Attitudinal Scores of Female Scholars towards Corruption.

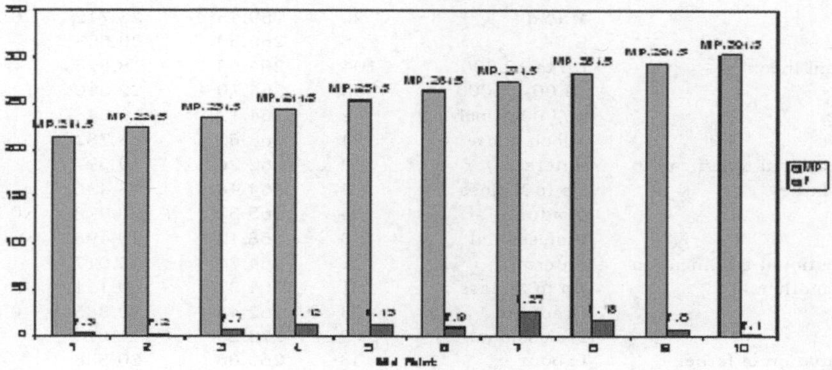

FIG. 6 : Frequency Polygon Showing the Frequency Attitudinal Scores of Female Scholars towards Corruption

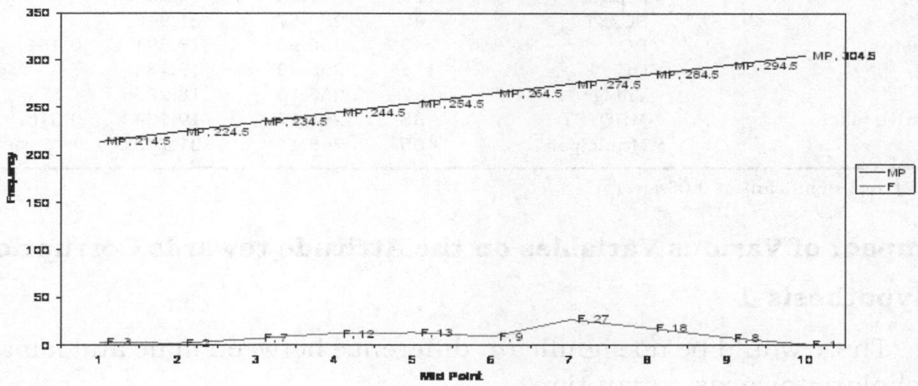

CONSOLIDATED MEANS, SDs, 't' AND 'F' VALUES OF VARIOUS VARIABLES:

TABLE 4 : Means and SDs of different variables and subgroups of scholars towards corruption in respective 't' and 'F' values

Variables	Categories	N	Mean	SD	't' value
Sex	Male	100	264.07	18.481	0.6158
	Female	100	265.77	20.507	@
Course of study	M.Phil.	38	263.76	18.749	0.419
	Ph.D.	162	265.19	19.705	@
Scholarship holder	No	122	265.20	19.356	0.256
	Yes	78	264.47	19.814	@

Variable	Category	N	Mean	SD	
Mother occupation	Labour/HW	191	264.92	19.454	0.004
	Employee	9	264.89	21.444	@
Educational qualification	M.A./M.Com	59	263.36	19.145	'F' value
	M.Sc.	95	266.61	18.439	
	M.Phil.	20	259.45	23.712	0.731
	B.Ed.	26	266.50	20.598	@
Annual income	Up to 12,000	104	264.63	18.825	
	12,00-25,000	30	264.10	22.310	
	25,000-1 loch	42	264.12	19.848	1.223
	1 loch above	24	268.62	18.782	@
Educational qualification of father	Illiterate	39	262.26	19.597	
	Up to X class	74	264.46	18.436	
	Graduate	54	265.52	20.998	0.547
	Professional	33	268.12	19.496	@
Educational qualification of mother	Illiterate	91	264.74	20.017	
	Up to X class	81	265.32	19.151	
	Graduate	23	262.43	20.385	0.390
	Professional	5	273.20	11.670	@
Occupation of father	Labour	33	260.06	20.538	
	Caste occu	84	265.99	17.786	
	Below Gazetted	49	264.59	20.866	1.487
	Gazetted	34	267.47	20.476	@
	Christian	6	265.00	22.307	
Religion	Muslim	7	267.29	25.519	0.29
	Hindu	189	264.88	19.282	@
	SC/ST	40	259.57	21.945	
Caste	BC	45	266.93	17.591	0.454
	OC	115	265.99	19.134	@
	Village	97	265.19	18.205	
Native place	MHQ/ST	38	263.87	19.154	0.546
	Municipal T	65	265.14	21.703	@

@ -'t' not significant at 0.05 level

Impact of Various Variables on the Attitude towards Corruption

Hypothesis-1

There would be no significant difference between male and female scholars towards corruption.

The above hypothesis is tested by employing 't' test and the results are shown in the table.

TABLE 5 : Mean and SDs of Attitudinal Scores of Scholars towards Corruption under the Variable Sex

Sex	N	Mean	SD	't' value
Male	100	264.04	18.481	0.6158
Female	100	265.77	20.507	@

@ 't' not significant at 0.05 level

It is clear from the table that the calculated 't' value 0.6158 is less than the table value 197 for 198 df at 0.05 level. It is not significant at 0.05 level. Hence, the null hypothesis is accepted. It is concluded that there is no significant difference between male and female scholars towards corruption.

FIG. 7 : Bar Graph Showing the Mean Attitudinal Scores of Male and Female Scholars towards Corruption

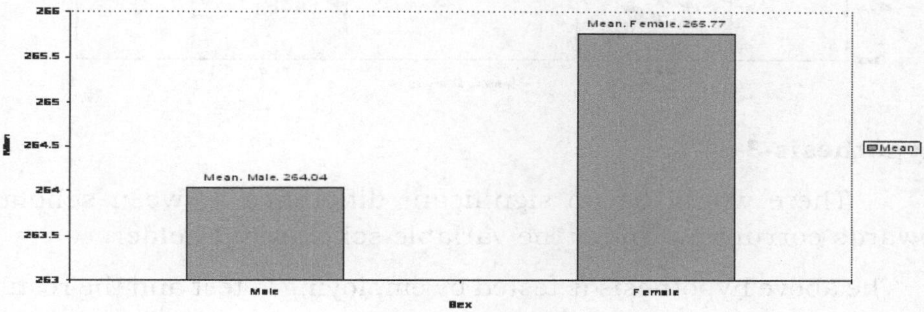

Hypothesis-2

There would be no significant difference between M.Phil. and Ph.D. scholars towards corruption.

The above hypothesis is tested by employing 't' test and the results are shown in the table.

Table 6 : Mean and SDs of Attitudinal Scores of Scholars towards Corruption under the Variable Course of Study

Course of study	N	Mean	SD	't' value
M.Phil.	38	263.76	18.749	0.419
Ph.D.	162	265.19	19.705	@

@ 't' not significant at 0.05 level

It is clear from the table that the calculated 't' value 0.419 is less than the table value 197 for 198 df at 0.05 level. It is not significant at 0.05 level. Hence, the null hypothesis is accepted. It is concluded that there is no significant difference between scholars towards corruption under the variable course of study.

FIG. 8 : Bar Graph showing the Mean Attitudinal Scores of Scholars under the variable Course of Study towards Corruption

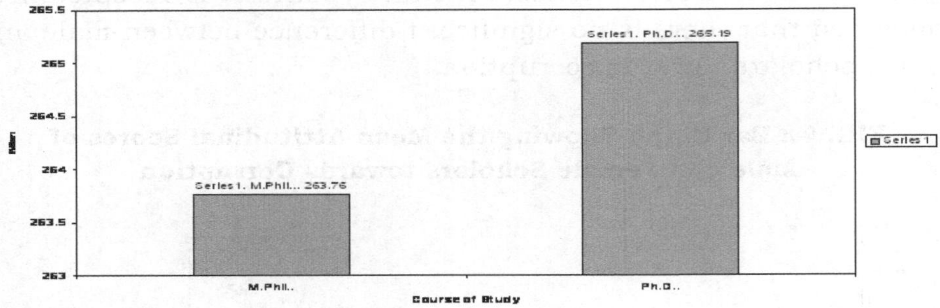

Hypothesis-3

There would be no significant difference between scholars towards corruption under the variable scholarship holder.

The above hypothesis is tested by employing 't' test and the results are shown in the table.

TABLE 7 : Mean and SDs of Attitudinal Scores of Scholars towards Corruption under the Variable Scholarship Holder

SSH	N	Mean	SD	't' value
No	122	265.20	19.356	0.256
Yes	78	264.47	19.814	@

@ 't' not significant at 0.05 level

It is clear from the table that the calculated 't' value 0.256 is less than the table value 197 for 198 df at 0.05 level. It is not significant

FIG. 9 : Bar Graph showing the Mean Attitudinal Scores of Scholars towards Corruption under the variable Scholarship Holder

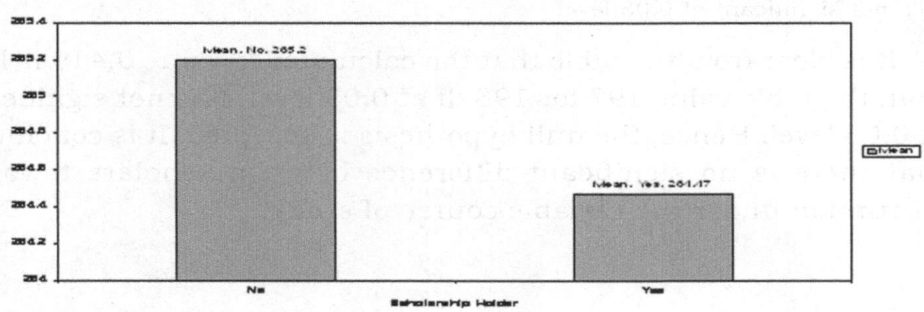

at 0.05 level. Hence, the null hypothesis is accepted. It is concluded that there is no significant difference between scholars towards corruption under the variable scholarship holder.

Hypothesis-4

There would be no significant difference between scholars towards corruption under the variable mother occupation.

The above hypothesis is tested by employing 't' test and the results are shown in the table.

TABLE 8 : Mean and SDs of Attitudinal Scores of Scholars towards Corruption under the Variable Mother Occupation

Mother Occu	N	Mean	SD	't' value
Labour/HW	191	264.92	19.454	0.004
Employee	9	264.89	21.444	@

@ 't' not significant at 0.05 level

It is clear from the table that the calculated 't' value 0.004 is less than the table value 197 for 198 df at 0.05 level. It is not significant at 0.05 level. Hence, the null hypothesis is accepted. It is concluded that there is no significant difference between scholars towards corruption under the mother occupation.

FIG. 10 : Bar diagram showing the Mean Attitudinal Scores of Scholars towards Corruption under the variable Mother Occupation

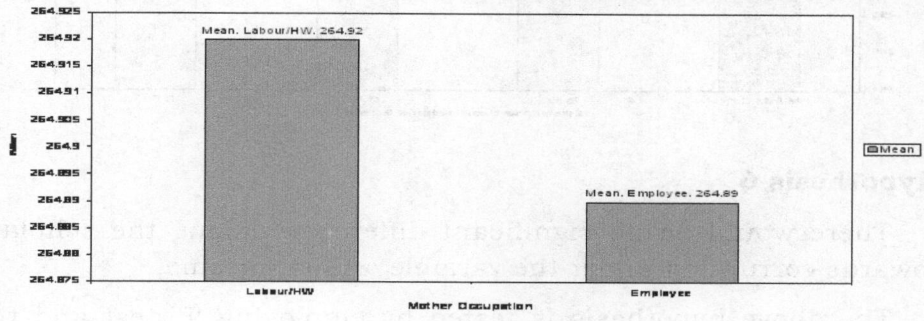

Hypothesis-5

There would be no significant difference among the scholars towards corruption under the variable educational qualification.

The above hypothesis is tested by employing 'F' test and the results are shown in the table.

TABLE 9: Summary of Analysis of variance (ANOVA) for the attitudinal scores of scholars towards corruption under the variable educational qualification of scholars

Score	SS	df	MS	'F' value
Between groups	99237.121	3	33079.040	
Within groups	8871832	196	45264.447	0.731
Total	8971069	199		@

@ 'F' not significant at 0.05 level.

It is clear from the table that the calculated 'F' value 0.731 is less than the table value2.65 for 3 and 196 df at 0.05 level. It is not significant at 0.05 level. Hence, the null hypothesis is accepted. It is concluded that there is no significant difference among scholars towards corruption under the variable educational qualification.

FIG. 11 : Bar Diagram showing the Mean Attitudinal Scores of different Scholars towards Corruption under the variable Educational Qualification of Scholars

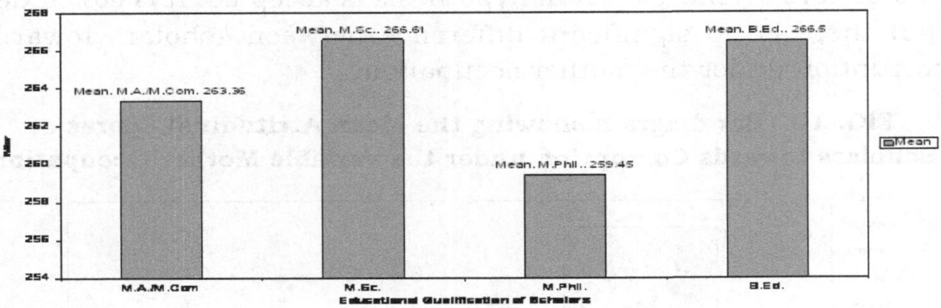

Hypothesis-6

There would be no significant difference among the scholars towards corruption under the variable annual income.

The above hypothesis is tested by employing 'F' test and the results are shown in the table.

It is clear from the table that the calculated 'F' value 1.223 is less than the table value2.65 for 3 and 196 df at 0.05 level. It is not significant at 0.05 level. Hence, the null hypothesis is accepted. It is concluded that there is no significant difference among scholars towards corruption under the variable annual income.

TABLE 10 : Summary of Analysis of Variance (ANOVA) for the Attitudinal Scores of Scholars towards Corruption under the Variable Annual Income

Score	SS	df	MS	'F' value
Between groups	1648656	3	54955.205	
Within groups	8806203	196	44929.608	1.223
Total	8971069	199		@

@ 'F' not significant at 0.05 level.

FIG. 12 : Bar Diagram showing the Mean Attitudinal Scores of Scholars towards Corruption under the variable Annual Income

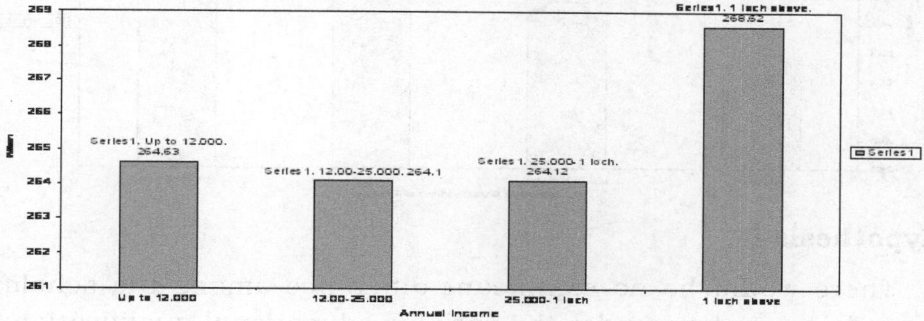

Hypothesis-7

There would be no significant difference among the scholars towards corruption under the variable educational qualification of father.

The above hypothesis is tested by employing 'F' test and the results are shown in the table.

TABLE 11 : Summary of Analysis of Variance (ANOVA) for the Attitudinal Scores of Scholars towards Corruption under the Variable Educational Qualification of Father

Score	SS	df	MS	'F' value
Between groups	74508287	3	24836.096	
Within groups	8896560	196	45390.614	0.547
Total	8971069	199		@

@ 'F' not significant at 0.05 level.

It is clear from the table that the calculated 'F' value 0.547 is less than the table value2.65 for 3 and 196 df at 0.05 level. It is not significant at 0.05 level. Hence, the null hypothesis is accepted. It is concluded that there is no significant difference among scholars towards corruption under the variable educational qualification of father.

FIG. 13: Bar Diagram showing the Mean Attitudinal Scores of Scholars towards Corruption under the variable Educational Qualification of Father

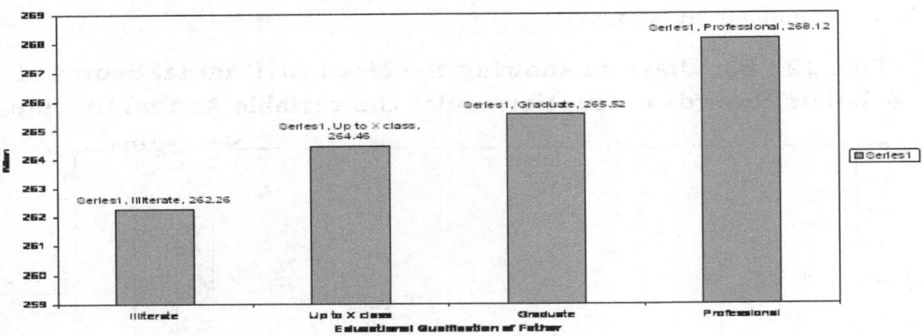

Hypothesis-8

There would be no significant difference among the scholars towards corruption under the variable educational qualification of mother. The above hypothesis is tested by employing 'F' test and the results are shown in the table.

TABLE 12 : Summary of Analysis of Variance (ANOVA) for the Attitudinal Scores of Scholars towards Corruption under the Variable Educational Qualification of Mother

Score	SS	df	MS	'F' value
Between groups	53299.624	3	17766.541	
Within groups	8917769	196	45498.822	0.390
Total	8971069	199		@

@ 'F' not significant at 0.05 level.

It is clear from the table that the calculated 'F' value 0.390 is less than the table value 2.65 for 3 and 196 df at 0.05 level. It is not significant at 0.05 level. Hence, the null hypothesis is accepted. It is concluded that there is no significant difference among scholars towards corruption under the variable educational qualification of mother.

FIG. 14 : Bar Diagram showing the Mean Attitudinal Scores of Scholars towards Corruption under the variable Educational Qualification of Mother

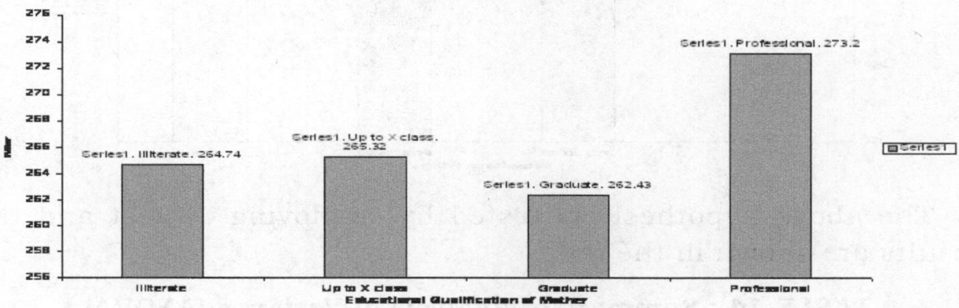

Hypothesis-9

There would be no significant difference among the scholars towards corruption under the variable occupation of father.

The above hypothesis is tested by employing 'F' test and the results are shown in the table.

TABLE 13 : Summary of Analysis of Variance (ANOVA) for the Attitudinal Scores of Scholars towards Corruption under the Variable Occupation of Father

Score	SS	df	MS	'F' value
Between groups	199672.5	3	66557.485	
Within groups	8771396	196	44752.022	1.487
Total	8971069	199		@

@ 'F' not significant at 0.05 level.

It is clear from the table that the calculated 'F' value 1.487 is less than the table value 2.65 for 3 and 196 df at 0.05 level. It is not significant at 0.05 level. Hence, the null hypothesis is accepted. It is concluded that there is no significant difference among scholars towards corruption under the variable occupation of father.

Hypothesis-10

There would be no significant difference among the scholars towards corruption under the variable religion.

FIG. 15 : Bar Diagram showing the Mean Scores of Scholars towards Corruption under the variable Occupation of Father

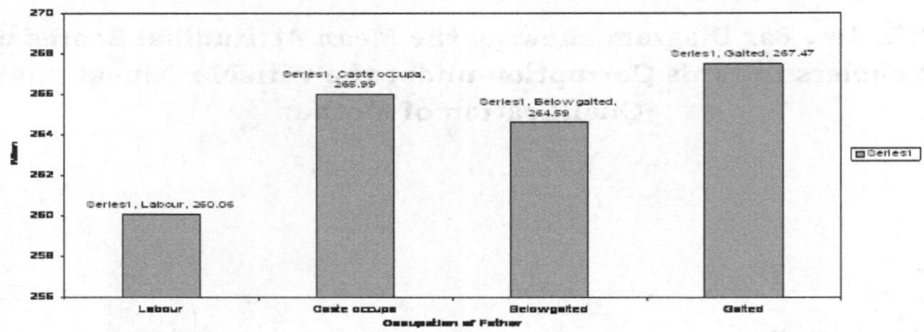

The above hypothesis is tested by employing 'F' test and the results are shown in the table.

TABLE 14 : Summary of Analysis of Variance (ANOVA) for the Attitudinal Scores of Scholars towards Corruption under the Variable Religion

Score	SS	df	MS	'F' value
Between groups	2622.372	2	1311.186	
Within groups	8968446	197	45525.108	0.029
Total	8971069	198		@

@ 'F' not significant at 0.05 level.

It is clear from the table that the calculated 'F' value 0.029 is less than the table value 2.65 for 2 and 197 df at 0.05 level. It is not significant at 0.05 level. Hence, the null hypothesis is accepted. It is concluded that there is no significant difference among scholars towards corruption under the variable religion.

FIG. 16 : Bar Diagram showing the Mean Attitudinal Scores of Scholars towards Corruption under the variable Religion

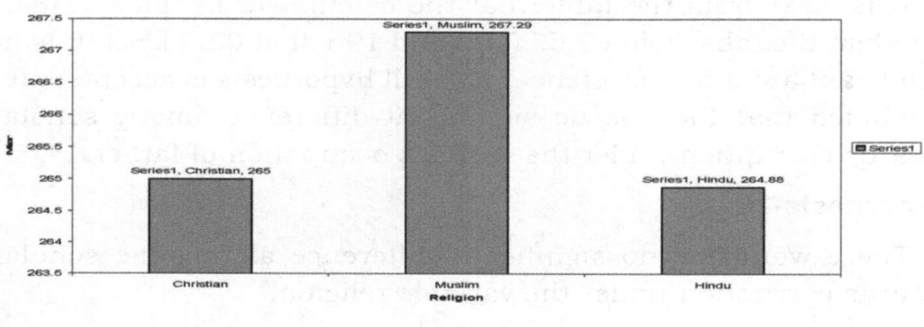

Hypothesis-11

There would be no significant difference among the scholars towards corruption under the variable caste.

The above hypothesis is tested by employing 'F' test and the results are shown in the table.

TABLE 15 : Summary of Analysis of Variance (ANOVA) for the Attitudinal Scores of Scholars towards Corruption under the Variable Caste

Score	SS	df	MS	'F' value
Between groups	41145.849	2	20572.925	
Within groups	8929923	197	45329.558	0.454
Total	8971069	198		@

@ 'F' not significant at 0.05 level.

It is clear from the table that the calculated 'F' value 0.454 is less than the table value 2.65 for 2 and 197 df at 0.05 level. It is not significant at 0.05 level. Hence, the null hypothesis is accepted. It is concluded that there is no significant difference among scholars towards corruption under the variable caste.

FIG. 17 : Bar Diagram showing the Mean Attitudinal Scores of Scholars towards Corruption under the variable Caste

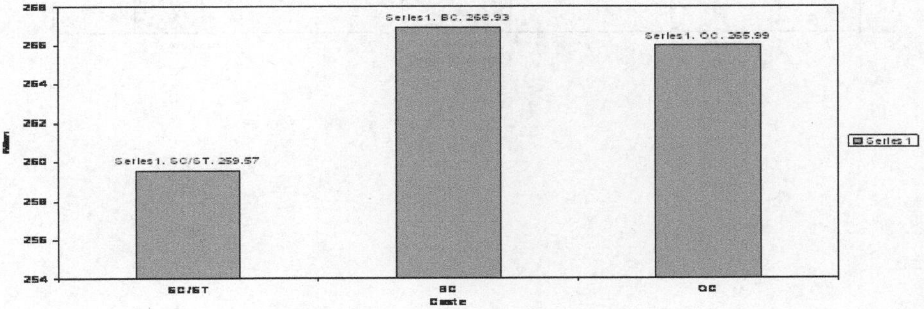

Hypothesis-12

There would be no significant difference among the scholars towards corruption under the variable native place.

The above hypothesis is tested by employing 'F' test and the results are shown in the table.

TABLE 16 : Summary of Analysis of Variance (ANOVA) for the Attitudinal Scores of Scholars towards Corruption under the Variable Native Place

Score	SS	df	MS	'F' value
Between groups	49428.871	2	24714.436	
Within groups	8921640	197	45287.512	0.546
Total	8971069	198		@

@ 'F' not significant at 0.05 level.

It is clear from the table that the calculated 'F' value 0.029 is less than the table value 2.65 for 2 and 197 df at 0.05 level. It is not significant at 0.05 level. Hence, the null hypothesis is accepted. It is concluded that there is no significant difference among scholars towards corruption under the variable native place.

FIG. 18 : Bar Diagram showing the Mean Attitudinal Scores of Scholars towards Corruption under the variable Native Place

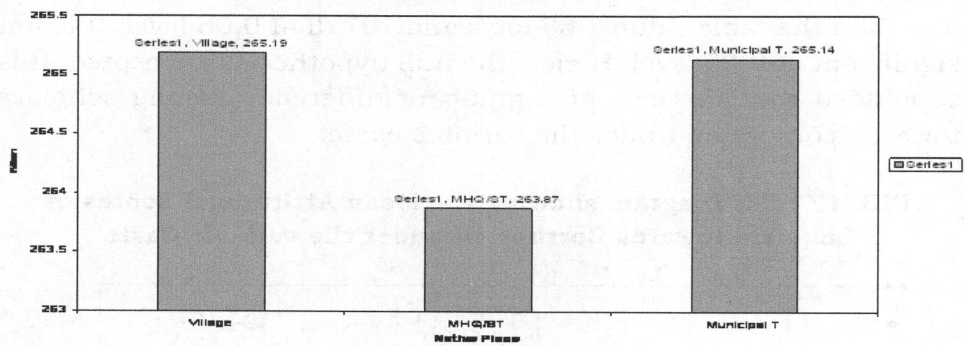

6

Summary, Conclusions and Suggestions

Summary

A shortage of basic decent human life in India has forced a common person to be corrupt. It is impossible for a common man to own a roof, provide good education to his children and hope for a peaceful retirement in India using normal and honest means. One has to bribe someone to get a good education, to get a deserving job and to avail services which one is entitled as being a citizen of India. A two percent growth rate in the GDP for two decades and explosive population growth in the last fifty years has brought corruption to every sphere of life in India. With such a huge population and massive government control, everything seems to be in short supply.

In India, government controls education, means of daily transportation, heavy industry like steel and automobile production, oil and gas production and distribution, public works departments, irrigation, banking, power generation and distribution, water purification and distribution, distribution of basic food commodities to individuals living below the poverty line, defense, hospitals, police, judiciary and dozens of other areas affecting its citizens' day-to-day life. Declining real wages has forced the government employees to use their position to extort money from other civilians to fulfill obligations towards their families. Criminalization of politics and poorly qualified politicians has further enabled sometimes forced these employees to misuse their authority. It is common to secure favors in various state and central government by bribing elected politicians. Ministers openly ask government employee to bring huge sums to return favors. A financially lucrative posting and award of government contracts are the big routes to funnel tax payer's money back to ruling party and politician's personal accounts. Domino effect of such bribes can be seen to the lowest level of the society. Government contracts run over budget. Hence the deficits in the government budgets keep on growing. On the other side, contractors performing these jobs squeeze the common labor to make their profits. Poor roads, inadequate drinking water supply in villages and acute housing shortage in various cities are few of a long list resulting from such government controlled environment. Farmers have to bribe government controlled bank officials to get an approval for a loan to buy tractors or other machinery. One has to bribe another set of government employees to get permits and basic supplies needed for developing any personnel and commercial property. Poor infrastructure and underdevelopment of villages is a direct result of such government control. Government's total failure in power generation and distribution has substantially added to such underdevelopment.

Corruption has also seeped in the poorly paid police and the judiciary system. Traffic laws in India seem to be the worst in the world. One can bribe a government official to get a driver's license without even taking a driving test. A small bribe on the spot to a traffic policeman can save a traffic ticket or a court trip. Most of the government controlled schools and colleges run short of teachers and other staff. Most of the teachers at the school level almost force students to take private lessons from them by avoiding any teaching in the schools. Colleges are run by poorly qualified or without any teachers at all. Poor quality of education provided in the government schools has forced individuals to pursue private schools out of their financial reach. This further forces individuals in power to be more corrupt. This in a long run has divided our society in distinct educated and totally illiterate groups.

Seniority or caste based promotions in government controlled jobs force most individuals to take bribes to fulfill their responsibilities otherwise impossible to cater on ever declining wages. With closed economy, quality products are in limited supply. Normal individuals have to bribe someone to buy quality products used in day-to-day life. Basically, such massive government involvement in an ordinary citizen's life has helped corruption to grow leaps and bound. With loose campaign financing rules, millions of rupees are funneled in various political parties' election fund from the major industrial houses. This results in higher prices of the goods used by the general public. Subsidies in the name of poor, which never reach to the one intended, facilitate corruption in more government employees. Government's funding of inefficient steel plants, oil refineries, fertilizer and chemical plants and other massive money losing public sector is a direct result of poorly managed and highly corrupt administration.

Corruption in India cannot be eradicated by questioning ethical standards of its population. Removal of corruption can only be achieved by right macro-economic policies and by reducing government control. Honest political leadership is a must as a first step. Opening the economy for the investors around the world can provide the needed capital. Fresh ideas and entrepreneurial spirit has to replace the beauracratic government control for a wealthier society. Supply of basic commodities has to be higher than the demand for general population to not bribe any government officials. Only skilled entrepreneurs hired by public shareholders can bring the money loosing monster public sector to profitability. An efficient tax collection mechanism supported by computerized revenue reporting systems of individual businesses would be a step in the right direction. Qualified political leadership is required to understand and implement such policies. Most importantly, political will of these leaders will be required to take such actions.

In conclusion, corruption in India exists because of the unfulfillment of the basic needs of the general population. To eradicate corruption, India has to implement right macro-economic policies rather than questioning the ethical standards of its population.

Towards Change

How then do we create change in the system so that it is more responsive to the people, more fulfilling to the employees and more effective for the nation? The following steps should be considered, in order of importance:

1. Reducing the size of the government and privatizing non-essential functions.
2. De-centralizing government functions away from large hierarchical bureaucracies and creating greater local accountability.
3. Simplifying laws, rules and procedures, taking into account the actual needs and practices of the people and creating a greater focus on customer service in public institutions.
4. Simplifying taxation, reducing duties on property taxes and property transfers and creating greater transparency and "buy-in" for the use of tax-proceeds by devolving more taxation and spending to local administration from the center and states
5. Tackling campaign finance reform – realizing that elections today involve large expenditures and creating rules for legal campaign contributions that take this into account while reducing the influence of criminal/black money clear performance-based reward system within the government to create greater incentive for honesty and performance.
6. More effective enforcement and prosecution of the remaining corrupt personnel to increase the cost for the corrupt.

The first fact to realize is that the answer is not more rules and larger bureaucracies, but a more transparent, accountable and responsive system. One option there is simply greater privatization where market demand and competition will drive accountability.

The telephone example is again a good one. If we are fundamentally corrupt, why is it that we do not have to pay a bribe in India to get a mobile phone? How would the situation have been different if mobile phones were to be a government monopoly instead? The answer is simple – in the case of competitive private enterprise, it is in the interests of the private operator to provide greater customer service – it is only in a monopoly where these interests are divergent. Some of these aligning of interests can also happen in semi-private models. In a recent journey on a local bus in Delhi, I was pleased to find courteous service and the conductor making sure that I got a ticket. Later I was told that the driver and conductor now get a percentage of the proceeds and both the quality of service and the revenue that is collected by the government has gone up as a result.

Secondly, a restructuring of government function needs to happen so that there is far greater local accountability. Let us take the example of education. Currently, appointments and administration of teachers for schools are centralized at the level of the entire state. This means that accountability flows into the state level bureaucracy that is itself only accountable to the ministers. Since the ministers are elected, it turns out that the loop of accountability to the consumers is closed only at the highest level. This is inefficient and frustrating at all levels. The teachers find that they are subject to arbitrary transfers by bureaucrats, the end consumers are not in the loop at all of teacher accountability or performance, the ministers find themselves deluged with personal requests for low-level appointments and the bureaucrats find themselves at the mercy of politicians. I recently met one of the senior-most bureaucrats in the state of Rajasthan with a reputation for honesty. A visit to his house showed that he had a very simple lifestyle. However, he was despondent about his lack of ability to make change. “Everything in this system is delegated upwards,” he said. “Even the transfer of a chapprassi will come as an order from the minister.” Clearly, the system serves no one well.

Taxation is another area of reform. Land and property transactions as well as local retail sales remain areas of high black money generation. There was a time when capital gains on sales of property were as high as 66%. No one in their right mind, after holding property for twenty years, would pay 66% of it in tax to the government – especially when the government appeared as a black hole of antagonistic incompetence, serving very little useful purpose. While this has been reduced, property transfers still remain expensive transaction with high stamp duties. Devolving more taxes down to the local community level, where the benefits of the government expenditures are both more visible and more accountable, will also help in this regard.

It is also worth noting that greater prosecution of corrupt officials has been placed last in this list even though it often receives the greatest emphasis from anti-corruption crusaders. This is because enforcement, while necessary, will remain ineffective in tackling the magnitude of the problem in the absence of systematic reform. At the present time, community activism can yield better long-term results when directed towards crafting a more responsive system than simply pursuing a few high-profile enforcement cases.

Similarly, continuing to harp on corruption as simply a moral problem without addressing first the issues of systemic reform exacerbates the problem of corruption rather than helping it. This is because if the problem is that we are corrupt, it becomes very difficult to change anything, since it is obviously very difficult to change who we are as people. It is no surprise that in the light of this belief; very few people in India believe that we can fix the problem of corruption. Realizing that much of it is a problem of the system can be an empowering and actionable idea, even while the road may be long. It is worth remembering that, even with all the problems in the Indian system, it still survives and functions because there remain a remarkable number of honest people trying to do their jobs, despite all the difficulties and disincentives. It is this honesty that we must build on and nourish as we create a blueprint for deep, systematic changes.

Views on Governance

I think definitely there is a need for improved Governance. Nowadays Governance has become a big buzzword ever since in the corporations started going under all kind of misuse coming in so the word corporate Governance has become very fashionable.

Also everybody is aware of the failure of the Governance of Government, as there is a lot of corruption, objectives are not being met, there are slippages and therefore the results don't trickle down. They might have excellent policy but when it comes to implementation it is just not reaching the people for whom it is meant. So everybody becomes very conscious of the need of better Governance by

Government and then I think logically it is coming down to the non-profit sector.

Till now everybody was content that it is going at enormous pace. There was need that government began realizing the need of Ngos to take up some services, which they are not successfully admitting. All of a sudden there was an increased inflow of funds and for that reason people became conscious of funds being properly utilized.

I think today there is far more awareness of the need to give on the part of the better off than there was so many years ago. The question of transparency and accountability started because of inflow of funds and therefore the question of Governance. It is about utilization of funds in not just pure accounting sense but it is also in the sense of achieving objectives.

It is inevitable in the sense that with Globalization coming, we are talking about increased efficiency particularly among corporate sector. Even Indian corporate were pretty content in a protective situation to produce what they want as they knew that there will be always a demand, so with the globalization coming in, competition came in and the also the realization of increasing the efficiency. I think the same thing is happening in the Ngos sector. Till now it was almost taken for granted that the non-profits were synonymous to dedication and commitment and cost flexibility was considered a good norm to achieve the end results. Sometimes the pendulum swung a little too far and lot of inefficiencies of all kind crept in. People tend to take things easy.

There were organizations that got lots of money and some did not so there was this question of having to improve the performance of the organization in order to attract founders. You will only be able to get money only if you are seen by your donors. Today, with more need of funding, NGOs have to raise the money from the public also and public will support you only if they think that you are good and honest.

Governance means are you giving satisfaction to all your stakeholders and not just the donors. Are you meeting all the commitments to your primary constituency, whoever it is? Are you complying with all the laws? Today, one has to look governance in all these lines.

Most of the times the members of governing body are too busy to get deeply involved in the organization. I think that also has to change even though they are voluntary board. They should take more responsibility if they want to be seen as Governing an organization because ultimately the authority rest in the governing body. From there it goes down to all other hierarchies in the organization. So I think definitely there is need and it will come and a lot of corporate practices will start getting incorporated to the extent they are relevant because of the same Globalization. There is a lot of cross-fertilization both internationally and between sectors and all that is going to reflect.

Indian culture is beautiful. World people like Indian culture. Unity in diversity is the special thing of India.

India is the richest country. But Indians are poor. There are many causes for this one viz., illiteracy, lack of communication and old traditions etc.

There are so many books regarding honesty, truth, peace and non-violence. But it is important to implement them. Otherwise there is no use.

If our behaviour is good then only we will see good behaviour in others. My opinion all problems have single solution that is education.

Swamy Vivekananda, Mahatma Gandhi, Nehru, Indira Gandhi, Rajiv Gandhi have given valuable speeches. Those are very important for us.

PROBLEM

From the past, value oriented education is existing in India. It takes diversified changes in the ancient, medieval and modern periods. When India freed from the Britishers in 1947, again various changes occurred in educational system. We studied about many honest persons in Puran and Vedas. At that time each and every person is honest. By increasing population and technology the selfishness of the person increases. It gives so many problems, some research work done on corruption. I liked to know the attitude of scholars towards corruption. So my problem is "The Analytical Study of Attitude of Scholars towards Corruption".

SAMPLE

The sample for the investigation was selected by a multistage stratified random sampling procedure, it consists of 200 scholars. All the scholars belonging to the various departments in the universities like Sri Venkateswara University, Padmavathi Mahila Viswa Vidyalayam and Samskrutha Vidya Peet.

TOOLS AND TECHNIQUES USED

An attitude scale specially designed and administered for the study of the attitude of scholars towards corruption was used to collect the data for the investigation. Present study aims at An Analytical Study of Corruption on different areas. To measure the attitude of scholars investigator used the five point scale comprises of 63 items. Against each of them five alternatives were given. They are SA, A, D, DA, SDA. In the scale among 63 items 19 are negative and all the remaining is positive.

Conclusion

The conclusions drawn from hypothesis is tested were as follows.

Hypothesis-1

An analysis of the mean attitudinal scores of male and female scholars showed that there was no significant difference between two groups with regard to this attitude towards corruption. Both have positive attitude towards corruption but there was no significant difference in this attitude.

Thus, the hypothesis-1 viz., “There was no significant difference between male and female scholars towards corruption” was accepted.

Hypothesis-2

An analysis of the mean attitudinal scores of scholars under the variable course of study showed that there was no significant difference between two groups with regard to this attitude towards corruption. Both have positive attitude towards corruption but there was no significant difference in this attitude.

Thus, the hypothesis-2 viz., “There was no significant difference between M .Phil. And Ph. D. scholars towards corruption” was accepted.

Hypothesis-3

An analysis of the mean attitudinal scores of scholars under the variable scholarship holder showed that there was no significant difference between two groups with regard to this attitude towards corruption. Both have positive attitude towards corruption but there was no significant difference in this attitude.

Thus, the hypothesis-3 viz., "There was no significant difference between scholars under the variable scholarship holder towards corruption" was accepted.

Hypothesis-4

An analysis of the mean attitudinal scores of scholars under the variable mother occupation showed that there was no significant difference between two groups with regard to this attitude towards corruption. Both have positive attitude towards corruption but there was no significant difference in this attitude.

Thus, the hypothesis-4 viz., "There was no significant different between scholars under the variable mother occupation towards corruption" was accepted.

Hypothesis-5

An analysis of the mean attitudinal scores of scholars under the variable educational qualification showed that there was no significant difference among four groups with regard to this attitude towards corruption. Four have positive attitude towards corruption.

Thus, the hypothesis-5 viz., "There was no significant difference among scholars under the variable educational qualification towards corruption" was accepted.

Hypothesis-6

An analysis of the mean attitudinal scores of scholars under the variable annual income showed that there was no significant difference among four groups with regard to this attitude towards corruption. Four have positive attitude towards corruption.

Thus, the hypothesis-6 viz., "There was no significant difference among scholars under the variable annual income towards corruption" was accepted.

Hypothesis-7

An analysis of the mean attitudinal scores of scholars under the variable father educational qualification showed that there was no significant difference among four groups with regard to this attitude towards corruption. Four have positive attitude towards corruption.

Thus, hypothesis-7 viz., "There was no significant difference among scholars under the variable father educational qualification towards corruption" was accepted.

Hypothesis-8

An analysis of the mean attitudinal scores of scholars under the variable mother educational qualification showed that there was no significant difference among four groups with regard to this attitude towards corruption. Four have positive attitude towards corruption.

Thus, hypothesis-8 viz., "There was no significant difference among scholars under the variable mother educational qualification towards corruption" was accepted.

Hypothesis-9

An analysis of the mean attitudinal scores of scholars under the variable father occupation showed that there was no significant difference among four groups with regard to this attitude towards corruption. Four have positive attitude towards corruption.

Thus, the hypothesis-9 viz., "There was no significant difference among scholars under the variable father occupation towards corruption" was accepted.

Hypothesis-10

An analysis of the mean attitudinal scores of scholars under the variable religion showed that there was no significant difference among four groups with regard to this attitude towards corruption. Three have positive attitude towards corruption.

Thus, the hypothesis-10 viz., "There was no significant difference among scholars under the variable religion towards corruption" was accepted.

Hypothesis-11

An analysis of the mean attitudinal scores of scholars under the variable caste showed that there was no significant difference among four groups with regard to this attitude towards corruption. Three have positive attitude towards corruption.

Thus, the hypothesis-11 viz., "There was no significant difference among scholars under the variable caste towards corruption" was accepted.

Hypothesis-12

An analysis of the mean attitudinal scores of scholars under the variable native place showed that there was no significant difference among four groups with regard to this attitude towards corruption. Four have positive attitude towards corruption.

Thus, the hypothesis-12 viz., "There was no significant difference among scholars under the variable native place towards corruption" was accepted.

Educational Implications

The foundation of every state is the education of its youth
– Diogenes

Education is a social process; Education is growth;
Education is not preparation for life; Education is life itself.
– John Dewey

Educated men are as much superior to uneducated men as the living are to the dead. **– Aristotle**

Education is a weapon, whose effect depends on who holds it in his hands and at whom it is aimed. **- Joseph Stalin**

Education is the learning of human souls to what is best, and making what is best out of them? **- John Ruskin**

Education makes people easy to lead, but difficult to drive; easy to govern, but impossible of enslave. **- Henry Peter**

Education means the acquisition of knowledge. There is no short-cut method to quire knowledge. There may be short-cuts to success or wealth or power or even a University degree but not to knowledge.

Curricular Activities

In this investigation; it was found that the study of attitudes of scholars towards Corruption. Due to liberalization, industrialization and globalization rapid changes are occurring in almost all social sciences. The value possessed and their attitudes according to the changes should be known up to date vast changes are occurring in the education. So called philosophical foundations of India are declining day to day with the country in a state of social turbulence, the goals and functions of formal education need to be reassessed and updated. Through education we can change the world.

The Educational implication of corruption through curriculum can be described as follows:

- o By giving a place for corruption in the curriculum.
- o Corruption can be explained through Stories and illustrations.
- o Corruption Education has mainly focused on training and educating civil servants and anti corruption practitioners.
- o By introducing a course on corruption and anti-corruption as part of its Master Degree in Developmental Administration.
- o Giving course training to students on identifying where corruption starts and develop strategies to reduce or eliminate corruption entirely.
- o By educating citizen through direct contact by setting up local offices across the religion.
- o Educate people through posters, advertisements and dramatizations; those are all a part in the curriculum.
- o By telling moral and ethical stories in the class room.
- o Role play of a good story in the lesson.

Co-curricular activities:

- o Arranging excursions, field trips and service camps and making the scholars/students to participate actively in them.
- o Organizing service agencies like JRC, Scouting, NSS, Clubs, Association, etc.
- o Arranging debates, discussions, essay writing competitions etc., on topics like National Integration, Literacy Mission.

- o Celebration birthdays of national leaders, important persons and events.
- o Arranging inter-collegiate and intra-university sports, athletics, games, etc.
- o Dramatization and role play.
- o Making the students responsible in various school managements and college activities-student/scholar participation.
- o Organization of science clubs, literary associations, music centers, recreational centers, adult education programs etc.
- o Organization morning prayers, celebrating certain socio-cultural festivals, anniversaries, school day, teachers' day, parent-teacher association meeting etc.
- o Encouraging values in the students by giving the talented and devoted persons awards, gifts, titles, rolling shields etc.
- o Telling about good stories about values and corruption.
- o Conducting different types of competitions regarding to corruption.
- o Giving suggestion to read good books regarding to corruption.

Limitations

- o In this investigation, an attempt was made to study the attitude of scholars towards corruption as viewed by the scholars themselves.
- o The investigation need not pointed out scholar's attitude with department wise towards corruption.
- o This investigation is done only 200 samples of scholars in Tirupati universities only. An analytical study may be done on large sample scholars' attitude towards corruption.
- o The investigation is done only scholars of M.Phil. and Ph.D.
- o This investigation is done only in Chittoor district.

Suggestions for Further Research

Scholars' attitude towards corruption further research may be done in the following areas.

- o The Attitude of High School children may be studied towards corruption.
- o The Attitude of Junior College Students may be studied towards corruption.
- o The Attitude of Degree College Students may be studied towards corruption.
- o The Attitude of M.Sc., M.Com. and M.A. Students may be studied towards corruption.
- o The Attitude of M.C.A. and M.B.A. Students may be studied towards corruption.
- o The Attitude of Engineering College Students may be studied towards corruption.
- o The investigation may be done in the other district and state.
- o The Attitude of Medical Students may be studied towards corruption.
- o The investigation can be carried out on a large sample belonged to different states in our country.
- o The Attitude in this study confirmed to only scholars but may be extended to various fields like teachers, PMT, TGT, PGTs towards corruption.

Investigator Thought

My opinion Education is a solution for all types of problems in the world. Corruption is difficult to prosecute because it is shrouded in a cloud of secrecy, protected by the very same individuals we consider victims of this crime. This is precisely because most of those who partake on this practice do not see themselves as "victims" nor "accomplices," but rather as business partners closing a "profitable" deal. While they perceive this habit as producing a win-win situation, they do not realize the hidden costs that are borne by society as a whole.

Creating a corruption-free government cannot be done if its citizens are also corrupt. Therefore, fighting corruption must be done by securing a partnership with the people and make them understand that everyone loses when they participate in corrupt practices. By raising their level of awareness about the ills of corruption and the extent of damage that it does to the community, the people themselves will act to eliminate this practice once and for all. Public education must focus on making people realize that everybody has a stake in fighting corruption.

Educating the people can be done using many avenues—the formal education system, religious communities, mass media, or direct face-to-face contact. In India, schools are the targets of an NGO's initiatives to promote moral and ethical education, whose curriculum includes good citizenship and democracy. In Cambodia, a group called "Transparency Task Force" has been formed, composing educators and anti-corruption pundits, which is developing a wide-ranging, counter-corruption curriculum, which will be adopted by the Ministry of Education in its formal educational program. It is based on putting forward traditional moral and ethical values that are advanced by Cambodian folk tales and Buddhist teachings.

In Australia, on the other hand, corruption education has mainly focused on training and educating civil servants and anticorruption practitioners. In 1998, the Australian National University introduced a course on Corruption and Anti-Corruption as part of its Masters Degree in Development Administration. By using its own anti-corruption agency as an example, the ANU course trains its students on identifying where corruption starts and develop strategies to reduce or eliminate corruption entirely.

The content and approach of each curriculum developed in these countries differ precisely because they are personalized to fit the culture and environment of its audience.

So it is important to educate everyone in the world. Then only all the people in the world live happy. So "each one teach one" is necessary for now a days.

REFERENCES

1. **Ahmed. B**. et. at. (1992). "Government Malpractices" Report of the Task Forces on Bangladesh: Development Strategies for 1990s. Vol. 2. Dhaka: University Publishers Limited (UPL), pp. 389-407.
2. **Alam, M.S.** (1996). "Corruption in Administration" (in Bangla), **Bangla Bazar Patrika** (a vernacular daily newspaper) January 28 and 29.
3. **Alfiler,** M.C.P. (1979). "Administrative Measures Against Bureaucratic Corruption: The Philippine Experience", **Philippine Journal of Public Administration (PJPA),** Vol.23, Nos.3 and 4: 321-349.

4. **Aminuzzaman, S.M.** (1996). "Accountability and Promotion of Ethics and Standard of Behaviour of the Public Bureaucracy in Bangladesh", **Asian Review of Public Administration**, Vol.8, and No.1: 13-27.
5. **Arora, D. (1993).** "Conceptualizing the Context and Contextualising the Concept: Corruption Reconsidered", **Indian Journal of Public Administration (IJPA),** Vol.39, No.1: 1-19.
6. **Blair, H.** et. al. (1992). The Bangladesh Democracy Program (BDP) Assessment: Final Report. Washington, DC: Bureau for Private Enterprise, USAID.
7. **Caiden, G.E. (1991a).** "What Really is Public Maladministration?", **IJPA**, Vol.37, No.1:1-16.
8. **Caiden, G.E. and N. Caiden (1977).** "Administrative Corruption", **Public Administration Review**, Vol.37, No.3.
9. **Caiden, G.E. and N. Caiden (1977).** "Administrative Corruption", **Public Administration Review**, Vol.37, No.3.
10. **de Zwart, Frank (1994**). The Bureaucratic Merry-Go-Round: Manipulating the Transfer of Indian Civil Servants. Amsterdam: Amsterdam University Press.
11. **Franda, M. (1982).** Bangladesh: The First Decade. New Delhi: South Asian.
12. Gould, D.J. (1980). **Bureaucratic Corruption and Underdevelopment in the Third World: The Case of Zaire.** New York: Pergaman.
13. **Gould, D.J. (1991).** "Administrative Corruption: Incidence, Causes, and Remedial Strategies in A. Farazmand ed. **Handbook of Comparative and Development Public Administration.** New York: Marcel Dekker, Inc., pp.467-480.
14. **Khan, M.M. (1979). Administrative Reform in Bangladesh.** New Delhi: South Asian.
15. **Khan, M.M. (1989a).** "The Electoral Process in Bangladesh", **Regional Studies,** Vol.7, No.3: 95-111.
16. **Kjellberg, F. (1992):** "Corruption as an Analytical Problem: Some Notes on Research on Public Corruption", Indian Journal of Administrative Science, Vol. III, No. 2: 195-221.
17. **Klitgaard, R. (1988). Controlling Corruption.** Berkeley, C. A.: University of California Press.
18. **Kochanek, S.A. (1993). Patron-Client Politics and Business in Bangladesh**. Dhaka: UPL.
19. **Kramer, J.J. (1997).** "Political Corruption in Post-Communist Russia: The Case for Democratization", paper presented at the XVIIth World Congress of International Political Science Association (IPSA) held in Seoul, Korea on August 17-21.
20. **Leff, H.N. (1979**). "Economic Development through Bureaucratic Corruption" in M.U. Ekpo ed. **Bureaucratic Corruption in Sub-Saharan Africa: Toward a Search for Causes and Consequences.** Washington, D.C.: University Press of America.

21. **Leys, C. (1970).** "What is the Problem about Corruption?" in A.J. Heidenheimer ed. **Political Corruption: Readings in Comparative Perspective**. New York: Holt, Rinehart and Winston.
22. **Lo, T.W. (1993). Corruption and Politics in Hong Kong and China.** Buckingham: Open University Press.
23. **Maloney, C. (1986). Behaviour and Poverty in Bangladesh.** Dhaka: UPL.
24. **Maniruzzaman, T. (1982). Group Interests and Political Changes: Studies of Pakistan and Bangladesh**. New Delhi: South Asian.
25. **Nye, J.S. (1979).** "Corruption and Political Development: A Cost-Benefit Analysis" in M.U. Ekpo ed. **Bureaucratic Corruption in Sub-Saharan Africa: Toward a Search for Causes and Consequences**. Washington, D.C.: University Press of America.
26. **Ouma, O.A. (1991).** "Corruption in Public Policy and its Impact on Development: The Case of Uganda since 1979", **PAD**, Vol.11, No.5: 473-489.
27. **Padhay, K.S. (1986). Corruption in Politics: A Case Study**. Delhi: B.R. Publishing Corporation.
28. **Paul, S. (1979a).** "Corruption: Who Will Bell the Cat?", **Economic and Political Weekly** June, 7:1350-1355.
29. **Paul, S. (1997).** "Corruption: Who Will Bell the Cat?" Economic and Political Weekly June 7; 1350-1355.
30. **Pope, J. (1996).** "National Integrity Programs" in P. Lengseth and K. Galt eds. **Partnership for Governance**. Proceedings of a Conference held in Copenhagen on May, 31, pp.23-26.
31. **Quah, J.S.T. (1995).** "Sustaining Quality in the Singapore Civil Service" in **Government in Transition**. London: Commonwealth Secretariat, pp.147-157.
32. **Rahman, M.H. (1994).** "Corruption and Patronage: The Social and Political Linkage" in Rahman, M.H. Decentralisation and Rural Society in Bangladesh: A Study of Bureaucratic Constraints on Access in the Upazilla Structure. Unpublished Ph.D. Thesis. Swansea: Centre for Development Studies, University College of Swansea, University of Wales.
33. **Rogow, A.A. and H.D. Laswell (1970).** "The Definition of Corruption" in A.J. Heidenheimer ed. **Political Corruption: Readings in Comparative Analysis**. New York: Holt, Rinehart and Winstan.
34. **Sarkar, J.N. (1935). Mughal Administration**. Calcutta: M.C. Sarkar and Sons Limited.
35. **Scott, J.C. (1972). Comparative Political Corruption**. Englewood Cliffs, N.J.: Princeton Hall, Inc.
36. **Siddiquee, N.A. (1997).** "Politics and Administration at the Upazilla Level: Problems of Access and Participation" in Siddiquee, N.A. Decentralisation and Development: Theory and Practice in Bangladesh. Dhaka: University of Dhaka.
37. **Thakur, U. (1979).** Corruption in Ancient India. New Delhi: Abhinav Publications.

38. **Theobald, R. (1990).** Corruption, Development and Underdevelopment. London: Macmillan.

39. **Tilman, R.O. (1970).** "Black Market Bureaucracy" in A.J. Heidenheimer ed. **Political Corruption: Readings in Comparative Analysis.** New York: Holt, Renehart and Winston.

40. **Vine, T.L.V. (1975). Political Corruption: The Ghana Case.** Stanford, CA: Hoover Institution.

41 **White-Harris, B. and White, G. eds. (1996).** Liberalization and the New Corruption. IDS Bulletin, Vol. 27, No. 2. Brighton: Institute of Development Studies, University of Sussex.

8

Modern Science Findings in Vedic Science

INRODUCTION

Now that India has been free for a number of decades from British rule, researchers, historians, and archeologists can all begin to take a new look at the true history of India. We can have a more unbiased view of the numerous new findings that keep cropping up that give an increasingly accurate understanding of how ancient and how advanced was the Indian Vedic civilization.

Marco Polo has written of India as the richest and noblest country in the world. A significant number of famous writers and high thinkers, such as Emerson, Thoreau, Schopenhauer and Sagan have praised the Vedic culture as the inspiration for many of the higher philosophical and scientific concepts the world has known.

The Scientific Verification of Vedic Knowledge by David Osborn (Swami Vishnu) presents empirical evidence proving the antiquity of Vedic civilization as well as it's many contributions. The History of Indian Science by Dr. Subash Kak gives an elaborate overview of the many sciences found in Vedic culture. Complex mathematical equations and computations can be easily solved within one's mind utilizing concepts inspired by the Vedas. This is elaborated by David Osborn in his article, Vedic Mathematics.

In modern science and Vedic Science, Dr. David Frawley (Pandit Vamadeva Shastri) explores the Indian concept of knowledge and explains the harmony between science and spirituality in Vedic culture.

SCIENCE

We live in an age in which science and technology continue their rapid progress that has been going on almost non-stop for the last two centuries. There are great advances in diverse fields, from genetics to physics, with practical applications through high tech and computer science that has reshaped our daily lives in amazing ways.

Yet science has unlocked not only many of the wonders but also many of the dangers of the outer world. In spite of all the scientific development, our civilization appears to be sinking further into a worsening crisis, with increasing ecological disruptions, health and psychological problems, spreading violence, hatred and brutality. Even with all our advances in communication, we seem to lack any true leadership, or any overriding spiritual or ethical direction that can bring peace and happiness to humanity. Our advanced global media seems happier to broadcast violence and promote divisions between people than to serve as a force for peace. Science does not seem to have the vision or the compassion necessary to link us to the greater universe and the whole of life in a meaningful and harmonious manner. If science is not entirely the cause of our current world problems, it does not seem to have the solution either.

While science has done well in terms of physics, its understanding of life and the biological science remains problematical. Its medicine, based largely upon drugs, does not seem able to create positive health for humanity. Its psychology, also increasingly drug based, seems to be causing more depression and unhappiness. In addition, the social science, including accounts of human history, remains questionable, caught in an outer model of the human being that lacks any deep spiritual meaning.

However, the 'outer' science that dominates our present culture is not the only measure of human knowledge of the universe. As we push the limits of science, another type of science is emerging – or reemerging – that can grant us a more authentic understanding of the true nature of ourselves and the vast cosmos in which we live.

Many ancient cultures and spiritual traditions speak of a higher science, an inner 'self-knowledge', through which we can know the cosmic reality not as an outer array of phenomena but as the very consciousness at the core of our own being. These sacred sciences have probably been best developed and preserved in India as the 'yogic' or 'Vedic' sciences, which remain to the present day well-researched, with clear teachings and practices, an extensive literature, millennia of experience, and can be made accessible and applicable to all humanity.

VEDIC SCIENCE

The word "**VEDA**" means **Knowledge**, deriving from the Sanskrit root 'vid' meaning to know, to see or to cognize. The Vedas are called Vidyas which means ways of knowledge or perception (a term cognate with Latin Video). The Vedas we might say are the Vidyas or videos of the sages shown on the inner screen of the meditative mind. They were said to have been cognized by the human mind in tune with the universal Being or Brahman. Vedas, the huge collection of knowledge include not only religious and spiritual knowledge, but also that of some of the branches known to modern science such as ***Architecture, Avionics, Astrobiology, Astronomy, Atomic Physics, Chronometry, Dietetics, Embryology, Gastroenterology, Health Sciences, Metallurgy, Meteorology, Psychophysiology, Science of warfare, Sociology etc.***

Vedic Science is the science and technology of consciousness. It is both ancient and modern. Veda means knowledge, and Vedic Science is the science of knowledge, self-referral knowledge, the knowledge of consciousness, and the knowledge of Natural Law, the intelligence that governs the universe.

The Vedic science, on the other hand, open the door to a cosmic intelligence, to a sense of self and reality that is universal, not bodily based but rooted in awareness, love and bliss. The Vedas reveal that we are a mini-universe, a microcosm of energy and intelligence, with all the secret forces of the greater cosmos at work within us accessible to our greater being. We are meat to function as a species to evolve a higher consciousness on the planet, not simply to enjoy ourselves at a mundane level.

MODERN SCIENCE FINDINGS IN VEDIC SCIENCE

Even with respect to science and technology, the people of the previous yoga's were more advanced than us, as they relied on science as described in the scriptures, rather than the speculative methodology used by many modern scientists.

Modern Science keeps changing as it's not the perfect. The Vedic science is timeless (unchanging) as it has the absolute truths. It is absolutely flawless. So when something is errorless it need not be changed. Vedas are coming from the person who is all knowing, who knows the past, the present, and the future. In other words, the Vedas are the word of God. Krishna says 'vedias ca sarvair aham eva vedyo' (from Chaitanya Charitamruta, Madhy lila 20.125). It means "By all the Vedas, I am known. Indeed I am the compiler of Vedanta, and I am the knower of the Vedas".

A vast number of statements and materials presented in the ancient Vedic literatures can be shown to agree with modern scientific findings and they also reveal a highly developed scientific content in these literatures. The great cultural wealth of this knowledge is highly relevant in the modern world.

Techniques used to show this agreement include:

- o Carbon and thermoluminiscence dating of archaeological artifacts
- o Scientific verification of scriptural statements
- o Linguistic analysis of scripts found on archaeological artifacts

Satellite imagery of the Dried up Sarasvati River Basin

Using modern scientific methods, such as satellite imagery and dating techniques, it can be shown that the ancient statements of the Vedas are factual, not mythical as erroneously propagated. High resolution satellite images have verified descriptions in the *Rig Veda* of the descent of the ancient *Sarasvati* River from it's source in the Himalayas to the Arabian Sea.

The mighty *Sarasvati* River and it's civilization are referred to in the *Rig Veda* more than fifty times, providing that the drying up of the *Sarasvati* River was subsequent to the origin of the *Rig Veda.* The drying up of the *Sarasvati* River around 1900 B.C. is confirmed archaeologically.

Evidence for the Ancient Port City of Dvaraka

Marine archaeology has also been utilized in India off the coast of the ancient port city of Dvaraka in Gujarat, uncovering further evidence in support of statements in the Vedic scriptures. An entire submerged city at Dvaraka, the ancient port city of Lord Krishna with its massive fort walls, piers and jetty has been found in the ocean as described in the *Mahabharata* and other Vedic literatures.

Dr. S. R. Rao, formerly of the Archaeological Survey of India, has pioneered marine archaeology in India. Marine archaeological findings seem to corroborate descriptions in the *Mahabharata* of Dvaraka as a large, Well-fortified and prosperous port city, which was built on land reclaimed from the sea, and later taken back by the sea. This lowering and raising of the sea level during these same time periods of the 15th and 16th centuries B.C. is also documented in historical records of the country of Bahrain.

Thirty five Archaeological Sites in North India

Apart from Dvaraka, more than thirty-five sites in North India have yielded archaeological evidence and have been identified as ancient cities described in the *Mahabharata.* Copper utensils, iron, seals, gold and silver ornaments, terracotta discs and painted grey ware pottery have all been found in these sites. Scientific dating of these artifacts corresponds to the non-aryan-invasion model of Indian antiquity.

Furthermore, the Matsya and Vayu Puranas describe great flooding which destroyed the capital city of Hastinapur, forcing its inhabitants to relocate in Kausambi. The soil of Hastinapur reveals proof of this flooding. Archaeological evidence of the new capital of Kausambi has recently been found which has been dated to the time period just after this flood.

The Iron Pillar of Delhi

The Vedic literatures contain descriptions of advanced scientific techniques, sometimes even more sophisticated than those used in our modern technological world. Modern metallurgists have not been able to produce iron of comparable quality to the 22 foot high Iron Pillar of Delhi, which is the largest hand forged block of iron from antiquity. This pillar stands at mute testimony to the highly advanced scientific knowledge of metallurgy that was known in ancient India. Cast in approximately the 3rd century B.C., the six and a half ton pillar, over two millennia has resisted all rust and even a direct hit by the artillery of the invading army of Nadir Shah during his sacking of Delhi in 1737.

Vedic Cosmology

Vedic Cosmology is yet another ancient Vedic Science which can be confirmed by modern scientific findings and this is acknowledged by well known scientists and authors, such as Carl Sagan and Count Maurice Maeterlink, who recognized that the cosmology of Veda parallels modern scientific findings.

Carl Sagan stated, "Vedic Cosmology is the only one in which the time scales correspond to those of modern scientific cosmology".

Nobel laureate Count Maurice Maeterlinck wrote of "a Cosmogony which no European conception has ever surpassed".

French astronomer Jean-Chaude Bailly corroborated the antiquity and accuracy of the Vedic astronomical measurements as "more ancient than those of the Greeks or Egyptians". And that, "the movements of the stars calculated 4,500 years ago, does not differ by a minute from the tables of today".

The ninety foot tall astronomical instrument known as Samrat Yantra, built by the learned King Suwai Jai Singh of Jaipur, measures time to within two seconds per day.

Cosmology and other scientific accomplishments of ancient India spread to other countries along with mercantile and cultural exchanges. There are almost one hundred references in the *Rig Veda* also to the ocean and maritime activity. This is confirmed by Indian historian R.C. Majumdar, who stated that the people of the Indus-

Sarasvata Civilization engaged in trade with Sooma and centers of culture in western Asia and Crete.

Vedic Mathematics

Vedic mathematics is the most perfect, easiest and the fastest one. This is the reason why Vedic Maths is used by students to crack competitive examinations like CAT, MAT etc. The modern day mathematics is not the most perfect method.

Voltaire, the famous French writer and philosopher, stated that "Pythagoras went to the Ganges to learn geometry", and Abraham Seidenber, Authour of the authoritative "History of Mathematics", credits the early Sulba Sutras as inspiring all mathematics of the ancient world from Babylonia to Egypt to Greece.

As Voltaire & Seidenberg have stated, many highly significant mathematical concepts have come from the Vedic culture, such as:

- The theorem bearing the name of the Greek mathematician Pythagorus is found in the Shatapatha Brahmana as well as the Sulba Sutra, the Indian mathematical treatise, written centuries before Pythagorus was born.
- The Decimal system, based on powers of ten, where the remainder is carried over to the next column, is first mentioned in the *Taittiriya Samhita* of the *Black Yajrveda.*
- The introduction of zero as both a numerical value and a place marker.
- The concept of infinity.
- The Binary number system, essential for computers, was used in Vedic verse meters. Binary numbers were known at the time of Pingala's Chhandahshastra. Pingala, who lived about the fifth century BCE. The knowledge of binary numbers indicates a deep understanding of arithmetic.
- A hashing technique, similar to that used by modern search algorithms, such as Google, was used in South Indian musicology. From the name of a raga one can determine the notes of the raga from this *Kathapayadi* system.

Ayurveda

In the Vedic sciences, human well-being is defined as the harmony of body, mind, prana and soul. Ayurveda, Vedic medicine, shows us how to find health and well-being through understanding the forces of nature and consciousness both within and around us.

The west is fond of proclaiming Hippocrates (460 – 377 BC) as the father of medicine, but way before him in 500 BC Maharishi Charaka wrote the famous Charaka Samhita or Physicians' Handbook. The Charaka Samhita went into great detail to describe human anatomy, pathology, diagnostic procedures, and treatment for various diseases. Charaka defined eight major medical disciplines of Ayur Veda: Shailya Chikitsa (surgery), Shaalakya Chikitsa (head, eye, nose, and throat), Kaaya Chikitsa (mental health), Kaumarbhrutya Chikitsa (pediatrics), Agada Tantra (toxicology), Rasaayana Tantra (Pharmacology), and Vaajeekarna Tantra (reproductive medicine). Charaka also described the functions of the heart and the circulatory system in great detail. The Charaka Samhita was widely translated in various languages and Charaka was a respected medical authority in both the Arab and Roman empires.

Shushruta describes the details of more than 300 operations such as extracting solid bodies, excision, incision, probing, puncturing, evacuating fluids and suturing. Ancient Indians were also the first to perform amputations, caesarean and cranall surgeries with 42 surgical processes. He worked with 125 kinds of surgical instruments including scalpels, lancets, needles, catheters, etc. Sushruta even devised non-invasive surgical treatments with the aid of light rays and heat. Sushrata & his team conducted complicated surgeries like cataract, artificial limbs, cesareans, fractures, urinary stones and also plastic surgery and brain surgeries.

Following is just a minute glimpse of the Timeless Vedas:

- o Using a variety of complicated instruments, gynecologists have gradually come to know how the embryo grows during the period of pregnancy. But *Srimad-Bhagavatam*, 3rd canto, 31st chapter, gives vivid description of the growth of the embryo in the mother's womb, exactly in conforming to their findings.
- o The Vedas state that cow dung, in spite of being the stool of an animal, is pure. This was proved to be true in 1940, when its antiseptic properties were discovered.

- o The Vedas have stated since time immemorial that plants have life. But till Jagadish Chandra Bose proved that plants have feelings, scientists believed that they were inanimate.
- o The Kurukshetra war involved many subtle celestial weapons like shabdavedi, vayavya, parthavya etc, which are more sophisticated than the gross weapons known to scientists today.
- o Sanskrit is grammatically the most perfect language and all the languages of the world are derived from it.
- o The power of Yogasanas, Ayurveda, and Meditation is unquestionable till date.
- o Modern science is yet to give a proper definition of the mind, intelligence and ego, their nature and function. But the *Vedas* explain these in minute detail.
- o Light traveled with a speed of 186,000 miles per second.
- o Blue Sky is nothing but scattered sunlight (*Markandeya Purana* 78.8).
- o "Seven horses draw the charot of Surya (Sun)". Further it states, these seven horses are the seven colors compromising light (*Rig Veda*). (Modern science: Sunlight is made up of all the colors of the rainbow: red, orange, yellow, green, blue, and violet. The gas molecules in the atmosphere interact with the sunlight before the light reaches our eyes.)
- o There are various sections of the Vedas that deal with science. (Such as "ayurveda" that deals with medicine). In the previous yoga's, we see that flying chariots (such as the pushpaka vimana) were used. It seems there is section in the scriptures called "Vimana shastra", that explains how to construct aeroplanes that run without fuel.
- o We have heard of warriors such as Arjuna using weapons such as the "Brahma astra" which were clearly superior to the present day nuclear missiles.
- o Big Bang model and mass-energy theory.
- o Sixty-four centuries before Isaac Newton, the Hindu Rig-Veda asserted that gravitation held the universe together. The Sanskrit speaking Aryans subscribed to the idea of a spherical earth in an era when the Greeks believed in a flat one.

- *Movement of the Earth*: "Earth rotates in two ways by the Will of Brahama, first it rotates on its axis secondly it revolves around sun. Days and Nights are distinguished when moves on its axis. Season change when it revolves around Sun"(*Vishnu Puran*).
- *Protection of the Earth*: After the formation of the earth planet, Brahama created atmosphere in group of seven, from that formation oceans began to exist, and the first form of life appeared on the earth planet. Atmosphere was created as protective skin of earth. The atmosphere surrounds the earth to the height of 60 miles, and clouds, lightning and the like are all phenomena connected with it (*Shrimad Bhagwatam*). (Modern science: Ozone is a relatively unstable molecule found in Earth's atmosphere. Most ozone is concentrated below a 30-mile (48-km) height. An ozone molecule is made up of three atoms of oxygen. Although it represents only a tiny fraction of the atmosphere, ozone is crucial for life on Earth. Depending on where ozone resides, it can protect or harm life on Earth. High in the atmosphere-about 15 miles (24 km) up—ozone acts as a shield to protect Earth's surface from the sun's harmful ultraviolet radiation. Without this shield, we would be more susceptible to skin cancer, cataracts, and impaired immune systems. Closer to Earth, in the air we breathe, ozone is a harmful pollutant that causes damage to lung tissue and plants. The amounts of "good" and "bad" ozone in the atmosphere depend on a balance between processes that create ozone and those that destroy it. An upset in the ozone balance can have serious consequences for life on Earth. Scientists are finding evidence that changes are occurring in ozone levels—the "bad" ozone is increasing in the air we breathe, and the "good" ozone is decreasing in our protective ozone shield.)
- Sun is the center of small system which includes 9 planets including earth, sun hold more that 98% mass of this small system in this giant universe which contains millions of suns (*Rig Veda*). (Modern science: Solar system. The Sun contains 99.85% of all the matter in the Solar System)

There are also many cases of modern scientists "discovering" things that were already known in the Vedic times. For example, modern science believed for a long time that the earth was flat and realized the truth (that the earth is round) much later. However, the Vedas always refer to the earth as "bhu-gol" (round earth).

CONCLUSION

In India, science and spirituality have always gone together. Spirituality through Yoga and Vedanta has always been conceived of as a science, a way of knowledge to be approached with reason and experimentation through Yoga and meditation leading to the direct perception of truth. Other Indic systems of thought like Buddhism and Jainism have shared similar views. The Vedas address all aspects of existence through Dharma, the natural laws that uphold the universe, which reflect not only matter and energy but life, mind and consciousness. As such, the Vedas constitute what could be called a science in the modern sense of the word and much more. We can find among the Vedic sciences a whole range of sciences from astronomy and chemistry to psychology and surgery, extending to astrology and to the science of Yoga itself. We can call this integral approach to both the spiritual and material sciences as 'Vedic science.' Many of the modern science findings are there in Vedas. It is our duty to preserve the great Indian heritage & culture and science & civilization. The present generation people are neglecting the study of Vedas. Vedas are real sources of knowledge. It is more important for all to know about inner knowledge (mind, soul) and outer knowledge (material world). Knowledge is power. Without knowledge, it is impossible to survive in the modern and globalized world.

REFERENCES

1. Dvid H. Obsborn (Swami B.B. Vishnu). (2009): "*Science of the Sacred-Ancient Perspectives for Modern Science*", Gosai Publishing.
2. *Markandeya Purana*
3. Rig Veda
4. *Shrimad Bhagwatam*
5. *Vishnu Puran*

9

Youth Participation in Nation's Development

INTRODUCTION

Young people need a chance to develop. They also need the opportunity to have their voices heard and to make decisions for themselves. It is only by working in true partnership with young people, by listening to their opinions and concerns, which we can ensure that services meet their needs and that society can benefit from their contributions. Youth participation is often used interchangeably with the term 'active involvement'. This means more than simply taking part in an activity. It refers specifically to the involvement in the process of identifying needs, exploring solutions, making decisions and planning action within communities and organizations that seek to support civil society. In relation to young people, youth participation is often regarded as the involvement of young people in decisions that are made that affect them. However many people believe that young people should be treated as citizens now and should be involved in all decisions that are made about the community and society in which they live. More than 40 per cent of youth are living in India. It is fortunate for India. Youth participation in development is important. Youth is power. Through this it is possible to solve all types of problems in the society. Swami Vivekanda has recognized the power of youth. It is our duty to follows the words of Vivekanadna on youth. The youth participation in nation's development is essential in the globalized world.

PARTICIPATION

Participation means voluntary choice, learning opportunity, challenging but bringing satisfaction, developing people's perception of social, political, economic and cultural contexts, mixing leisure and training.

According to UNDP (1993:21) "Participation means that people are closely involved in the economic, social, cultural and political processes that affect their lives". Therefore, participation is a process by which the beneficiaries influence the direction and execution of a development programme to enhance prosperity in terms of income, personal growth, self-reliance or other values that they cherish. Article 12 of the United Nations Convention on the Rights of the Child (UNCRC) is the main driver for children and young people's participation, and states: "Children and young people have the right to say what they think should happen when adults are making decisions that affect them, and to have their opinions taken into account" (Funky Dragon, 2006). People may, in some cases, have complete and direct control over these processes-in other cases, the control may be partial or indirect. The important thing is that people have constant access to decision- making and power. Participation in this sense is an essential element of human development.

Participation, certainly not a new term, has been a part of the development vocabulary since the 1960s, or even before. But it has generally referred only to people's involvement in particular projects or programmes. The critical difference is that participation is an overall development strategy-focusing on the central role that people should play in all spheres of life. Human development involves widening their choices, and greater participation enables people to gain for they access to a much broader range of opportunities.

People can participate as individuals or as groups. As individuals in a democracy, they may participate as voters or political activists—

or in the market as entrepreneurs or workers. Often, however, they participate more effectively through group action-as members of a community organization, perhaps, or a trade union or a political party.

People everywhere are certainly demanding much greater access to political, economic and social opportunities. They might not expect "full participation"-but they do want a steady advance towards it.

FORMS OF PARTICIPATION

- Economic participation
- Political participation
- Social participation
- Cultural participation

Participation is, after all, a process, not an event. Since participation requires increased influence and control, it also demands increased empowerment-in economic, social and political terms. In economic terms, this means being able to engage freely in any economic activity. In social terms, it means being able to join fully in all forms of community life, without regard to religion, colour, sex or race. And in political terms, it means the freedom to choose and change governance at every level, from the presidential palace to the village council. All these forms of participation are intimately linked. Without one, the others will be incomplete and less effective. Participation, from the human development perspective, is both a means and an end. Human development stresses the need to invest in human capabilities and then ensure that those capabilities are used for the benefit of all. Greater participation has an important part to play here: it helps maximize the use of human capabilities and is thus a means of increasing levels of social and economic development. But human development is also concerned with personal fulfillment.

Implementation of any development project is not possible without the active and widespread participation of the people. It becomes the responsibility of the administrative authority to spot active persons in the local population, awaken their interest and mobilize their initiative. Then only any programme will be succeeded.

NEED OF YOUTH PARTICIPATION

Youth participation in EEEE (Education, Economy, Employment and Environment) is more important for any nation's development. The development of any nation depends on its' three Ps (PPP) i.e., People, Policy and Participation. India is a developing country. We have a huge number of youth. Youth is the major source for development. Youth is power. There is nothing impossible for youth in the world. The given below information regarding education, economy, employment and environment tells us that, we need more youth participation in these sectors. The situation is better than some of the developing countries and poorer than developed countries.

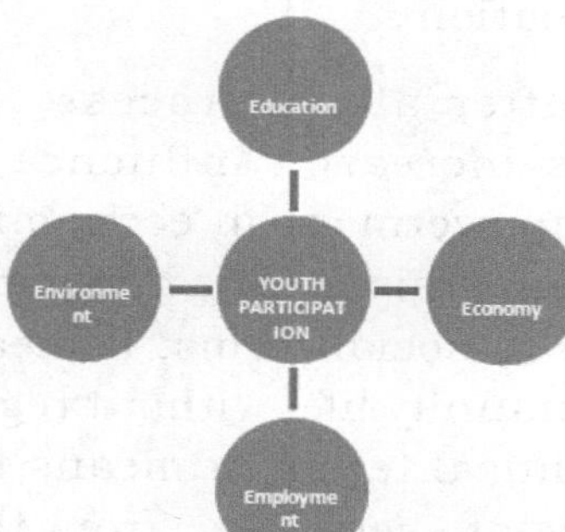

Fig-1: Areas of Youth Prettification

Education

Literacy in India is a key for socio-economic progress, and the Indian literacy rate grew to 68% in 2007 from 12% at the end of British rule in 1947. According to the latest survey by the National Sample Survey Office (NSSO) in June 2008, the literacy rate among the population with age 7 and above was 72% whereas the adult population (age 15 and above) had a literacy rate of 66%.

Although this was a greater than fivefold improvement, the level is well below the world average literacy rate of 84%, and India currently has the largest illiterate population of any nation on earth. Despite government programs, India's literacy rate increased only "sluggishly," and a 1990 study estimated that it would take until 2060 for India to achieve universal literacy at then-current rate of progress. The 2001 census, however, indicated a 1991-2001 decadal literacy growth of 12.63%, which is the fastest-ever on record.

There is a wide gender disparity in the literacy rate in India: adult (15+ years) literacy rates in 2009 were 76.9% for men and 54.5% for women. The low female literacy rate has had a dramatically negative impact on family planning and population stabilization efforts in India. Studies have indicated that female literacy is a strong predictor of the use of contraception among married Indian couples, even when women do not otherwise have economic independence. The census provided a positive indication that growth in female literacy rates (14.38%) was substantially faster than in male literacy rates (11.13%) in the 1991-2001 decadal period, which means the gender gap appears to be narrowing.

Education in India is seen as one of the ways to upward social mobility. Good education is seen as a stepping stone to a high flying career. Education System in India currently represents a great paradox. On the one hand we have IIMs & IITs that rank among the best institutes in the world and on the other hand there are number of schools in the country that don't even have the basic infrastructure. Even after more than 50 years after independence we are far away from the goal of universal literacy. But on a positive note, Indian professionals are considered among the best in the world are in great demand. This signifies the inherent strength of Indian education system.

Enrollment at primary and secondary level schools is very low. Wastage and stagnation is high at primary level schools. Only 15 per cent of total students are going to study higher education. It is very less when compared to developed countries. The number of universities is also less. Youth participation in higher education is important.

Economy

The Economy of India is the eleventh largest in the world by nominal GDP and the fourth largest by purchasing power parity (PPP). The country's per capita GDP (PPP) is $3,290 (IMF, 127th) in 2010. Following strong economic reforms from the socialist inspired economy of a post-independence Indian nation, the country began to develop a fast-paced economic growth, as free market principles were initiated in 1990 for international competition and foreign investment. Economists predict that by 2020, India will be among the leading economies of the world.

India was under social democratic policies from 1947 to 1991. The economy was characterized by extensive regulation, protectionism, public ownership, pervasive corruption and slow growth. Since 1991, continuing economic liberalisation has moved the country toward a market-based economy. A revival of economic reforms and better economic policy in first decade of the 21st century accelerated India's economic growth rate. In recent years, Indian cities have continued to liberalize business regulations. By 2008, India had established itself as the world's second-fastest growing major economy. However, as a result of the financial crisis of 2007–2010, coupled with a poor monsoon, India's gross domestic product (GDP) growth rate significantly slowed to 6.7% in 2008–09, but subsequently recovered to 7.2% in 2009–10, while the fiscal deficit rose from 5.9% to a high 6.5% during the same period.

India's large service industry accounts for 57.2% of the country's GDP while the industrial and agricultural sector contribute 28% and 14.6% respectively. Agriculture is the predominant occupation in India, accounting for about 52% of employment. The service sector makes up a further 34% and industrial sector around 14%. The labour force totals half a billion workers. Major agricultural products include rice, wheat, oilseed, cotton, jute, tea, sugarcane, potatoes, cattle, water buffalo, sheep, goats, poultry and fish. Major industries include telecommunications, textiles, chemicals, food processing, steel, transportation equipment, cement, mining, petroleum, machinery, information technology-enabled services and pharmaceuticals. However, statistics from a 2009-10 government survey, which used a smaller sample size than earlier surveys, suggested that the share of agriculture in employment had dropped to 45.5%.

Previously a closed economy, India's trade and business sector has grown fast. India currently accounts for 1.5% of world trade as of 2007 according to the WTO. According to the World Trade Statistics of the WTO in 2006, India's total merchandise trade (counting exports and imports) was valued at $294 billion in 2006 and India's services trade inclusive of export and import was $143 billion. Thus, India's global economic engagement in 2006 covering both merchandise and services trade was of the order of $437 billion, up by a record 72% from a level of $253 billion in 2004. India's total trade in goods and services has reached a share of 43% of GDP in 2005–06, up from 16% in 1990–91.

Employment

The unemployment rate for 2009–2010, according to the state Labour Bureau, was 9.4 percent nationwide, rising to 10.1 percent in rural areas, where two-thirds of the 1.2 billion population live.

Labour Force: 478 million (2009)

Labour force by Occupation: Agriculture (52%), Industry (14%), Service (34%) (Estimated)

Population Below poverty line 37% (2010)

Environment

Air and water pollution and lack of sanitation, garbage and sewage disposal and other basic urban services severely hamper the development of India's cities. The prime ecological worries in India's rural areas are soil erosion, deforestation, water pollution and the scarcity of safe drinking water. In the cities, up to one-third of household wastes are never collected by municipal services. The situation is particularly bad in slums, which house at least one-fifth of India's urban population. Up to three quarters of Indian city dwellers lack sanitation.

Overall, India's environmental situation is in bleak. J. Mohan Rao claims that 60 percent of agricultural land is degraded to varying degrees. Semi-arid and fragile soils have been brought under the plough. Waterlogging, erosion, salinization and overgrazing add to the depletion. While the government targets one-third of the nation's land to be covered by forest, the ratio had dropped below 20 percent by the late 1980s. Seventy percent of surface waters are seriously polluted. Eighty percent of the population does not have permanent access to safe drinking water.

The "multiple environmental crises that confront our country have created an alarming situation", Prime Minister Manmohan Singh said on Tuesday (August 18th 2009), while asking state governments to curtail pollution, clean rivers and fight climate change. "Climate change is threatening our ecosystems, water scarcity is becoming a way of life and pollution is endangering our health," said Singh after opening a daylong conference of environment ministers from all state governments. "We have to make fundamental choices about our lifestyles," the prime minister said, assuring his audience that the "challenges are not insurmountable". Describing climate change as a "major global challenge", he said India was conscious of its "responsibility to present and future generations" and would ensure the "ecological sustainability of its development path". Singh sought the cooperation of all state governments to implement the eight missions that the centre has outlined under the National Action Plan on Climate Change. He asked the assembled ministers to have state-level action plans in concordance with the national plan. He also called upon state governments to modernize their forest departments and to fill up vacant posts, pointing out that many states would now get huge funding for compensatory afforestation projects, as the Supreme Court has recently unfrozen over Rs.9,000 crore meant for this. The money was lying in escrow accounts for over seven years.

Reasons for Youth Participation

These are the most commonly stated reasons for involving young people actively in the development:

- It is young people's right to be involved and have their voice heard in decisions that will impact on them. This right is enshrined in the UN Convention of the Rights of the Child, article 12;
- Participation of all citizens is essential to a healthy democratic society. This obviously includes the participation of young people. This is a particularly relevant reason given the context of declining engagement of young people with traditional political processes;
- Improved, better targeted and more effective services and projects. By involving young people in the planning and management, services can remain relevant and effective as

they are based on young people's reality as opposed to a professional's perceptions; and

- o Skills development for young people. Young people can gain a huge amount of confidence from seeing their opinions and experiences valued and directly contribute to positive change in their community. Many skills are also developed which can directly lead to improved educational performance and better prospects of gaining employment in the future.

YOUTH PARTICIPATION - DEVELOPMENT

The youth are a major human resource for development, and thus key agents of social change, economic development and technological innovation. There is, therefore, a need for youth involvement and participation in the socio-economic, cultural, political environment of a country, in its development programmes, as well as in activities based on the youth's specific needs, desires and aspirations.

If children are the future of a nation, its youth are its present resource. The dynamic role of youth in the growth and prosperity of any society is extremely vital. A constructive and active work culture of the youth lends a nation its integrity and character. But the profile of the youth in India has been rather low and its role extremely mediocre especially after India achieved Independence.

The former Union Home Minister, Mr. L.K. Advani has said Indians should set their goal to ensure the 21st century belongs to India.

"Just as the last century belonged to Europe, the 21st century can very well be that of India", Mr. Advani said addressing the Indian community.

"Just as the single goal of the Indians early last century was to achieve Independence, they now have to define their new goal and work towards achieving it", he said.

Too often, young people are portrayed in negative ways - as gang members, juvenile delinquents, or reckless troublemakers seeking to inflict damage on "adult" society. As persuasive as these views of youth may appear, they are frequently very far removed from the truth: the majority of the world's youth are often more interested in leading productive and meaningful lives rather than in harming or undermining their communities. In various regions and varying situations around the world, hundreds of thousands of young people are spearheading positive social change - leading community initiatives, operating small businesses, and reshaping political processes.

More can be done to nurture these productive behaviors, as young people constitute clear assets to development when they are positively empowered to be active citizens. Supporting and including young people in development processes is critical for several reasons. Firstly, and fundamentally, youth have experience, knowledge and ideas that are unique to their situation, enabling them to offer key insights and perspectives on development that adults cannot. Secondly, in many communities, youth make up the majority of the local population; as a result, youth voices can be crucial expressions of overall community needs. Finally, regardless of their current status, young people are the future custodians of their environments and future leaders of their peers. The lessons learned today influence tomorrow, and already the majority of youth around the world counter real world issues of childbirth, disease and unemployment. Although "youth" by definition, they are wise to the roles government and economics play in their life and community. It is therefore imperative that young people are given opportunities to develop the values, attitudes and skills they need to actively participate and succeed in the spheres of family, workplace and community both today and tomorrow. A failure to promote youth development - and roles for youth in development - will have disastrous effects on countries across the world, both in the short- and long-term.

Youth participation is a way to provide opportunities for youth to take on greater responsibilities and, through these real world experiences, to build competencies and develop into successful adults. Participation in social groups fosters a feeling of connectedness and belonging, helping young people to develop a sense of identity. The experience of contributing to a cause, a decision, and/or a group can be crucial part to the development of sense of responsibility, purpose and self-worth. Creativity and innovation are stimulated by challenging youth to take on clear tasks and then providing the coaching needed along the way as obstacles or unexpected results are encountered.

Promoting youth participation can take many forms, from encouraging youth volunteering in community development projects, to empowering young people to offer their perspectives on world issues, to having youth serve as members of advisory boards, become peer mentors, and lead development programs, non-profit organizations and small businesses. However, what is most important is that in all these cases, attention is paid to the quality of this participation - to ensure that young people are not just token figures, but that they are meaningfully engaged in ways that strengthen their problem-solving, decision-making and leadership skills. This prepares and engages young people today to actively build a both a better future and a better present. It also illustrates one of the most effective forms of sustainable development- achieved only when the processes cultivated today last for generations to come.

CONCLUSION

Today we are hearing healthy words regarding the status of India like..... *We are shining, we will be the 2nd largest economy by 2020, we are the largest pool of skilled man power on the earth, we are the emerging global IT superpower, we are the outsourcing hub of the world, we offer one of the largest consumer market across the world for MNC's, we boast of rich and varied heritage, we are growing at the GDP rate of impressive 8-9% per annum and aiming for a glittering double digit growth rate soon, we are India!* It seems that the above facts are in our favor; we are shining, but are we really? Or our mindset of estimating standard of living of the population just by the glittering GDP growth rates is a sign of our biased mentality? The other side of the story – 25 per cent population still living below poverty line, most of the cities and villages without even suitable condition for a healthy living, proper health care centers, electricity, UNESCO is concerned about the child mortality rate in India, we are in the top countries from below in the Human Development Index and still we ignoring the reality or over shadowing the face of our country's ugly face. The cause of the above problems is lack of youth participation or less youth participation in development. More than 40 per cent of youth are living in our country. It is our duty to utilize youth in the right manner. Without youth participation it is not possible for India to recognize developed country status by 2020. It is important to establish some more institutions like Rajiv Gandhi National Institute of Youth Development for nation's development.

REFERENCES

1. "*A Profile of Youth in India*", National Family Health Survey (NFHS-3) 2005-06, Ministry of Health and Family Welfare, Government of India, New Delhi.
2. "*Youth in India: Situation and Needs 2006-07*", Ministry of Health and Family Welfare, Government of India, New Delhi.
3. Report of UNDP-2003, United Nations, New York.
4. Reports of RGNIYD, Sriperumbudur, Tamil Nadu.

10

Women and Food Security in India

INTRODUCTION

Hunger is on the rise. A food crisis is hurting the poor all over the world, hitting the landless and women the hardest. It struck even before the current global economic meltdown and rising food prices aggravated people's access to food. Those who were already food insecure find themselves in worsening conditions. They are joined by millions more of newly food-insecure people. Misguided agricultural and trade policies have contributed to the current food crisis, including the failure to recognize women's crucial roles in agricultural production and food security.

The right to food is a fundamental human right. Yet, millions of people suffer the "ravages of hunger and malnutrition or the consequences of food insecurity". It is paradoxical that one of the most claimed fundamental of human rights is the one violated more than any other right. As the 1980 Presidential Commission on World Hunger stated, without the right to food, "the protection of other human rights becomes a mockery for those who must spend all their energy merely to maintain life itself. The role of women is crucial in the process of food production and food security not only in India but also in other parts of the world.

FACTS OF INDIA

People

Total population (millions): 1134.4

Life expectancy at birth: 63

Urban population: 29 %

Agricultural labour force (thousands): 559 656

Number of people undernourished (millions): 251.5

Proportion of undernourished in total population: 22

Per capita daily calorie intake: 2 330

Per capita daily protein intake (% kcal): 9 %

Child malnutrition, underweight: 43 %

Child malnutrition, stunting: 48 %

Child mortality rate (per 1 000 live births): 87

Land

Land area (1 000 ha): 297 319

Arable land (1 000 ha): 160 555

Permanent crops (1 000 ha): 9 200

Pastures (1 000 ha): 11 040

Irrigated land: 55 808

Share in total water use by

Agricultural: 86.5 %

Industrial: 5.5 %

Domestic: 8.1 %

Forest area (1 000 ha): 67 701

Economic

Agriculture as percentage of Gross Domestic Product: 18

Value of agricultural exports (US $million): 7 058

Share of agricultural exports (percentage of total exports): 9.83

Value of agricultural imports (US $ million): 5 108

Share of agricultural imports (percentage of total imports): 5.43

Production

Cereals (1 000 tonnes): 232 630

Meat (1 000 tonnes): 6 032

Fish (1 000 tonnes): 7 308

Woodfuel (1 000 m3): 303 839

Industrial roundwood (1 000 m3): 19 146

Source: FAO, UN on 1st December, 2010.

WOMEN IN AGRICULTURE

In any economy, women play a prominent role at various levels. They are the backbone of the village economy in rural India. Women take up different works to eke out their livelihood and the majority of the rural women depend on agriculture, which is the major, unorganized sector in India. Many of these laborers are landless, homeless and belong to the socially depressed classes of the society. Despite the seasonal nature of employment in the field of agriculture, enormous growth is witnessed in the size of the agricultural labourers since the beginning of this century.

Ours is basically an agricultural country. It is a source of livelihood for over 70 per cent of the population. Agriculture, therefore, has become a family enterprise. The whole family of men, women and children work on it and earn their livelihood. Men's role in agriculture is widely known, but women's role is not that open, though they mostly work for more number of hours, with fewer privileges, tedious activities and with painful postures. It is only in the recent times that their role is being recognized, though there is a possibility that the women themselves are not aware of their contributions, hardships and above all, over-burden of not only the household jobs but jobs related to agriculture and allied fields. The condition is worse when they work on fields not of their own but on others. On others field, they work as labourers with no facilities for their selves or for their children. Children are left on the fields under the umbrella of sun, dust, rain, cold. Women do not know their rights; do not know how to fight for their rights.

Regardless of the level of development achieved by the respective economies, women play a pivotal role in agriculture and in rural development in most countries of the Asia-Pacific region. Evidently there are serious constraints which militate against the promotion of an effective role for women in development in those societies which were bound by age-old traditions and beliefs. Patriarchal modes and practices motivated by cultures and/or interpretations of religious sanctions and illiteracy hinder women's freedom to opt for various choices to assert greater mobility in social interactions. Resulting from these situations, women's contribution to agriculture and other sectors in the economy remain concealed and unaccounted for in monitoring economic performance measurement. Consequently, they are generally invisible in plans and programmes. They were, in fact, discriminated against by stereotypes which restrict them to a reproductive role, and denied access to resources which could eventually enhance their social and economic contribution to the society.

In India, nearly 70 per cent of the male and 87 per cent of the female workers are dependent upon agriculture, livestock, forestry etc. for their livelihood. Women are engaged in a number of farm operations along with men. Activities such as application of manure, land preparation, seed grading, sowing, dabbling, planting, irrigation, fertilizers application, plant protection, harvesting, threshing, shelling, hulling, winnowing, cleaning and storing grain, feeding cattle, looking after milk animal, poultry and kitchen gardening are the main occupations of farm women.

WOMEN – FOOD PRODUCTION

In developing country like India, most women's work is devoted to agriculture. Women are involved in every stage of food production. Although men usually plough the fields and drive draught animals, women do most of the work involved in sowing, weeding, fertilizing and harvesting the staple crops – such as rice, wheat and maize – which allows for more than 90 per cent of the rural poor's diet. Women's contribution to secondary crops, such as legumes and vegetables, is even greater. Most of these crops are grown in home gardens, tended almost exclusively by women. These gardens are often remarkably productive and critically important to nutritional and economic well-being.

FOOD SECURITY

Food Security, at the individual, household, national, regional, and global levels [is achieved] when all people, at all times, have physical, social, and economic access to sufficient, safe, and nutritious food to meet their dietary needs and food preferences for a healthy and active life. ...FAO (2001)

Food security is essentially built on three pillars: food availability, food access, and food utilization. An individual must have access to sufficient food of the right dietary mix (quality) at all times to be food secure. Those who never have sufficient quality food are chronically food insecure. Those whose access to an adequate diet is conditioned by seasonality are food insecure and are generally called seasonally food insecure. Individuals who normally have enough to eat but become food insecure in the face of disasters triggered by economic, climatic, and civil shocks (war and conflict) are transitorily food insecure. The "at all times" element of the food security definition makes risk and associated vulnerability an important element of the food security concept.

The definition of food security is often applied at varying levels of aggregation, despite its articulation at the individual level. The importance of a pillar depends on the level of aggregation being addressed. At a global level, the important pillar is food availability. Does global agricultural activity produce sufficient food to feed all the world's inhabitants? The answer today is yes, but it may not be true in the future given the impact of a growing world population, emerging plant and animal pests and diseases, declining soil productivity and environmental quality, increasing use of land for fuel rather than food, and lack of attention to agricultural research and development, among other factors.

When food security is analyzed at the national level, an understanding not only of national production is important, but also of the country's access to food from the global market, its foreign exchange earnings, and its citizens' consumer choices. Food security analyzed at the household level is conditioned by a household's own food production and household members' ability to purchase food of the right quality and diversity in the market place. However, it is only at the individual level that the analysis can be truly accurate because only through understanding who consumes what can we appreciate the impact of socio-cultural and gender inequalities on people's ability to meet their nutritional needs.

The third pillar, food utilization, essentially translates the food available to a household into nutritional security for its members. One aspect of utilization is analyzed in terms of distribution according to need. Nutritional standards exist for the actual nutritional needs of men, women, boys, and girls of different ages and life phases (that is, pregnant women), but these "needs" are often socially constructed based on culture. For example, in South Asia evidence shows that women eat after everyone else has eaten at a meal and are less likely than men in the same household to consume preferred foods such as meats and fish.

Hidden hunger commonly results from poor food utilization: that is, a person's diet lacks the appropriate balance of macro- (calories) and micronutrients (vitamins and minerals). Individuals may look well nourished and consume sufficient calories but be deficient in key micronutrients such as vitamin A, iron, and iodine. People may live in unhealthy environments with inadequate hygiene and sanitation, which results in frequent illnesses and compromised nutritional outcomes despite sufficient food being available. Infants and very young children may have mothers who are so time constrained, particularly at peak times in the agricultural calendar, that they are unable to feed a child as often as necessary to provide good nutrition. Malnutrition is economically costly: it can cost individuals 10 per cent of their lifetime earnings and nations 2 to 3 per cent of gross domestic product (GDP) in the worst-affected countries (Alderman 2005).

WOMEN – FOOD SECURITY

Agricultural interventions are most likely to affect nutrition outcomes when they involve diverse and complementary processes and strategies that redirect the focus beyond agriculture for food production and toward broader consideration of livelihoods, women's empowerment, and optimal intra-household uses of resources. Successful projects are those that invest broadly in improving human capital, sustain and increase the livelihood assets of the poor, and focus on gender equality. **...** *World Bank (2007b)*

Women are crucial in the translation of the products of a vibrant agriculture sector into food and nutritional security for their households. They are often the farmers who cultivate food crops and produce commercial crops alongside the men in their households as a source of income. When women have an income, substantial evidence indicates that the income is more likely to be spent on food and children's needs. Women are generally responsible for food selection and preparation and for the care and feeding of children. Women are the key to food security for their households (Quisumbing and others 1995).

Women are responsible for half of the world's food production, and in most developing countries they produce between 60 and 80 per cent of the food. Yet, women continue to be regarded as home producers or assistants on the farm, and not as farmers and economic agents on their own merit. Women receive a small fraction of assistance for agricultural investments; women in Africa receive less than 10 per cent of small farm credit and 1 per cent of total credit to the agricultural sector. Empowering women farmers is vital to lifting rural communities out of poverty, especially as many developing nations face economic crisis, food insecurity, HIV/AIDS, environmental degradation and increasing urbanization.

Agricultural productivity and income gains are necessary but not sufficient to eliminate hunger and malnutrition. Women are responsible for nutrition in most homes, including the purchase and preparation of food. However, because of traditional norms, they often have limited access to education and control over resources. When given the opportunity to manage household finances, studies show that women are more likely than men to spend on their family's nutritional needs, healthcare, and school fees for children. Therefore, empowering women to increase access to and control over resources is critical to attaining food security in the developing world.

WOMEN'S MULTIPLE ROLES IN FOOD SECURITY IN INDIA

Women play important roles in food security as food producers, keepers of traditional knowledge and preservers of biodiversity, food processers and preparers and food providers for their families. Because of their multiple roles, women are key players in overcoming food insecurity.

Women as farmers and food producers

Women produce a large part of the world's food. Exact data is very hard to come by but FAO estimates that women are the main producers of the world's staple foods: maize, wheat and rice. Overall, women are responsible for about 50 per cent of the world's food production and, in some countries of sub-Saharan Africa and India women provide between 60 and 80 per cent of the food for household consumption, mainly as unpaid labourers on family plots. Women's contribution to agricultural production varies from country to country, crop to crop and task to task. Women are also found in agricultural wage labour.

Majority rural Indian women are experts in the field of food production. Women perform many tasks in household crop production, including sowing seeds, weeding, applying fertilizers and pesticides, and harvesting and threshing of the crops. They are also responsible for post-harvest food processing, storage, transport and marketing. In addition to producing staple crops, women in many countries also grow legumes and vegetables to feed their families. They also play an important role in raising poultry and small livestock such as goats, rabbits and pigs. They also feed and milk larger livestock. Small-scale fisheries, which provide more than 25 per cent of the world's fish food catch, depend on women's contributions. Women play critical roles in fisheries in India, particularly in the pre- and post-harvest sector. In the marine sector, according to the Marine Fisheries Census, 2005, of the 756,391 fisher folk involved in fishing and allied activities, 365,463 are women. There are 152,692 women engaged in marketing of fish, as against 54,670 men, which indicates that women predominate in fish marketing.

Women as preservers of biodiversity

Women are often the preservers of traditional knowledge of indigenous plants and seeds. As the ones responsible for supplying their families with food and care, they have a special knowledge of the value and diverse uses of plants for nutrition, health and income. They grow traditional varieties of vegetables, herbs and spices in their home gardens. Women also often experiment with and adapt indigenous species. They are involved in the exchange and saving of seeds. This has important implications for the conservation of plant genetic resources. Unfortunately, the importance of women's knowledge and expertise on biodiversity is often overlooked or ignored by development planners. The present UPA Government has taking some steps towards in this direction.

As providers of basic foods, fuel and water for their families, women have an important stake in the preservation of the environment and combating environmental degradation. Women recognize the importance of forests as a source of food, fodder, medicine and many other products. Mainly responsible for providing water for the household, women are acutely aware of the importance of water sources. Consequently, women have a particular interest in natural resource management, sustainable development and preservation of the environment.

Women as food processors, preparers and providers

Women are universally responsible for food preparation for their families and engaged in various stages and steps of processing this food. In many cultures and countries including India, women have the main responsibility for the provision of food—if not by producing it, then by earning income to purchase it. This applies to urban and non-farming women as well as women farmers, and is not limited to the large percentage of female-headed households in the world.

This gender division of responsibilities is often unrecognized by development planners. False assumptions about households as a unit can have detrimental effects on food security. Development planners often assume that the increase of household income through the employment of men in cash crop production will benefit everyone and enable the household to purchase food. But in many cases, incomes are not pooled although women remain responsible for supplying the food.

Obstacles Women Face in Food Security

- In many developing countries, land is predominantly owned by men and transferred inter-generationally to males. Therefore women may lack access to land, water rights and livestock. In addition, even when women are able to access land, lack of ownership creates a disincentive to invest time and resources into sustainable farming practices, which in turn lowers production and results in less income and food for the household.

- o Women and girls do not receive adequate education and training opportunities. Education has proven to be an important tool to increase agricultural productivity and reduce poverty and malnutrition. However, girls in developing countries often have less access to basic education and women receive only five per cent of agricultural extension services worldwide.
- o Women have less access to credit than men, as well as less control over financial resources. Women in Africa access only one per cent of available credit in the agricultural sector, in part because women often do not have the necessary collateral. This lack of credit limits their ability to purchase agricultural tools, seeds, fertilizers or hire labor that could increase their crop production.
- o Women often do not have the appropriate technology, tools and inputs for farming productively. Studies in Burkina Faso, Kenya, Nigeria and Zambia showed that due to differential control over resources, when men and women grew the same crop on individual plots, women were at a disadvantage. Most inputs, such as labor and fertilizer, went to the men's plots. Some experts estimate that if women had the same inputs as men, household agricultural output in sub-Saharan Africa could increase between 10 to 20 percent.
- o Time is a major constraint for women. In many instances, women have to spend a great deal of time traveling on foot to collect water and firewood, preparing meals and feeding the family, and traveling between the home and fields, forcing them to make difficult trade-offs.
- o Women's mobility may be constrained because they are tied to their homes and are the primary care takers of children. They may also lack access to transportation and roads. Furthermore, women may be confronted with risks to their safety, especially in conflict and post-conflict environments; violence against women is a serious problem around the world.

- o Households affected by HIV/AIDS have increased vulnerability to food insecurity. Illness due to HIV/AIDS impedes a family's capacity to grow food while their nutritional needs are even more critical. Additionally, burdens on women as caretakers are increased.

Interventions

- o Include women as well as men in the design of agriculture and nutrition programs.
- o Encourage property, divorce and inheritance laws that allow women to hold title to land and provide a mechanism for enforcing the laws.
- o Provide women and girls with access to primary education as well as training on agricultural production, resource management and conservation.
- o Ensure agricultural extension agents understand and consider the needs of women farmers; and recruit more female extension workers.
- o Facilitate lending to women entrepreneurs working in agriculture; make financial services more accessible to rural women.
- o Ensure that agricultural programs consider the needs and preferences of both men and women when developing and introducing new varieties and technologies.
- o Provide rural women with greater mobility and market information by facilitating access to roads, transportation, water and information technology services.
- o Include gender specific monitoring and evaluation indicators in food security programs.
- o Provide training for agriculture and nutrition specialists on how to apply gender methodologies to the design and implementation of programs.
- o Build local leadership (PANCHAYAT) and leverage relationships with government ministries and other institutions to create responsible food security policies that prevent crisis, integrating gender considerations into policies using evidence-based advocacy.

KEY FACTS

- o In developing countries, women tend to work far longer hours than men. In Asia and Africa, studies have shown that women work as much as 13 hours more per week.
- o On average, rural women and girls spend almost an hour each day gathering fuel and carrying water needed to prepare meals. In some communities, these activities may take up to four hours a day.
- o A study in Africa found that, over the course of a year, women carried more than 80 tonnes of fuel, water and farm produce for a distance of 1 km. Men carried only one-eighth as much, an average of 10 tonnes for 1 km each year.
- o Studies have shown that women use almost all they earn from marketing agricultural products and handicrafts to meet household needs. Men use at least 25 per cent of their earnings for other purposes.

CONCLUSION

Women's contributions to food production and food security would be far greater if they enjoyed equal access to essential resources and services. In many societies, tradition and laws bar women from owning land. In South and Southeast Asia more than 60 per cent of the female labour force is engaged in food production but, in India, Nepal and Thailand for example, less than 10 per cent of women farmers own land. Without lands to serve as collateral, women are also cut off from access to credit. And without credit, they often cannot buy essential inputs – such as seeds, tools and fertilizer – or invest in irrigation and land improvements. It is the main duty of government to recognize the role of women in food production and food security in India. The former Chief Minister of Andhra Pradesh, Dr. Y.S. Rajasekhara Reddy had given more importance for women in general and women formers in particular. He provided loans with Rs. 0.25 interest and free current for cultivation for the welfare of all human beings including women. India is taking good steps towards food security along with International Organizations like; FAO and SAARC. Without food security it is not possible for India to become developed country status in the world.

REFERENCES

1. Daman Praksh. (2003): "*Rural Women, Food Security and Agricultural Cooperatives*", Rural Development and Management Centre, New Delhi, India.
2. FAO. (2006): "*The State of Food and Agriculture*", FAO Information Division, Rome.
3. FAO. (2010): "*Global Food Security Review*", Rome, 13th December 2010.
4. FAO. "*GIEWS Country Briefs-India*", Rome, 2nd September-2010.
5. FAO. "*Module-1: Gender and Food Security*", Rome.
6. FAO. "Quick Country Facts-India", Rome, 1st December-2010.
7. FAO. "*Women, Agriculture and Food Security*", Fact Sheet of Food and Agriculture Organization of the United Nations, Rome.
8. Marilee Karl. (2009): "*Inseparable: The Crucial Role of Women in Food Security Revisited*".
9. Nilabja Ghosh and Basudeb Guha Khasnobis. (2006): "*Looking for Answers to the Food Security Problem – India under Current Compulsions*", World Institute for Development Economic Research, United Nations University, Tokyo.
10. Nira Ramachandran. (2006): "*Women and Food Security in South Asia – Current Issues and Emerging Concerns*", World Institute for Development Economic Research, United Nations University, Tokyo.
11. Radhika, K. and Amareswaran, N. (2009): "*Women in Agriculture*", Paper Presented in the National Seminar on 'Work Participation and Training Opportunities for Women: Status and Strategies', Dept. of Adult and Continuing Education, Sri Venkateswara University, Tiruapti, 5th -6th December, 2009.
12. Rekha Mehra and Mary Hill Rojas. "*Women, Food Security and Agriculture in a Global Market Place*", International Centre for Research on Women.
13. Report of the Workshop on "*Gender Concerns in Food Security*", M. S. Swaminathan Research Foundation, Chennai, 2007.
14. Report on "*Enhancing Women's Roe in Fisheries in India*", YUVA Centre, Navi Mumbai, India, 2010.
15. Susan Lynn Robers. (2001): "*Women: The Key to Food Security*".
16. USAID. "*Food Security and Gender*", Fact Sheet, International Development, United States Agency, USA.

11

Malnutrition Among Children and Women in India

INTRODUCTION

In the scientific and modern world, it is not difficult to know information in the world related to Education, Health, Economy and Entertainment. Globalization, privatization and liberalization have been giving better opportunities to get job and money. There is no doubt at all 'the economic development of individual and society are taking place simultaneously', but the position of tribes is as usual

The Indian economy has recently grown at historically unprecedented rates and is now one of the fastest-growing economies in the world. Real GDP per head grew at 3.95% a year from 1980 to 2005, and at 5.4% a year from 2000 to 2005. Measured at international prices, real per capita income in India, which was two-thirds of Kenya's in 1950, and about the same as Nigeria's, is now two and a half times as large as per capita income in both countries. Real per capita consumption has also grown rapidly, at 2.2% a year in the 1980s, at 2.5% a year in the 1990s, and at 3.9% a year from 2000 to 2005.

Approximately 60 million children are underweight in India. Given its impact on health, education and productivity, persistent under-nutrition is a major obstacle to human development and economic growth in the country, especially among the poor and the vulnerable, where the prevalence of malnutrition is highest. The progress in reducing the proportion of undernourished children in India over the past decade has been modest and slower than what has been achieved in other countries with comparable socioeconomic indicators. While aggregate levels of under-nutrition are shockingly high, the picture is further exacerbated by the significant inequalities across states and socioeconomic groups – girls, rural areas, the poorest and scheduled tribes and castes are the worst affected –and these inequalities appear to be increasing.

In India, child malnutrition is mostly the result of high levels of exposure to infection and inappropriate infant and young child feeding and caring practices, and has its origins almost entirely during the first two to three years of life. However, the commonly-held assumption is that food insecurity is the primary or even sole cause of malnutrition.

Consequently, the existing response to malnutrition in India has been skewed towards food-based interventions and has placed little emphasis on schemes addressing the other determinants of malnutrition. Maximum number of youths is living in India. 'Health is wealth'. It is our duty to take care about health. Without good health any one can't do anything. Because of science and technology enormous changes were occurred in the field of medicine. It is the right time to take right action towards malnutrition of citizens of India in general and tribal children and women in particular.

NUTRITION OF CHILDREN AND WOMEN

The well articulated analysis of child malnutrition in India (June 22, 2009) has rightly concluded that linkages of child malnutrition with women's health and well-being are strong. As for the contention that the focus should shift from enhancing incomes and food availability to understanding how members of a household establish command over food, health and care.

The National Family Health Survey (NFHS-3) 2005-06 was released recently by the Ministry of Health and Family Welfare. This report offers a comprehensive picture of the health, nutrition and population status in the country. The report paints a mixed picture of India's overall reproductive health status. On the one hand, women are having fewer children and infant mortality has dropped in the seven-year period since the last NFHS survey in 1998-99. On the other hand, anaemia and malnutrition are still widespread among children and adults.

The NFHS survey is based on a sample of households that is representative at the national and state levels. It conducted interviews with around 2, 00,000 women age 15-49 and men age 15-54 throughout India. NFHS-3 also tested more than 1, 00,000 women and men for HIV and 2, 15,000 adults and young children for anaemia. The data set on key indicators provides a trend that includes information on several new topics, such as HIV/AIDS related attitudes and behaviour, male involvement in family welfare and attitudes about family life and education for children in school.

Malnutrition and Anaemia major problem in children and women

Malnutrition continues to be a significant health problem for children and adults in India. While there have been some improvements in the nutritional status of young children in several states, nutritional deficiencies are still widespread. There has been the increase in wasting (excessively thin), or weight per height, among children under age 3 years. Around 23% of children were wasted. At the same time, there has been very marginal change in the percentage of children who are underweight (43% in NFHS-2 and 40% in NFHS-3).

NFHS-3 also found high prevalence of anaemia – 70% – in children aged 6-59 months. Anaemia in India is primarily linked to poor nutrition. Women and men suffer a dual burden of over-nutrition and under-nutrition. More than one third of women are too thin, while 13% are overweight or obese. In all, nearly half of the married women are either underweight or overweight. One-third of men are too thin, and 9% are overweight or obese. The states with the largest percentage of overweight women and men are Punjab, Kerala, and Delhi, especially among the more educated.

Anaemia is also disturbingly common among adults. More than half of women in India (55%) are anaemic. Anaemia among pregnant women has also increased. Even though men are much less likely women to be anaemic, anaemia levels in men are at around 24%.

Diarrhoea continues to be a major health problem for many children. Although knowledge about Oral Rehydration Salts (ORS) for the treatment of diarrhoea is widespread among mothers, only 58% of children with diarrhoea were taken to a health facility, down from 65% seven years earlier.

The data not only presents the stark reality but is an urgent call to action. It is a call not only to make policies or programmes which are focussing on children and women, but also to allocate resources for all those proclamations and focus on implementation and monitoring of all that is proclaimed.

Malnutrition and Anaemia Rates are high among Children

- o 38.4% of children under age three are stunted, that is too short for their age and 46% are underweight that is too thin for their age. Both indicators have slightly improved from 1998-99.
- o Wasting, defined as an abnormally low weight for the child's height affects 19% of children under age three with a slight deterioration from 1998-99.
- o Overall, girls and boys are about equally likely to be undernourished. Under-nutrition is higher in rural areas and is strongly correlated with the level of maternal education showing a two-fold difference between non-educated mothers and 10-year and above educated mothers. This may be linked to a stark difference in access to a nutritious diet and complementary feeding at 6-9 months.
- o Most children under age three are anemic (79.2%). The prevalence is slightly higher in rural areas and among non-educated mothers. High prevalence of anaemia may be linked to poor variety of diet, poor hygienic conditions and limited access to iron supplementation.

Improvements Needed in Infant and Child Feeding and Micronutrient Intake

- o While breastfeeding is nearly universal in India, less than half of children (46%) are fed only breast milk for the first 6 months, as recommended. Exclusive breastfeeding is slightly higher among the non-educated mothers and in rural areas. Work conditions and access to breast milk substitutes may impact the feeding pattern among urban and better educated mothers.

- o Only 23.4% of children are breastfed within one hour of birth and the prevalence is significantly lower among the non-educated mothers and in rural areas. However, there has been an overall improvement from 9.5% in 1992-93 and 16% in 1998-99.
- o Only 55.8% of children aged 6-9 months receive solid or semisolid food and breast milk. Although the percentage is significantly lower among non-educated mothers and in rural areas, the prevalence in urban areas and among well-educated mothers is still less than 70% making complementary feeding a high-priority to be addressed.
- o Only 44 percent of breastfeeding children 6-23 months are fed at least the minimum recommended number of times per day (twice a day for children 6-8 months and three times for children 9-23 months) and only 36 percent are given food from at least 3 food groups, as recommended to ensure adequate diversity in their diet.
- o Just 25% of children age 6-35 months received vitamin A supplements in the six months before the survey. The Government of India recommends twice yearly vitamin A supplements for children age 6-59 months.

A significant percentage of Women and Men are either too thin or too fat

- o Malnutrition and anaemia are common among Indian adults. Both malnutrition and anaemia have increased among women since 1998-99.
- o 33% of married women and 28% of men are too thin, according to the body mass index (BMI), an indicator derived from height and weight measurements. Underweight is most common among the poor, the rural population, adults who have no education and scheduled castes and scheduled tribes.

- o Overweight and obesity, the other side of malnutrition, is a growing problem in India, affecting almost 15% of women and 12% of men. Overweight and obesity are most common in urban areas, in wealthier households, and among older adults, Sikhs and those with more education.

Anaemia is Widespread

- o 56.2% of women and 24.3% of men suffer from anaemia, and have lower than normal levels of blood haemoglobin. Anaemia has increased in ever-married women from 1998-99. Among pregnant women, anaemia has increased from 50% to almost 58%.
- o Only 22.3% of pregnant women consume Iron and Folic Acid supplementation for 90 days and the percentage is less than 10% among the non-educated women compared to 50% among the well-educated. Also the disparity between rural and urban areas is significant (18% and 34.5% respectively)

Many Households are Vulnerable to Iodine Deficiency

- o Iodine deficiency, which can lead to mental retardation, goitre, and complications of pregnancy, is easily prevented by using salt fortified with iodine. Only 51 percent of Indian households use adequately iodized salt, however.

FACTS RELATED TO NUTRITION

- o Malnutrition kills 5 million children every year.... one child every 6 seconds.
- o 47 percent of India's children below the age of three years are malnourished (underweight). The World Bank puts the number – probably conservatively – at 60 million this is out of a global estimated total of 146 million.
- o 47 percent of Indian children under five are categorized as moderately or severely malnourished.
- o The UN ranks India in the bottom quartile of countries by under-1 infant mortality (the 53rd highest), and under-5 child mortality (78 deaths per 1000 live births).6 According to the 2008 CIA fact book, 32 babies out of every 1,000 born alive die before their first birthday.

- o At least half of Indian infant deaths are related to malnutrition, often associated with infectious diseases.
- o Malnutrition impedes motor, sensory, cognitive and social development 8, so malnourished children will be less likely to benefit from schooling, and will consequently have lower income as adults.
- o The most damaging effects of under-nutrition occur during pregnancy and the first two years of a child's life.
- o These damages are irreversible, making dealing with malnutrition in the first two year crucially important.
- o A close reading of available statistics shows the problem to be far from uniform.

CONCLUSION

Two factors govern a common man's diet in India. The first is misconception about nutrition. A lot of us associate nutrition with costly food. Most of our cooking processes drain the food of essential nutrients. The food is mainly carbohydrate rich and protein deficient. The second factor is the failure of the public distribution system. Basic food commodities are becoming costlier and out of the reach of the common man. To complicate matters, the new fad of having processed food threatens to push traditional foods, which are quite nutritious, into oblivion. To improve the health status of child and women, village panchayats should register all health cases. Pregnant women should be taken care about theirs' health. A mobile medical unit should visit them for pre-natal and post-natal checkups. Secondly, a pregnant woman should be given cereal food equivalent to her wage for three months. She should not be allowed to work for these three months one-and-a-half months before and after delivery. Such minimum social security measures will go a long way in helping women. It is the duty of government to conduct awareness programmes related to nutritional food. Majority of citizens have no idea about National Rural Health Mission. Mini nutritional food stalls should be established for better health of child and women in general and rural child and women in particular.

REFERENCES

1. "*National Family Health Survey-3*" (2005-06), Ministry of Health and Family Welfare, Government of India.
2. "*National Family Health Survey-2*" (1998-99), Ministry of Health and Family Welfare, Government of India.
3. "*National Family Health Survey-1*" (1992-93), Ministry of Health and Family Welfare, Government of India.

12

Senior Citizens in India – National Development

INTRODUCTION

The development of any country depends mainly on its human resources. India is a developing country. Now we are living in the scientific, technological modern world. We have more human resources after China. Increased human life span as witnessed in the preceding decades has not been accompanied by good quality of life for majority of older Indians. Of the many determinants of the quality of life: financial security, emotional security and health and wellbeing, the last one occupies the prime position, as all other issues become irrelevant in poor health. Research in social gerontology and geriatrics in past decades have provided insight into various aspects of the status of older people in India. Large volume of authentic data on demographic trends, impact of changes in the family structure and migration, physical and behavioral status, organization and dynamics of health systems exist in Indian literature. However, very little effort has been made to develop a model of health and social care in tune with the changing need and time. As no model for older people exists in India, as well as most other societies with similar socioeconomic situation, it may be a challenge as well as an opportunity for innovation in social and health system development.

DEMOGRAPHY OF IN INDIA

According to the 2001 Census, India's population was 102.9 crores. Viewed in a global context, India constitutes 16.9 per cent of world population and 2.4 per cent of the global land area. Currently, India's population is estimated to be around 111.2 crores. The population of India grew by 21.6 per cent in the first decade following Independence; the rate rose to 24.8 per cent during the next decade. The growth began declining from the third decade onwards and in between 1991 and 2001; it declined to 21.5 per cent. The high population growth rate in some parts of the country is due to the large size of the population in the reproductive age group, higher fertility due to lack of contraception, and high wanted fertility due to the high infant mortality rate (IMR). The population of India is expected to increase from 1,029 million to 1,400 million during the period 2001-2026-an increase of 36 per cent in 25 years at the rate of 1.2 per cent annually. With declining fertility and increase in life expectancy, the number of older people is expected to more than double, from 71 million in 2001 to 173 million in 2026.

DEFINITION

The elderly are defined as those who are 60 years old and above. This definition is based on that made at the World Assembly on Aging in Vienna in 1982. Elderly are also known as senior citizens.

DEMOGRAPHY OF SENIOR CITIZENS

As per Census 2001, the number of older persons in 2001 was 70.6 million (6.9%) which was projected to be 83.5 million in 2006 (7.5%). As per the projections the percentage of older persons will be 94.8 million in 2011 (8.3%), 118 million in 2016, (9.3%) 143.7 million in 2021(10.7%) and 173.1 million in 2026 (12.4%).

The gender position of the elderly reveals that the life expectancy of women is expected to remain higher. For the period 2006-2010 the life expectancy of female is 68.1 against 65.8 of males which will rise to 72.3 for female against 69.02 for males during the period

2011-2016. This indicates that the population of elderly women will account for a larger chunk compared to their male counterpart in 60+ age bracket.

In absolute terms, the projection for male population in 60 + age group was 35 million in 2001, projected to be 40.7 million in 2006 and 48 million in 2011 as against the female population in same age group was 36 million in 2001, 42 million in 2006 and 50.2 million in 2011. From the projected figures for the year 2006-2011 and 2016, 2021 and 2026, it is also clear that percentage of female population in 70 + age group will outnumber their male counterpart in the same age group. This accounts for a larger female population in the overall 60 + age group compared to the male population in the years to come. Many of women in the 70 + age group would be either widow or single without any ostensible support for themselves.

A comparison of rural elderly and the urban establish the fact that around 74.97 per cent of older persons live in rural areas and 25.02 in urban areas. This involves planning for post retirement socio-economic security through continued skill up-gradation, employment and participation in other creative and gainful activities.

With the changing lifestyle of modern society the young generation are migrating from not only rural to urban area rather one country to another as well; leading to increase in old age dependency ratio. The old age dependency ratio (number of old persons 60+ years) to the working age group (15-59 years) has increased from 9.8 per cent in 1981 to about 12.6 per cent by the year 2001. (Census of India, 2001)

Other Significant Facts – No Specific Interventions:

- o 58% of women 60+ are widows/ unmarried/ divorced (2000).
- o 70.3% of elderly are illiterate (2000).
- o Labour force participation of 65+ in 2000 -32%.
- o 90% from the unorganised sector –No pensions or provident fund

Emerging Scenario

- o Increase in life expectancy
- o Increase in 'old -old' segment

- o Feminisation of elderly population
- o Urbanisation
- o Changes will be at a rapid pace in infrastructure. Access friendly and Mobility for all in New Infrastructure
- o Grant in Aid (Rs. 18.79 crores) 04-05
- o Separate Department in China for Older Persons

Other Significant Facts:

	Rural	**Urban**
Old-age dependency ratio	125	103
Sex-ratio among the aged	985	1046
Living arrangements (%)		
Living Alone	5	4
With spouse	58	58
Children	33	33
Others	4	5
Immobile and Confined to bed (%)		
Male	6.7	6.8
Female	8.8	10.0
Persons	7.7	8.4

Challenges Posed By Ageing:

1. *Health*

- o By 2020, it is projected that three-quarters of all deaths in developing countries could be ageing-related. 16% of the world's elderly population will be in India.
- o Visual impairment and vision loss increase dramatically with age. Cataract mostly related to the ageing process. 8.1 million are blind in India out of which 6.5 million is due to cataract.
- o Over 10% of India's elderly suffers from depression and 40-50 % of elderly requires psychiatric or psychological intervention at some point in their twilight years.

2. *Financial Insecurity*

- o As many as 70% aged depend on others for their day-to-day maintenance. The situation is worse for elderly females where 85-87% is economically dependent either partially or fully.

- o Among the aged who were once employed either as wage/ salaried employees or as casual labour, about 79% in the rural areas and 35% in urban areas do not receive any benefit on their retirement.

SENIOR CITIZENS - NATIONAL DEVELOPMENT

In each family, it's the old people who act as a bridge to connect traditional and modern values. They also hold a key position in preserving and developing traditional occupations.

Many elderly people are making use of their wealth of experience to continue contributing to the society. Majority of elderly are running their own businesses or farms. Thousands of retire and intellectual are teaching at community-based education centres, or continue their research work.

Elderly people in India can now live longer with better health as their living conditions have been improved much thanks to the country's economic growth and specially-designed policies of the government. The average life expectancy has extended to 66.43 years.

No one is useless thing in the world. Elderly are resources of values and traditions. Their experiences and knowledge are very useful for national development. By proper utilizing their services we can develop in all the fields within the goal period.

SUGGESTIONS AND CONCLUSIONS

The implementation of programmes and activities related to the elderly by every individual and group, voluntary organisation, local community, government agency and the private sector based on the National Policy on Older People.

For the success of the implementation of the National Policy on Older People, integrated and comprehensive efforts have to be taken by the concerned agencies, including:

- o Education – Education and training are to be made available for the elderly to develop their potential to the optimum. The school curriculum is to include education on the family to enable the younger generation to understand and appreciate the elderly.

- o Employment – The elderly are encouraged to continue contributing to national development through employment according to their respective experience and skills. In this way, they are able to be independent with respect to income and their well-being.
- o Participation in society – The elderly are encouraged to involve themselves in family and societal activities to enable them to play their role in their family and society besides interacting among themselves.
- o Recreation – Suitable facilities are to be provided to the elderly to carry out recreational activities in housing areas, recreational parks and sports centres.
- o Transport – The public transport system is to provide suitable facilities to enable the elderly to move comfortably from one place to another.
- o Housing – Existing and future houses should include facilities suitable for the elderly to enable them to live comfortably.
- o Support system for the family – To ensure that the elderly can continue to live with their family, a support system for the family needs to be established in housing areas to assist families in caring for the elderly. Certain incentives need to be introduced to enable family members to continue caring for their elderly members.
- o Health – Health and medical facilities appropriate and specific to the elderly are to be provided to ensure that their health is well taken care of.
- o Social security – A comprehensive social security scheme is to be provided to secure the future of the elderly.
- o Media – The print as well as electronic media are to play active roles to increase the society's awareness of the elderly.
- o Research and development – Studies are to be carried out to obtain information to enable better planning for the senior citizens. The Social Welfare Department under the Ministry of Women, Family and Community Development has been identified as the agency responsible for the coordination of the implementation of the action plan.

REFERENCES

1. Arjun Adlakha (2003). "Population Trends: India", International Brief.
2. Dey, A.B. (2006). "Emerging Challenges Old Age Care in India", Journal of the Indian Academy of Geriatrics, Vol.2, No.4.
3. HELPAGE INDIA, non-profit organization, NGO, www.helpageindia.org.
4. National Policy on Older People, Government of India, New Delhi.

13

Attitude of Older People Towards Policies on Ageing in India

INTRODUCTION

"Age to me means nothing. I can't get old; I'm working. I was old when I was twenty-one and out of work. As long as you're working, you stay young. When I'm in front of an audience, all that love and vitality sweeps over me and I forget my age".

—George Burns (1896-1996)

Ageing is a universal biological fact and a natural process. It begins from the day we are born, or perhaps even before. The perception of age, however, is socially constructed. Isolation, exclusion and marginalization of older persons are the consequences of age discrimination. It not only undermines the status of older persons in society but also threatens the overall development of a society. The quality of life of the older person, however, can be improved by mainstreaming their concerns systematically into the overall developmental agenda.

NATIONAL POLICY ON OLDER PERSONS (NPOP)

Government of India announced the National Policy on Older Persons in 1999 to reaffirm its commitment to ensure the well-being of the older persons in a holistic manner. Reiterating the mandate enshrined in Article 41 of the Constitution of India, the Policy has brought the concern for older persons on top of the National Agenda. The NPOP while promising to safeguard their interest in terms of financial security, health, legal, social and psychological security, also envisages a productive partnership with them in the process of development by creating opportunities for their gainful engagement and employment. The Policy also appreciates special needs of older persons and therefore lays emphasis on empowerment of community as well as individuals to adequately meet the challenges of the process of ageing.

The NPOP broadly provides for the following to fulfill these objectives:

- Financial security
- Health Security:
- Recognizing Shelter as basic human need,
- Education/information needs
- Welfare and Institutional Care: Institutional Care
- Protection of Life and Property of Older Persons:
- Training of Human Resource to care for Older Persons
- Media

Available Support Services

- National Social Assistance Programme (NSAP)
- The National Old Age Pension Scheme (NOAPS)
- Annapurna Scheme
- Concessions/Tax Rebate/Other Incentives
- Insurance Coverage

STATEMENT OF THE PROBLEM

The present study aimed at study the attitude of elderly (both in rural and urban areas without considering their economic status) towards policies on ageing, social problems, social status and social welfare activities.

TITLE OF THE PROBLEM

The title of the present study is stated as "***ATTITUDE OF OLDER PEOPLE TOWARDS POLICIES ON AGEING IN INDIA***".

NEED AND IMPORTANCE OF THE STUDY

In the modern times, the role of family has been undergoing significant changes. Even in traditional societies of Asia or Africa there is a visible change taking place so far as the role and function of family is concerned. The traditional joint family system is gradually making way for nuclear family mode. Family, nevertheless, occupies a unique place in the traditional as well as modern societies even today. As a result of demographic changes and the changing family context, it can no longer be assumed that the older persons live comfortably at home receiving care from family members. Given the trend of population ageing in India, the older persons face a number of problems ranging from absence of ensured and sufficient income to support themselves and their dependants, to ill-health, to absence of social security, to loss of a productive social role and recognition, to non-availability of opportunities for creative use of free time. The trend clearly reveals that ageing poses a major challenge, and vast resources are required towards the support, care and treatment of the older person. There is an emerging need to pay greater attention to ageing issues and to promote holistic policies and programmes for dealing with an ageing society. Care of older persons is a growing concern of every individual and social security of the elderly is one of the prime responsibilities of the State.

PURPOSE OF THE STUDY

The present study aims at investigating the attitude of elderly towards policies on ageing. The purpose of the study is an attempt to answer the following aspects:

1. What is the position of elderly in India?
2. What is the status of implementation of policies on ageing?
3. What type of programmes we want?

OBJECTIVES OF THE STUDY

1. To find out the status of implementation of Policies on Ageing in India.
2. To find out real economic status of elderly in India.
3. To find out the social status of elderly in India.
4. To find out the role of family in the process of welfare of elderly.

SAMPLING

Two point scale questionnaire was used to collect the data. Random sampling technique was used. The size of the sampling was 60. 30 females and 30 males were taken in rural and urban areas.

RESULTS

1. Old Age Pension Amount

The government is giving old age pension under National Old Age Pension Scheme (NOAPS). Data was collected about amount of old age pension. The results age showed in the below table-1.

Table-1 Old Age amount

S.No.	Sex	Old Age amount	
		Is Normal	Will be increased
1	**Male**	-	100%
2	**Female**	-	100%

An analysis of the data table-1 shows that 100% of elderly male and female are feeling that the old age amount will be increased. The expressed their feeling that the amount is very less.

2. Status of Government Programmes

Table-2

S.No.	Sex	Government Programmes	
		Good	Not Good
1	**Male**	30%	70%
2	**Female**	40%	60%

From the above table we conclude that 30% male and 40% of female are feeling that the government programmes of ageing are good. Overall 35% of elderly are supporting government programmes, remaining 65% have no good feelings about government programmes of elderly.

3. New Policies of Ageing

Table-3

S.No.	Sex	New Policies of Ageing	
		Necessary	**Not necessary**
1	**Male**	86.66%	13.33%
2	**Female**	73.33%	26.66%

The result shown as about 80% of elderly (both male and female) are feeling that new policies of ageing are necessary. Only 20% of elderly are supporting to continue present policies.

4. Corruption

Table-4

S.No.	Sex	Corruption	
		Yes	**No**
1	**Male**	33.33%	66.67%
2	**Female**	30%	70%

The results from the Table-4 shown that, there are 31% of corruption is abstracting the effective implementation of policies of ageing.

5. Economic Position

In this category two cases were taken; economically dependent and economically independent.

Table-5

S.No.	Sex	Economic Position	
		Dependent	**Independent**
1	Male	66.66%	33.32%
2	Female	53.32%	46.66%

The above table shows that 60% of elderly are economically dependent either sons or daughters or relatives. Only 40% of elderly are economically independent. Females are better than males.

6. Department Co-operation

Table-6

S.No.	Sex	Department Co-operation	
		Good	Not Good
1	Male	73.32%	26.66%
2	Female	46.66%	53.32%

The analysis of the above table shows that 73.32% of males and 46.66% of females are feeling that they are getting full co-operation from government officials. Overall 60% of elderly are feeling that they are living happily. Only 40% of elderly are feeling they are not getting full co-operation from officials.

MAJOR FINDINGS

1. 100% of elderly male and female are feeling that the old age amount will be increased.
2. Only 35% of elderly are supporting government programmes.
3. 60% of elderly are living with good social status and getting full co-operation from government officials.
4. 60% of elderly are economically dependent on sons, daughters or relatives.
5. 100% of elderly are supporting joint family system.

CONCLUSION

The problems of the aged are related to other social problems in our society. There are a number of specialized NGOs coming up to join hands with the efforts of the government towards creating an elderly friendly environment in the country. The Senior Citizen Forums and Welfare Associations have been formed by the elderly themselves in various localities in India. By minimizing corruption and strengthening the policies it is possible to give good life for elderly in India. Our policies are good, but there is a lack of implementation. Elderly are resources of our traditions, culture and values. By utilize senior citizens experiences and ideas India will become developed country as early as possible.

REFERENCES

1. Bali, A. (1997). "Socio-economic status & its relationship to morbidity among elderly". Indian Journal of Medical Research. 106, pp 349-360.
2. National Policy on Older Persons (1999), Government of India, New Delhi.
3. Satyendra Prakash (2007). "Policies and Programmes on Population Ageing: Indian Perspective".

14

Gandhian Principles for Rural Development

You cannot build nonviolence on a factory civilization, but it can be built on self-contained villages. Education should be so revolutionized as to answer the wants of the poorest villager, instead of answering those of an imperial exploiter. ....M.K. Gandhi.

INTRODUCTION

There are no universally accepted approaches to rural development. It is a choice influenced by time, space and culture. The term rural development connotes overall development of rural areas to improve the quality of life of rural people. In this sense, it is a comprehensive and multidimensional concept, and encompasses the development of agriculture and allied activities, village and cottage industries and crafts, socio-economic infrastructure, community services and facilities and, above all, human resources in rural areas. As a phenomenon, rural development is the end-result of interactions between various physical, technological, economic, social, cultural and institutional factors. As a strategy, it is designed to improve the economic and social well-being of a specific group of people – the rural poor. As a discipline, it is multi-disciplinary in nature, representing an intersection of agriculture, social, behavioural, engineering and management sciences.

In the Indian context rural development assumes greater significance as 72.22 per cent (according to the 2001 census) of its population still live in rural areas. Most of the people living in rural areas draw their livelihood from agriculture and allied sectors (60.41 % of total work force), and poverty mostly persists here (27.1 % in 1999-2000). At the time of independence around 83 per cent of the Indian population was living in rural areas. Accordingly, from the very beginning, our planned strategy emphasized rural development and will continue to do so in future. Strategically, the focus of our planning was to improve the economic and social conditions of the underprivileged sections of rural society. Thus, economic growth with social justice became the proclaimed objective of the planning process under rural development. It began with an emphasis on agricultural production and consequently expanded to promote productive employment opportunities for rural masses, especially the poor, by integrating production, infrastructure, human resource and institutional development measures. Mahatma Gandhi, the Father of Indian Nation has paid special attention towards rural development. Village industry, model village and sarvodaya are the best concepts of Gandhi for rural development of India.

RURAL DEVELOPMENT

Rural development is defined as a "process which leads to a continuous rise in the capacity of the rural people to control their environment, accompanied by a wider distribution of benefits resulting from such a control.

Rural development must aim at reducing poverty by increasing production and raising productivity. It recognizes that improved food supplies and nutrition, together with basic services such as health and education, cannot only directly improve the physical well-being and quality of life of the rural poor, but can indirectly enhance their productivity and their ability to contribute to the national economy. It is concerned with the modernization and monetization of rural society, and with its transition from traditional isolation to integration with the national economy.

Objectivities of Rural Development

In a nutshell, the objectives of rural development are as under:

1. Providing certain social goods and services in terms of social and economic infrastructure.
2. Increasing the income of every rural family and to see that those who are below the poverty line are enabling to come above that line in coming years.
3. Improving the quality of rural poor.
4. Creating of additional employment opportunities in rural areas.

RURAL DEVELOPMENT – GANDHIAN PRINCIPLES

Rural development as a slogan came to the fore only in Gandhiji's time. He was a practical idealist who proclaimed for the first time that India was a country of villages and, consequently, the real development of her villages. Most of the leaders, who preceded him, had either an urban elite base or a semi-feudal base or a religious base. Gandhiji spoke in clear terms about the importance of Indian Village. "*To serve our Village is to establish Swaraj. Everything else is but an idle dream*". Gandhi further stated, "*If the village perishes, India too will perish. It will no more be India. Her own mission in the world will get lost*". According to Gandhi, "*We have to make a choice between India of the villages that are as ancient as her and India of the cities which are a creation of foreign domination. Today, the cities dominate and drain the villages so that they are crumbling to ruin. My Khadi mentality tells me that cities must sub-serve villages when that domination goes. Exploitation of villages is itself organized violence; we will have to give the villages their proper place*". Gandhiji was the first practical economist who diagnosed the human sufferings in our country and suggested pragmatic remedies; which were however, not given a fair trial by Indian planners.

Rural development programmes can be broadly classified into three categories – poverty alleviation, infrastructural development and structural programme, in which science and technology are vital for creating assets. The question is if the Gandhian view, in this context is obscurantist, why should P. Jyoti Rao (Joint Secretary, Ministry of Rural Development, Government of India), in 1994, make a categorical statement that Rural Development in India, as a conceptualized vision was the dream of Mahatma Gandhi, and it continues to be the guiding philosophy of rural society. Starting from Community Development Programme, which was launched in 1952, to today's poverty alleviation and employment generation programmes, all along the emphasis has been on rural development. Gandhiji's concept of '*Bread Labour*' was an essential component of '*sarvodaya society*'; Swadeshi was another Gandhian concept which added to the quality of life in rural India. His pleas for Basic Education emphasized the need for quality of life. The aim of his concept of Panchayat Raj, a sarvodaya principle, was to remove the social inequalities which still constitute a great danger to the quality of life. Gandhiji wanted the development process to start with the village. As Dr. G.S. Herbert maintains that Gandhiji did not prescribe rules for rural development, but gave us principles which are relevant today and will be relevant also in the twenty first century.

Science was definitely given top priority in Nehruvian model of rural development, and the history of difference between Gandhiji and Jawaharlal Nehru dates back to several decades. The questions were whether Gandhiji abhorred principle of mechanization of the West from a sense of despise. Prof. D.S. Ganguly contends that Gandhiji was not against the machinery altogether, he welcomed machinery of simple operation and saving individual labour. Gnadhiji exhorted; "*Scientific truths and discoveries should first of all cease to be the mere instruments of greed. Then labourers will not be overworked, and machinery, instead of becoming a hindrance, will be a help. I am aiming not at eradication of all machinery, but limitation*". Again he observed: "*I am against all destructive machinery, as saves individual labour, lightens the burden of the million of cottagers, I should welcome*".

We must not forget that Gandhiji placed rural development at the core of India's future destiny. His concept of Gram Swaraj was an oceanic circle, whose centre was the ever humble villager. Above all, there has to be a re-examination of the modern thrust of science and technology on ecology and local environment. But we need not accept Gandhiji's suggestions that to hasten the rural resurgence, we have to turn ourselves scavengers. However, it is to be borne in mind that Mahatma Gandhi proclaimed the victory of ultimate truth in man, and let him remain as guide to the last step of ascent.

Mahatma Gandhi and Mao Zedong, who differed radically in both philosophy as well as strategy, shared a common vision for rural development. Both leaders felt the need for ensuring that the masses had adequate employment so that their basic minimum needs in food, clothing, shelter, education and health care were met. Both stressed the role of mass participation and involvement and the need for the leadership to identify with the masses. Mahatma Gandhi writing in 1920 says: "*Every village's first concern will be to grow its own crops and cotton for its cloth. It should have a reserve for its cattle, recreation and playgrounds for adult and children. Then if there is more land available it will grow useful money crops. They will maintain a village theatre, school and public hall. It will have its own waterworks ensuring clean supply. This can be done through controlled wells and tanks. Education will be compulsory up to the final basis. There will be no castes as we have today, with their graded untouchability. Non-violence with its technique of 'Satyagraha' and non-cooperation will be the sanction of the village community. There will be a compulsory service of village wards who will be selected by rotation from the register, maintained by the village. The government of the village will be conducted by the Panchayat of five persons, annually elected by the adult villagers, male and female, possessing minimum prescribed qualifications. These will have all the authority and jurisdiction required. Since there will be no system of punishments in the accepted sense, this 'Panchayat' will be the legislature, judiciary, executive combined to operate for its years of office*".

Mahatma Gandhi had repeatedly focused his main attention on rural development and had offered a series of programmes to improve the well-being of the large number of rural population. In his oft-quoted phrase "*India does not live in its towns but in its villages*" he showed great concern for the people living outside the urbanized areas.

In "*Young India*" (23-04-1930) Mahatma Gandhi wrote: *If the cities want to demonstrate that their populations will live for the villagers of India, the bulk of their resources should be spent in ameliorating the condition of and befriending the poor. We must not lord it over them, we must learn to be their servants. When the cities realize that they must live for the welfare of the poor, they will make their palaces and institutions and the life of their inhabitants correspond somewhat to our villages.*

Mahatma Gandhi believed emphatically that an individual works for the family, the family for the village, the village for the district, the district for the province and the province for the nation. To this the script at Rajghat is an eloquent exposition. Gandhiji wanted that the rural communities should be integrated with the main economic stream. He offered to the rural people avenues for non-farming occupations by consciously advocating the adoption of cottage and small scale industries. He wanted rural areas to be accessible by good, clean roads and advised people on sanitary wells. He wanted electricity to reach the homes of all in the villages. Gandhiji strongly believed in self help and enthused people to organize themselves around viable institutions e.g. cooperatives, panchayats and the like so as to improve the quality of rural life and well-being. His conception of model village is described as follows: "*An ideal Indian village will be so constructed as to lend itself to perfect sanitation. It will have cottages with sufficient light and ventilation but of material obtainable within a radius of five miles of it. The cottages will have courtyards enabling the householders to plant vegetables for domestic use and to house their cattle. The village lanes and streets will be free of all avoidable dust. It will have wells according to its needs and accessible to all. It will have houses of worship for all, also a common meeting place, a village common for grazing its cattle, a cooperative dairy, primary and secondary schools in which industrial education will be the central factor, and it will have panchayats for settling disputes. It will produce its own grains, vegetables and fruits and its own khadi. This is roughly my idea of a model village*".

Gandhiji envisioned the establishment of a new civilization called Ram Rajya. He says, "*by Ram Raj, I do not mean Hindu Raj. I mean by Ram Raj a kingdom of God on earth*".

Gandhiji did not approve at all the western civilization which is urban in character. He said that "*a big country with a teeming population, with an ancient rural tradition, which has hitherto answered its purpose, need not and must not copy the western model. What is good for one nation situated in one condition is not necessarily good enough for another differently situated*".

The myth or misassumption about Gandhian view of Rural Development needs to be examined in depth. We have to remember that he was an emblem of what Max Weber would call charismatic authority, and that he was not a leader of '*machine politics*'. The distinguished author of Individuals and Societies: A Methodological Inquiry observes: "*In a pseudo scientific vein, it is often said that one's ideology has little or nothing to do with one's personal life, and could very well be assessed impersonally and objectively. This attitude betrays a series of misunderstanding about Science and Reason, and its hollowness has been exposed in recent years among others by Polanji and Hayek*".

It is a point to ponder that Gandhiji had no firsthand knowledge of the ideas of Einstein, though the great scientist found in the former's life, a profound ethical core with added new dimensions to an ideology, unheard of before. Practice is said to be the '*acid test*' of an idea. Gandhiji put his ideals of rural development process to a test, unheard of before, and it is here that one encounters the moral challenge of his ideology. Gandhiji's critique is directed not against science. He found the paradox of rural development process reflecting the ethical tension suffered by the alienated poor of the poorest in Indian villages-alienated under the pressure of westernized rural elite and the institutionalized man in the name of science and technology. Wrote Gandhiji: "*Let us not be obsessed with catchwords and slogans from the West. All that comes from the West on this subject is tarred with the brush of violence. I object to it because I have seen the wreckage that lies at the end of this road...And I owe whatever influence I have in the West, to my ceaseless endeavour to find a solution which promises an escape from the vicious circle of violence and exploitation. I have seen a sympathetic student of the Western Social order, and I have discovered that underlying the fever that fills the soul of the West, there is a restless search for truth...Let us study our Eastern institutions in that spirit of scientific enquiry and we shall evolve a truer socialism and a truer communism than the world has yet dreamed of*".

Prof. Sumit Sarkar goes astray when he asserts that Gandhian concept of rural development was '*undoubtedly unrealistic and even obscurantist'*, and it never had much appeal for sophisticated urban groups, which by the 1930s and 1940s were turning increasingly to modern industrialization and scientific technological measures and missions. Prof. Sumit Sarkar builds up his symphony of arguments on the *'Gandhian social, utopia'*, solely on the basis of Gandhiji's book entitled *'Hind Swaraj'* which was published in 1919. Prof. Sumit Sarkar maintains that the Gandhian idiom of rural resurgence was a full-scale repudiation of modern industrial civilization.

Gandhiji wanted the rural areas to hum with various types of activities and desired that rural living be made more pleasant and respectable. Rural development for Gandhi is a "*Self-sufficient village economy and self-sufficient village community*". He emphasized the utilization of local resources for development. He endeavoured to set up society that is self-supportive and self-governing. Gandhi wanted to make the affairs of the rural development the work of the rural people itself.

Revival of the Village

Gandhi's idea to develop the Indian society was based on his understanding of the society and hence based on the village system. Talking about the importance of village, he wrote in 1936, "*I would say if the village perishes, India will perish too. It will be no more India. His one mission in the world will get lost.*"

The revival of the village is possible only when it is no more exploited. Industrialization on a mass scale will necessarily lead to passive or active exploitation of the villagers as the problems of competition and marketing come in. Therefore we have to concentrate on the village being self-contained, manufacturing mainly for use. Provided this character of the village industry is maintained, there would be no objection to villagers using even the modern machines and tools that they can make and can afford to use. Only they should not be used as a means of exploitation of others.

He was aware of the realities of the village life and knew the plight of half starved masses of India. He often acknowledged the same in his vivid descriptions of Indian villages. He wrote, "*instead of having graceful hamlets dotting the lands, we have dung-heaps. The approach to many villages is not a refreshing experience. Often one would like to shut one's eyes and stuff one's nose, such is the surrounding dirt and offending smell*". (Gandhi: Constructive programmes – its meaning and place). His understanding of the plight of the people has been extremely well brought out in his writings, identifying his emphasis on removal of poverty over aesthetics.

Rural Reconstruction – Ideal Village

Gandhiji concept of rural reconstruction is a comprehensive one, emphasizing on the economic, political, social, educational, ecological and spiritual dimensions. He ceaselessly insisted on a pattern of village life, which will be man-centered and non-exploiting. The decentralized village economy should provide full employment to all on the basis of voluntary cooperation and work for achieving self-sufficiency in its basic requirement of food, clothing and shelter. In short, it can be said that rural reconstruction, according to Gandhi should not be merely concerned with raising the standard of living of village folk, though that was important. Talking specifically about an ideal village, where in he outlined the objectives of rural reconstruction: - he said, *My idea of an ideal village is that of complete republic independence of its neighbor for its own vital wants, and yet dependent for many others in which dependence is necessity. Such village will contain intelligent people. First concern of the village should be to grow its own food. Then only all communities will live together in harmony.*

The curse of untouchability, intoxicating drinks and drugs will not exist. Women will enjoy the same right as the men. People in villages will not live in dirt and darkness as animal. No one will wallow in luxury. The village community should take up the responsibility for providing work to all able bodied people and every one will have to contribute his quota of manual labour.

Non-violence with its techniques of Satyagraha and non-cooperation will have the sanction of village community. The government of the village will be conducted by the panchayat of five persons annually elected by the villagers (Harijan 26.07.42). Such an ideal society, he stated is "*necessarily highly cultured because every man and women in that society knows what he or she wants and also no one should want anything that others could not have. Such a society will be an*

"Oceanic Circle" where the centre will be the individual who will always be ready to perish for the village, later ready to perish for the circle of villagers, till at last the whole becomes a life comprised of individuals".

Affluence of people was, not in Gandhi's mind. He believed that there was sufficient to meet the needs of all people, but not their greed. He considered, that the type of development, Europe had achieved was the result of a systematic colonization and exploitation of both people and nature. In addition, it had contributed to imbalance in the levels of development of different areas, monopolization of benefits by a few families, and increase of poverty and violence. He, therefore rejected not only supportive mechanism of development seen as bureaucracy, technology, elitist education, but also the whole idea of development as conceived by the builders of the western industrial society.

Truth, non-violence, freedom, equality, full employment, bread labour, trusteeship, decentralization, swadesh and cooperation were perceived as cardinal principles for rural reconstruction.

CONCLUSION

The great soul of all human beings is Gandhiji. There is nothing in the world untouched by Gandhi for the welfare of all men and women including children. His every word is valuable. His principles on rural development are more valuable. He has given solutions for all types of problems in the rural India. It is the duty of our governments to follow his principles for rural development. There is no short cut route for rural development. Sustainable development of village is necessary for India to reach the status and goal of developed country. Without rural development it is impossible. The philosophical mind of Gandhi said valuable remarks. He was the man of clarity in mind and purity in heart. Every view of Gandhi reflects his greatness. It is our duty to establish 'Rama Rajyam' dreamed by Mahatma Gandhi.

REFERENCES

1. Gandhi, M.K. (1927): "*Autobiography: The Story of My Experiments with Truth*", Navajivan Mudranalaya, Ahemadabad-380014, India.
2. Lea, A.M., & Chaudhri, D.P. (1983): "*Rural Development and the State*", University Press, Cambridge, Great Britain.

3. Misra, R.N. (2002): "*Rural Development and Population*", Anmol Publications Pvt. Ltd., New Delhi.
4. Prasad, B.K. (2003): "*Rural Development: Concept, Approach and Strategy*", Sarup & Sons Publication, New Delhi.
5. Prasad, B.K. (2004): "*Rural Development and Village Democracy*", Anmol Publications Pvt. Ltd., New Delhi.
6. Ravindra Kumar. (2004): "*Mahatma Gandhi-at the close of Twentieth Century*", Anmol Publications Pvt. Ltd., New Delhi.
7. Shah, S.M. (1985): "*Growth Centres for Rural and Urban Development*", Abhinav Publications, New Delhi.
8. Sing, C.P. (1998): "*Relevance of Gandhian Thought in 21st Century-Rural Development: The Gandhian Experiences*", research paper published in 'Gandhi and 21st Century' edited by Janardan Pandy, Concept Publishing Company, New Delhi.
9. Tendulkar, D.G. (1934-38): "*Mahatma*" Vol.4, 'The Collected Works of Mahatma Gandhi', Navjivan Publishing House, Ahmedabad.
10. Tripathy, S.N. (2000): "*Rural Development*", Discovery Publication, New Delhi.

15

Nehru's Role In Industrial and Scientific Development of India

INTRODUCTION

Science has brought all these mighty changes and not all of them have been for the good of humanity. But the most vital and hopeful of the changes that it has brought about has been the development of the scientific outlook in man. ...Pandit Jawaharlal Nehru

In the present globalized world the development of any nation depends mainly on the standards of its Industrial and Scientific development. India is a developing country. We have a lot of human resource next to China. Without industrial and scientific development, it is not possible to provide/fulfill all types of requirements to each and every citizen. A vision is important for any political leader. The views and visions of our First Prime Minister Pt. Jawaharlal Nehru were excellent. He was the man behind the excellent development of India in the fields of Industry and Science. Nehru started his career as the Prime Minister of independent India in 1947, and immediately launched a number of economic reforms. Nehru was a firm believer in state control over the economic sectors. His socialist ideals revealed themselves in the way he introduced laws for land redistribution, in order to curtail the economic disparity in India among the landed and the land-less classes. One of Nehru's key economic reforms was the introduction of the Five Years Plan in 1951. It was introduce to determine the mode of government expenditure and grants in important development sectors like agriculture, industry and education.

POSITION OF INDIA BEFORE 1947

When India gained its independence after a long period of subjugation, its land and people were a picture of distress, removed from great events of its past glory and splendour. A whole creative side of Indian civilization had shrunk under the foreign rule. Common man, burdened by poverty, hunger and ignorance, had lost the will to exercise its productive might. Out of the dust, they had to be raised by men of great vision, like Gandhi and Nehru. In his memorable speech delivered to the Constituent Assembly on 14th August, 1947, Nehru said: "The future is not all of ease and resting, but of incessant striving..."

India was a stagnant economy at the time of independence. The economy was predominantly agrarian with little industrial development. Most people lived in villages, in hunger and despair. Bullock carts, wooden ploughs, spinning wheels and thatched huts - life made of small things, unimaginatively hard, dull and cruel. Agricultural growth was around 0.3% per annum in the first half of the century. The colonial government took little interest in the improvement of cultivation practices, except in the case of export crops like cotton, jute and tea. The railway system was built only for connecting the ports with the export production centres and the import markets; all other infrastructural facilities were lacking. Local enterprise was confined largely to trade and commerce, mainly in and around port cities like Bombay, Calcutta and Madras. A few industrial centres grew around these cities through private entrepreneurship. There had been an adverse impact on the artisan sector under British rule. The old crafts were left to languish and decay - ill prepared to modernise. Large factories, few in number, produced mainly consumer goods, like textiles and sugar. Intermediates like steel, cement and jute machinery were mostly imported. The extremely narrow base of industrialisation remained confined to a very few cities and states and was the monopoly of a few privileged families. The export strategy was not conducive to the country's interests. Exports were seen as a mechanism to transfer raw materials cheaply to the metropolitan cities in the United Kingdom, which, in turn, processed them into final goods for exporting back to the colonies.

Social indicators were equally poor; illiteracy was as high as 84%; public health services were inadequate to face even epidemics such as influenza, malaria and cholera. Some efforts were made by the state to prevent epidemics like malaria which continued to revisit again and again. The mortality rate remained high at around 27 per thousand in 1947. Children cried for milk but mothers could not feed them. Famines devastated human lives, adding to the interminable misery in a barren wasteland.

NEHRU- INDUSTRIAL DEVELOPMENT

Nehru

Nehru is among the most distinguished Indians of the 20th century. As one of the makers of modem India, his life merges with the life of the nation. Nehru (1889-1964): The bare facts about Nehru's life can tie told quickly. Born to rich Kashmiri parents, he had an exclusive education, first at home at the hands of governesses and then at Harrow and Cambridge and the Inner Temple. Soon after his return from England he plunged into the nationalistic struggle, went to jail a number of times, became President of the Indian National Congress, took a leading part in the negotiations that culminated in the freedom of the country and headed the Interim Government. He was Prime Minister of free India from August 1947 till his death on 27 May 1964.

Industrial Development

Nehru presented the first five-year plan to the Parliament of India on 8th December 1951. The first plan sought to get the country's economy out of the cycle of poverty. The plan addressed, mainly, the agrarian sector, including investments in dams and irrigation. The agricultural sector was hit hardest by the partition of India and needed urgent attention. The total planned budget of 206.8 billion

(US$23.6 billion in the 1950 exchange rate) was allocated to seven broad areas: irrigation and energy (27.2 per cent), agriculture and community development (17.4 per cent), transport and communications (24 per cent), industry (8.4 per cent), social services (16.64 per cent), land rehabilitation (4.1 per cent), and for other sectors and services (2.5 per cent). Nehru had given fourth priority for industry in the first five year plan period.

The conditions in India at the time of Independence were more or less, similar to those prevailing in the Soviet Union. It could develop both light and heavy industry. But the Indian planners opted for the development of heavy industry in the first stage. It may be clarified that heavy industry includes all industries producing capital goods, which enlarge the productive capacity of the economy. In this sense, it also includes railways and infrastructure in the form of hydro and thermal electric power projects. This policy of developing heavy industry was incorporated in the Industrial Policy of 1956.

Professor P.C. Mahalanobis, who was the architect of the Second Plan, clearly favoured the development of heavy industry as the basic strategy of Indian economic development. He was supported by Jawaharlal Nehru, the first Prime Minister of India who considered the development of heavy industry to be synonymous with industrialisation. Nehru categorically stated: "If we are to industralise, it is of primary importance that we must have the heavy industries which build machines". In another reference, he mentioned: "There are some who argue that we must not go in for heavy industry but for lighter ones. Of course, we have to have light industries also but it is not possible to industralise the nation rapidly without concentrating on the basic industries which produce machines which are utilised in industrial development." Nehru's philosophy of industrialisation was incorporated in the Second Five Year Plan, which clearly stated:

"In the long run, the rate of industrialisation and the growth of the national economy would depend upon the increasing production of coal, electricity, iron and steel, heavy machinery, heavy chemicals and heavy industries generally –which increase the capacity for capital formation. One important aim is to make India independent as quickly as possible of foreign imports of producer goods so that the accumulation of capital would not be hampered by difficulties in securing supplies of essential producer goods from other countries. The heavy industry must, therefore, be expanded with all possible speed."

Since private sector was not willing to invest in heavy industry, which had a long gestation period and a relatively low rate of return, the task of development of heavy industry was assigned to the public sector. It was, therefore, argued that public sector would be the engine of growth. However, private sector was expected to supplement the efforts of the public sector.

Hydroelectric power projects and five steel mills at Bhilai, Durgapur, and Rourkela were established by Nehru. Coal production was increased. More railway lines were added in the north east.

The Atomic Energy Commission was formed in 1958 with Homi J. Bhabha as the first chairman. The Tata Institute of Fundamental Research was established as a research institute. In 1957 a talent search and scholarship program was begun to find talented young students to train for work in nuclear power.

The third plan stressed on agriculture and improving production of rice, but the brief Sino-Indian War of 1962 exposed weaknesses in the economy and shifted the focus towards the Defence industry.

NEHRU – SCIENCE AND TECHNOLOGY

Article 51 A of our constitution which deals with fundamental duties makes it a duty of every citizen to develop a scientific temper. This is a good enough reason for young citizens to first of all, find out what exactly is scientific temper, and then to try and cultivate it. But, even though it is important to carry out the duties laid down in the constitution, there are reasons other than formal and legal for understanding and practicing scientific temper. If we have a scientific temper, we can understand and solve our problems with much less difficulty or stress, and we would be reasonable in our decisions and creative in our activities. However, scientific temper is no magical formula for success in life; nor can it be acquired suddenly by going through a lesson; it may, infact, take a life time of careful attention and examination of our own motivations and actions to acquire it.

Nehru's Scientific Attitude

Nehru's understanding of science in relation to the country's development was penetrating. He, unlike some of his senior contemporaries, viewed science with an unbiased and realistic attitude. His belief in the scientific method was unshakable. He thought of an advanced India with a heavy commitment to industrialization through science and technology. But the most striking aspect of his scientific thinking was the importance he attached to the scientific outlook. The major conflict in the world, according to him, was between the method of science and the methods opposed to it. In the early period of the development of science, there was a serious conflict between religion and science. Nehru did not find any real conflict between the two: "Religion must put on the garb of science and approach all its problems in the spirit of science", he used to say.

The last few decades have transformed all societies and development has become synonymous with scientific advance. And what is needed of a leader is the appropriate scientific attitude. Few men at the top of political affairs even in the most advanced countries can boast of such an outlook. And one wonders what a man like Nehru would have achieved if he had the requisite scientific techniques at his command.

J.B.S. Haldane, when he left Britain and settled in India, said that he was doing so because of the Indian Prime Minister's scientific attitude.

After Independence India made some very important commitments to science, under Nehru's leadership. He agreed that countries like ours should go in for expenditure on scientific research and development equivalent to at least one per cent of the national income, if anything concrete is to be achieved, though even now, India's scientific budget provisions are nowhere near this target. Nehru wanted to achieve it. His keen interest in the affairs of the Council of Scientific and Industrial Research and the Atomic Energy Commission is a clear indication of his scientific aspirations.

He was the main inspiration behind the adoption of a national science policy and the formulation of the Science Policy Resolution.

He invited the top scientists of the world to visit India and give their appraisal of what our country should do in the field of science. He would miss any appointment but never a gathering of scientists. Scientists like P.M. S. Blackett and J.D. Bernal were always welcome in Nehru's India: Blackett, in fact, influenced Nehru considerably in evolving his approach to such important issues as disarmament and nuclear weapon. The way he once called a visiting British scientist and science writer at quick notice because he was coming from China and Nehru wanted to have a clear idea of what was happening in Mao's land to promote science, was remarkable. Even several eminent scientists were not aware of the visitor's presence in New Delhi whereas Nehru took pains to be posted with his views.

The meetings of the Scientific Advisory Committee to the Cabinet were extremely lively during Nehru's time and the decisions were implemented immediately after they were taken. After the Chinese aggression in 1962, there was too much pressure on the government to divert part of the allocation for scientific research to the Defence needs. It was almost unanimously agreed that a ten per cent cut would not make any considerable difference in our scientific activity. Nehru intervened and saw to it that no such step was taken. For, the research itself could be made Defence-oriented instead of depriving it of a portion of its meager resources.

At the onset of independence, Nehru called science "the very texture of life" and optimistically declared that "science alone . . . can solve problems of hunger and poverty, of insanitation and illiteracy, of superstition and deadening customs." Under his leadership, the government set out to cure numerous societal problems. The Green Revolution, educational improvement, establishment of hundreds of scientific laboratories, industrial and military research, massive hydraulic projects, and entry into the frontiers of space all evolved from this early decision to embrace high technology.

One of the early planning documents was the Scientific Policy Resolution of 1958, which called for embracing "by all appropriate means, the cultivation of science and scientific research in all its aspects—pure, applied, and educational" and encouraged individual initiatives. In 1983 the government issued a similar statement, which, while stressing the importance of international cooperation and the diffusion of scientific knowledge, put considerable emphasis on self-reliance and the development of indigenous technology. This goal is still in place in the mid-1990s.

Science & Technology

Science & Technology (S&T) has always been an integral part of the Indian culture. Natural Philosophy as it was termed in those ancient times was pursued vigorously at institutions of higher learning. The contributions made by the scholar-scientists Aryabhatta, Bhaskara, Brahmagupta, Dhanvantari and Nagarjuna, to name a few, to the fields of mathematics, astronomy, medicine and chemistry during the prehistoric period are legendary and invaluable not only to Indian S&T but also to the knowledge base of the humanity at large.

The innate ability to perform creatively in science came to be backed with an institutional set-up and strong state and political support after country's independence in 1947. Since then the Government of India has spared no effort to establish a modern S&T organization in the country. India's first Prime Minister Pandit Jawaharlal Nehru gave whole-hearted support to a concerted programme for the promotion of S&T in the country. As a result, many new S&T departments and laboratories were set up and the pursuance of scientific research started in an organized manner.

Jawaharlal Nehru firmly believed that Science and Technology can be the twin tools that would help bring about social equity and economic development to enable India join the mainstream of the world community. This conviction was reflected in the Scientific Policy Resolution (SPR) of 1958, the aim of which was "to foster, promote and sustain the cultivation of sciences and scientific research in the country and to secure for the people all the benefits that can accrue from the acquisition and application of scientific knowledge".

Nehru was established four Indian Institute of Technology to promote science and technology in India. Indian Institute of Technology (IITs) is a group of 4 autonomous engineering and technology-oriented institutes (at present 16 IITs in India) of higher education established and declared as Institutes of National

Importance by the Parliament of India. The IITs were created to train scientists and engineers, with the aim of developing a skilled workforce to support the economic and social development of India. In order of establishment, they are located in Kharagpur (1950; as IIT 1951), Mumbai (1958), Chennai (formerly Madras) (1959), Kanpur (1959), Delhi (1961; as IIT 1963).

Consequently, the growth of science and technology in India has been partial and superficial. The scientific temper in society, which Nehru tried to develop, is yet to take roots. The vast majority of people, not being exposed to science and technology, are unable to understand its implications or benefit from the gains of development. They still look towards traditional ideas and beliefs for guidance, and solution of their problems. Having grown up in age old traditions, cultural ethos and outlook, their hold on traditional beliefs becomes stronger when they feel insecure and threatened. This explains the growth of irrationalism and obscurantism even as India has moved into the 21st Century.

CONCLUSION

Science should unite and not break-up India. 'I love India, not because I have had the chance to be born on its soil but because she has saved through limitless ages the living words that have issued from the illuminated consciousness of her great sons'. So wrote our great poet Rabindranath Tagore several years ago but few among the modern generation of intelligent youth have bothered to get even a glimpse of what that glorious heritage of India was. Valmiki, Vyasa, Kalidasa and Bhavabhuthi are just names. The masses of India, however, are better informed, Ramayana and Mahabharatha have impressed on their mind the oneness of India. In the same manner the impact of Nehru is very much on all the politicians in the country. Every village, at least till recently, had a Bhajan Mandal where the entire village would participate. Pilgrimages were undertaken with great religious favour to holy places like Varanasi, Gaya, Rameswaram, Dwarka, Puri and Haridwar, Badrinath and Amarnath. These inculcated in the minds of the people the vastness and variety of their homeland and welded them as one human entity. This tradition of unity and integrity of the country is being destroyed by the self-serving politicians jockeying for power and sowing seeds of hatred in an otherwise peaceful population. Science has barely tried to perpetuate this unifying influence. 'The Discovery of India' by Nehru had given more importance to science in the process of national development. We want political leader like Nehru. The commitment and strong vision of Nehru is excellent. The role of Nehru in the development of industry and science & technology is incomparable and inseparable.

REFERENCES

1. Alvares, C. Homo Faber (1979): "Technology and Culture in India, China and the West 1500-1972". Bombay: Allied Publishers.
2. Barber, B. (1952): Science and the Social Order. New York: The Free Press.
3. Barnes, B., and D. Edge, eds. (1982): "Science in Context: Readings in the Sociology of Science". Milton Keynes: Open University Press.
4. Hull, D. (1988): "Science as a Process". Chicago: University of Chicago Press.
5. Jawaharlal Nehru (1946): "Discovery of India".
6. Krishna, V., and Jain, A. "Country Report: Scientific Research, Science Policy and Social Studies of Science and Technology in India." Paper presented at the First Workshop on the Emergence of Scientific Communities in the Developing Countries, 22-27 April 1990, Paris: ORSTOM.
7. Nandy, A. (1980): "Alternative Sciences". New Delhi: Allied Publishers.
8. Nandy, A. (1987): "Traditions, Tyranny and Utopias". Delhi: Oxford University Press.
9. Radhakrishna, B.P. (2009): "Nehru's 'Discovery of India' the role of science in India's development", Journal of Geographical Society of India, VOL.73.

16

Social Entrepreneurship in India

The reasonable man adapts himself to the world; the unreasonable one persists in trying to adapt the world to himself. Therefore all progress depends on the unreasonable man. ...George Bernard Shaw.

INTRODUCTION

India is the most civilized country in the world. We have thousand years of tradition and culture. We have a large number of human resources in the world next to China. The GDP growth is increasing year by year. But at rest majority of the Indian populace are living below poverty line when compared to any other developing country in the world. The role of non-profit organizations is important to eradicate poverty in the society. Nothing is impossible for human beings. A true entrepreneur can change the world through his/her thoughts and actions. Entrepreneurs see the opportunities rather than the problems created by change. India has a huge number of young people in the world. Innovative programmes and reforms are necessary in the social sector. The government has a pivotal role in the process of providing healthy and wealthy facilities for all its citizens in the country. Along with government the NGOs have a prominent role in the development of nation in general and society in particular.

ENTREPRENEUR

An entrepreneur is a person who has possession of a new enterprise, venture or idea and assumes significant accountability for the inherent risks and the outcome. The term is originally a loanword from French and was first defined by the Irish-French economist Richard Cantillon. Entrepreneur in English is a term applied to the type of personality who is willing to take upon himself a new venture or enterprise and accepts full responsibility for the outcome. Jean-Baptiste Say, a French economist, is believed to have coined the word "entrepreneur" first in about 1800. He said an entrepreneur is *"one who undertakes an enterprise, especially a contractor, acting as intermediatory between capital and labour."*

Qualities of Entrepreneurs

1. ***Passion*** - entrepreneurs have a strong passion for their idea or concept, so much so that their work is their play. If you don't like what you do, you won't stick it out when challenges come along, as they inevitably will.
2. ***Curiosity*** - entrepreneurs need to understand how things work. They ask a lot of questions. Curiosity therefore triggers innovation.
3. ***Hunger*** - entrepreneurs are sponges. They devour information about their industry and are always current on new and emerging trends and technologies, not only in their specific industry but in closely related industries. Entrepreneurs are ALWAYS looking for new markets, applications, products or twists on an old concept.
4. ***Optimism*** - entrepreneurs think of problems as opportunities for improvements and new ideas.
5. ***Forward looking*** - entrepreneurs are never satisfied with the status quo and are always proactively carving out their future.
6. ***Careful about money*** - entrepreneurs are careful with money and have a firm grasp on what things cost and their value to

the business. This allows them to recognize a true bargain when they see one.

7. ***Start earning at a young age*** - entrepreneurs commonly display entrepreneurial leanings as teenagers seeking out entrepreneurial activities such as babysitting, selling craft, running errands.
8. ***Competitive*** - entrepreneurs are naturally competitive and don't let the grass grow under their feet.
9. ***Time conscious*** - entrepreneurs know the value of time and how to make the best use of it.
10. ***Risk takers*** - entrepreneurs are not afraid of taking calculated risks. They typically trust their hunches and act on them.
11. ***Professional*** - entrepreneurs are professional in their approach to work. They operate as they would in a corporate environment and don't allow themselves to be distracted by outside influences.
12. ***High energy*** - entrepreneurs have a plan and a vision and they work it. Entrepreneurs are often health-conscious too, recognizing that the fitter they are, the better their minds work. So entrepreneurs will take time from their schedule to work out and eat well.
13. ***Flexible*** - entrepreneurs are nothing if not responsive to change. Although they appreciate the importance of having a plan and working that plan, they allow themselves room to react and respond to opportunities that may suddenly reveal themselves.
14. ***Confident goal-setters*** - entrepreneurs are confident and set long-term goals, both for themselves personally and their businesses.
15. ***Persistent*** - entrepreneurs never give up. They persist until they succeed.
16. ***Learn from failure*** - entrepreneurs learn from their failures and those of others. Failure to an entrepreneur is nothing more than an opportunity waiting to be discovered.
17. ***Self responsibility*** - entrepreneurs take the initiative and personal responsibility for their success or failure (which is always a merely temporary state).

18. ***Resource utilization*** - entrepreneurs utilize ALL of their available resources.
19. ***Internal control*** - entrepreneurs don't believe in luck. They firmly believe that success and failure lies within their personal control or influence.

Among these the following characteristics are also important

1. Need for Achievement
2. At least average intelligence
3. Good communicator
4. Sense of efficacy
5. Open to feedback and learns from experience
6. Need for independence
7. Hope of success
8. Procreative
9. Action oriented
10. Need for influencing others
11. Problem-solving rather than problem avoiding attitude
12. New initiative-taking rather than conforming attitude
13. Concern for society
14. Creative and innovative
15. Opportunity seeker
16. Realistic
17. Not too discouraged by failures
18. Sensitive and perceptive
19. Assertive
20. High tolerance of ambiguity
21. Family and friends second to business
22. Good problem solver
23. Knowledge of the business

Six Qualities of Successful Entrepreneurs

- Willingness to self connect
- Willingness to share credit
- Willingness to break free of established structures

- o Willingness to cross disciplinary boundaries
- o Willingness to work quietly
- o Strong ethical impetus

ENTREPRENEURSHIP

The term, entrepreneurship, today might refer to a young academic discipline or, to a set of activities or practice intended to create a new/renewed enterprise for generating economic and/or social effects. The word entrepreneurship is a mixed blessing. On the positive side, it connotes a special, innate ability to sense and act on opportunity, combining out-of-the-box thinking with a unique brand of determination to create or bring about something new to the world. On the negative side, entrepreneurship is an ex-post term, because entrepreneurial activities require a passage of time before their true impact is evident.

According to Webster, an entrepreneur is a person who "*organizes, manages and assumes the risks of a business enterprise.*" In a 1998 column for *Inc.* magazine, Norm Brodsky expanded on the definition. "*Starting with nothing more than an idea or a prototype,*" he wrote, "*entrepreneurs have the ability to take a business to the point at which it can sustain itself on internally generated cash flow.*"

More recently, management guru Peter Drucker described entrepreneurs and entrepreneurship this way; "*The entrepreneur always searches for change, responds to it, and exploits it as an opportunity*". Entrepreneurs see the opportunities rather than the problems created by change.

SOCIAL ENTREPRENEURSHIP

The most commonly quoted definition of "*social entrepreneurship*" today was formulated by Prof. J. Gregory Dees of Stanford University in 1998, but his essay contained a fundamental oversight. He outlines five factors that define social entrepreneurship:

1. *Adopting a mission to create and sustain social value (not just private value).*
2. *Recognizing and relentlessly pursuing new opportunities to serve that mission.*

3. *Engaging in a process of continuous innovation, adaptation, and learning.*
4. *Acting boldly without being limited by resources currently in hand; and*
5. *Exhibiting a heightened sense of accountability to the constituencies served and for the outcomes created.*

A social entrepreneur is any person, in any sector, who uses earned income strategies to pursue a social objective, and a social entrepreneur differs from a traditional entrepreneur in two important ways:

- o Traditional entrepreneurs frequently act in a socially responsible manner: They donate money to nonprofits; they refuse to engage in certain types of businesses; they use environmentally safe materials and practices; they treat their employees with dignity and respect. All of this is admirable, but their efforts are only indirectly attached to social problems. Social entrepreneurs are different because their earned income strategies are tied directly to their mission: They either employ people who are developmentally disabled, chronically mentally ill, physically challenged, poverty stricken or otherwise disadvantaged; or they sell mission-driven products and services that have a direct impact on a specific social problem (e.g., working with potential dropouts to keep them in school, manufacturing assistive devices for people with physical disabilities, providing home care services that help elderly people stay out of nursing homes, developing and selling curricula).
- o Secondly, traditional entrepreneurs are ultimately measured by financial results: The success or failure of their companies is determined by their ability to generate profits for their owners. On the other hand, social entrepreneurs are driven by a double bottom line, a virtual blend of financial and social returns. Profitability is still a goal, but it is not the only goal, and profits are re-invested in the mission rather than being distributed to shareholders.

Since Bowen (1953) wrote his seminal book Social responsibilities of the Businessman, claiming that the obligations of the businessman are to pursue those policies, to make those decisions, or to follow those lines of action which are desirable in terms of the objectives and values of our society (1953, p.16), the field concerning the role and responsibilities of business in society has grown significantly. Society and business, corporate social responsibility, social issues in management, corporate citizenship, and stakeholder approach are just some of the terms used to describe the relationship between business and society.

Despite this growth, little attention has been devoted to those organizations existing expressly to respond to social demand in an entrepreneurial way. Although progress toward defining the domain of the field is still slow, social entrepreneurship (SE), as an unusual ‘contact point’ among entrepreneurship, innovation, and social change, has attained wider and more enthusiastic acceptance in corporate thinking and practice than in the scholarly literature.

IMPORTANCE OF SOCIAL ENTREPRENEURSHIP

The developed world has a vast, under-utilized asset that is not being leveraged to its best advantage: idealistic people who want to make the world a better place. For most of a century, idealistic people have been encouraged to use anger, protest, lobbying, and legal action in order to make the world a better place. While most certainly some of these behaviors and activities were necessary, we have reached the point at which the social benefit of such behaviors is decreasing. We have reached the point at which creation, rather than attack, ought to be the first obligation of reformers. The social entrepreneurship movement is the first tip of this iceberg. We want to create a world in which all idealists realize that the creation of new enterprises is the most powerful way to make positive change in the world. If all the energy that is currently invested in zero-sum political conflict was gradually transferred to the committed creation of sustainable enterprises, the cumulative impact on behalf of the good would be extraordinary. **...Michael Strong**

Social Entrepreneurship is fundamentally a merge of two concepts; socially responsible action and entrepreneurship. Put together, the term implies applying business principles to improve society. The benefits of giving and helping the less fortunate are obvious. Both for-profit and not-for-profit organizations can practice social entrepreneurship to generate funds to help those in need and can also help by teaching and enabling those in need to help themselves.

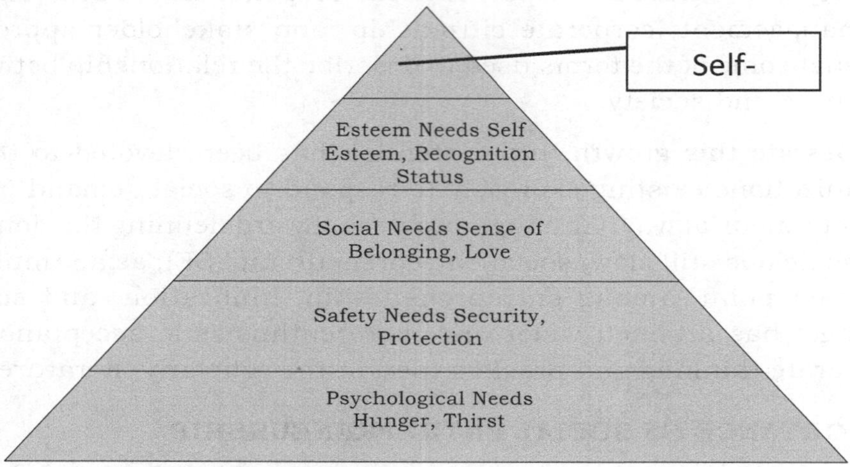

Fig-1: Abraham Maslow, Motivation and Personality

We all have basic needs – food, shelter, security, etc. Many of these needs can be satisfied with money. So in a capitalist society, driven by money, we can take care of these basic needs relatively easily. But there is more to life than that. The old adage – "*Money can't buy happiness*" is true indeed, and directly correlates to what Abraham Maslow postulated in his hierarchy of needs. Interestingly, the higher level needs are not dependant on financial means. Consequently, failure to satisfy these higher level needs will result in an unfulfilled life in some form or another. This is why we see some wealthy, powerful, and/or popular people living seemingly unhappy lives.

We all go through life wondering why we are here. What is our purpose? We ask these questions because of our desire to satisfy our higher level needs of belonging, self-esteem and self-actualization.

The wealth of tomorrow will be redistributed to those who embark in the Global Entrepreneurial Movement. These new rich will easily satisfy their basic needs but will quickly realize they don't have a deeper purpose in their lives if they haven't already found it. They will have more money than they need and as a result, they will seek to satisfy their higher level needs by using their wealth and helping the less fortunate.

They will realize why social entrepreneurship can help them gain self-esteem and actualization, and will feel good by "giving back". In addition, they will also notice other new rich entrepreneurs among them and feel a sense of kinship by supporting common causes and developing socially responsible projects together. This will also help them to achieve a sense of belonging.

So we see not only why social entrepreneurship is important to those in need of help, but the underlying motivations for those who will practice it are driven by a desire to be living with purpose and fulfillment in their own lives.

SOCIAL ENTREPRENEURSHIP IN INDIA

Emerging field of social entrepreneurship is growing rapidly and attracting increased attention from many sectors. The term itself shows up frequently in the media, is referenced by public officials, has become common on university campuses, and informs the strategy of several prominent social sector organizations, including Ashoka and the Schwab and Skoll foundations.

The reasons behind the popularity of social entrepreneurship are many. On the most basic level, there's something inherently interesting and appealing about entrepreneurs and the stories of why and how they do what they do. People are attracted to social entrepreneurs like Muhammad Yunus for many of the same reasons that they find business entrepreneurs like Steve Jobs so compelling – these extraordinary people come up with brilliant ideas and against all the odds succeed at creating new products and services that dramatically improve people's lives.

But interest in social entrepreneurship transcends the phenomenon of popularity and fascination with people. Social entrepreneurship signals the imperative to drive social change, and it is that potential payoff, with its lasting, transformational benefit to society, that sets the field and its practitioners apart.

When Muhammad Yunus, 2006 Nobel Peace Prize awardee and founder of Grameen Bank, was contacted by the Nobel Foundation for the customary winner interview, he remarked, "*...poverty is an* *artificial creation. It doesn't belong to human civilization, and we can change that, we can make people come out of poverty (sic). The only thing we have to do is to redesign our institutions and policies.*"

That's what social entrepreneurship is about: creating business models revolving around low-cost products and services to resolve social inequities. And the realization that social progress and profit aren't mutually exclusive has led to many social ventures taking root in India as well.

Examples of successful social projects like Amul or SEWA were few and far between. However, with the slowdown taking the shine off urban, higher-income target markets, organizations focusing on 'bottom of the pyramid' audiences have become a reality. But the days of easy funding are over. Given the employment squeeze, it would be natural for aspiring social entrepreneurs to stick to their secure jobs instead. Surprisingly, they continue to launch social enterprises with a vengeance.

In May 2008, 27-year old Rajnish Sinha and his IIM-Kozhikode batchmate Siva Cotipalli started Bangalore-based DhanaX. A fascination with microfinance and the idea of clubbing it with person to person (P2P) lending led them to quit their jobs to launch DhanaX, a platform where people contribute small amounts online as loans. NGOs take up the task of disbursing these loans to needy communities in their areas of operation.

Interest is charged at 24%, of which DhanaX keeps approximately 6%. This model has worked in other countries as well. So far, DhanaX has helped its four partner NGOs acquire loans of Rs 20 lakh. While yet to recover their initial investment of Rs 25 lakh, Sinha is confident of success. "*In future, we may partner with wealth management companies or treasury departments of large corporations to keep the pipeline running,*" he says.

Richa Pandey, a marketing MBA, was a media sales professional in New Delhi for eight years. But her calling was rural India, partly because of her roots—her grandfather was a farmer in Uttar Pradesh. "*The retail and BPO sectors were creating job opportunities in a big way. I zeroed in on vocational training for rural youth in these areas,*" Pandey recalls. In October 2007, she approached the Rural Technology Business Incubator (RTBI) at IIT-Madras with a business plan outline. "The RTBI platform helped add magnitude to my plan," Pandey says, adding, "*Prof Ashok Jhunjhunwala assisted me in launching a pilot programme in three districts of Tamil Nadu under the banner of eJeevika.*" Around the same time, she got a lucrative offer to head the marketing division of a large media firm. Pandey turned it down and continued focusing on designing course content and online training programmes in three areas: retail sales, data entry and security services.

eJeevika subjects candidates to psychometric tests to determine where they'd fit in best and trains them accordingly. But Pandey's chosen path hasn't been easy. She currently doesn't take home a salary, preferring instead to plough everything back into the business. In the past year, eJeevika trained 160 people, is on the verge of signing up four BPOs as partners and is growing both in terms of scale and size, aiming to train 1,500 people by March-end. "*If the slowdown has affected companies like ours, I'm yet to see evidence of it,*" she says, "*Our team consists of eight highly-experienced people and we still get enquiries from people who want to work with us.*"

Experts like Kallol Borah, CEO, Headstart Foundation, feel that social-focus startups will continue to thrive in India. "*Bringing low-cost services such as banking, healthcare, finance, etc. to underprivileged sections of society is definitely a big opportunity as well as a necessity. Rural, small-town and lower-income consumers constitute a large market waiting to be tapped, but it is necessary for social entrepreneurs to get past language, literacy and geographical barriers.*"

The current environment has also complicated the mix. Adrienne Villani, associate at Intellectual Capital Advisory Services (Intellecap), is cautious, "*No market is immune to the global meltdown. I would think that people earning between 2-12 dollars a day will indeed be affected.*" If that is true, companies working for this block of the pyramid would be affected as well. The answer may well lie in technology. Hi-tech social startups are banking on 'smart' models to bring services to people at affordable costs.

Social Entrepreneurs in India

Social entrepreneurship is quietly revolutionizing the less privileged sections of India. Here are some of the more prominent social entrepreneurs in India.

- ***Vinoba Bhave*** - Founder and leader of the Land Gift Movement, he caused the redistribution of more than 7,000,000 acres (28,000 km^2) of land to aid India's untouchables and landless. Mahatma Gandhi described him as his mentor.
- ***Dr Govindappa Venkataswamy and Thulasiraj D Ravilla*** established Aravind Eye Hospital in 1976. Till date, it has treated more than 2.3 million outpatients and carried out more than 2.7 lakh operations in 2006-07, about two-thirds of them free.
- Barefoot College, started by ***Bunker Roy*** in 1972, has made innumerable school dropouts in villages into "barefoot" doctors, engineers, architects, teachers, designers and communicators.
- Self-Employed Women's Association (SEWA) started by ***Ela Bhatt*** in 1972 provides financial, health, insurance, legal, childcare, vocational and educational services to poor self-employed women, who comprise its members.
- Bhartiya Samruddhi Investments & Consulting Services (BASIX) started by ***Vijay Mahajan*** is the first microfinance project to lend to the poor.
- Narayana Hrudayalaya Institute of Medical Sciences and its network of hospitals run by ***Devi Shetty*** perform about three dozen surgeries a day. Of these, 60% are carried out at nominal cost or free of charge.
- Technology Informatics Design Endeavour (TIDE) run by ***S Rajagopalan and Svati Bhogle*** supports the development of financially rewarding and environmentally-friendly methods invented by leading research institutions into thriving enterprises.
- ***Dr. Abraham M. George*** - Founder of The George Foundation (TGF).

List of Enterprises in India

Key Social Enterprises operating or supporting in India – Helping people have their lives.

1. Ashoka India
2. Bandhan

3. BASIX India
4. Bharatiya Yuva Shakti Trust
5. Crafts Bridge
6. Centre for Civil Society
7. Datamation Consultants Pvt. Ltd
8. Desi Power
9. Drishtee Dot Com Pvt. Ltd
10. Indus Tree Craft Foundation
11. International Development Enterprises (India)
12. Jiva
13. Mann Deshi Mahila Sahakari Bank
14. Meghdoot Gramodyog Sewa Sansthan
15. National Innovation Foundation
16. Pardada Pardadi
17. RangSutra
18. Rural Innovation Network
19. Sankalp Forum
20. Satin Creditcare Network
21. Sasha
22. Shri Mahila Griha Udyog Lijjat Papad
23. Selco India
24. Soma Shop
25. Unltd India
26. Think Change India
27. Tiny Tech India
28. Youth Social Enterprise Initiative

CONCLUSION

The development of any nation depends mainly on the standards of its educational institutions. Education is power. Education gives knowledge and strength. Individual development leads to national development. It is the duty of government and non-government organizations to take care about individual development without considering caste, religion, region and colour. We are living in the highly scientific and industrialized modern world. Many organizations are working for the development of society. Social entrepreneurs are working hardly to change the world. Seventy per cent of Indian populace is living in the rural areas. According to the Father of Nation M.K. Gandhi, village development is the only way for national development. We want healthy society without poverty. The World Economic Forum is an independent international organization committed to improving the state of the world by engaging business, political, academic and other leaders of society to shape global, regional and industry agendas. The role of social entrepreneurs is important in the process of national development.

REFERENCES

1. Bill Drayton (2005): "*The Social Entrepreneur*", US News & World Report.
2. David Bornstein, "*How to Change the World: Social Entrepreneurs and the Power of New Ideas*", Oxford University Press.
3. Francesco Perrini (2006): "*The New Social Entrepreneurship – What Awaits Social Entrepreneurial Ventures?*" Edward Elgar Publishing Limited.
4. Gregory Dees, J. (1998): "*The Meaning of Social Entrepreneurship*".
5. Gregory Dees, J. "*Social Entrepreneurship: Mobilizing Resources for Success*".
6. Jerr Boschee and Jim McClurg, "*Towards a Better Understanding of Social Entrepreneurship-Some Important Distinctions*".
7. Stanford University Social Entrepreneurship Report (2003): "*Light Up the World – INDIA*", University of Stanford.
8. Thompson, J.L. (2002): "*The World of the Social Entrepreneur*", The International Journal of Public Sector Management, 15(4/5), p.413.
9. World Economic Forum (2009): "*List of Social Entrepreneurs*".

17

Poverty Alleviation and Inclusive Growth in India

INTRODUCTION

Science and technology has put a land mark in the history of mankind. Industrialization and globalization have changed the life styles of human beings. Radio, computer, internet, mobile phone, satellite and robot are helping more and more for human development. It is possible to know any type of information within seconds throughout the world. The life expectancy of human being is increasing. The living standards are also increasing. All these developments are one face of a single coin. The other face of a coin is more terrible. Majority of people in the developing countries including India are suffering for primary needs. The gap between the poor and the rich is gradually increasing. Poverty leads to many problems. Poverty is a sin. It is an obstacle for national development. Honourable Prime Minister Dr. Manmohan Singh said to press reports on 6th September 2010 that, 37 per cent of total population is living below poverty line. It is foremost duty of government to provide food and shelter for all people of Below Poverty Level (BPL). All human beings are equal. All of them have equal rights to live. Without inclusive growth it is not possible for India to become a developed country in the modern world.

ECONOMY OF INDIA

The economy of India is the eleventh largest economy in the world by nominal GDP and the fourth largest by purchasing power parity (PPP).Following strong economic reforms from the socialist inspired economy of a post-independence Indian nation, the country began to develop a fast-paced economic growth, as free market principles were initiated in 1990 for international competition and foreign investment. India is an emerging economic power with a very large pool of human and natural resources, and a growing large pool of skilled professionals. Economists predict that by 2020, India will be among the leading economies of the world.

India is enjoying a period of unprecedented growth, with real GDP rising at over 8 per cent per year for the past few years, making it one of the world's fastest growing economies. Yet, India still has the largest concentration of poor people in the world. The quality of life in India continues to be appalling with the country ranked poorly at 134 among 182 countries on the Human Development Index of the United Nations Development Programme (UNDP) that was released globally on October 5th 2009.

POVERTY

'No family will lack basic needs like food, clothing and shelter and all will enjoy a better quality of life and will be able to lead a comfortable life, filled with opportunities to learn and develop skills and earn a livelihood'. ...The Mission of Velugu Programme

Poverty can be defined as a social phenomenon in which a section of the society is unable to fulfill even its basic necessities of life. Poverty is hunger. Poverty is lack of shelter. Poverty is being sick and not being able to see a doctor. Poverty is not having access to school and not knowing how to read. Poverty is not having a job, is fear for the future, living one day at a time. Poverty is losing a child to illness brought about by unclean water. Poverty is powerlessness, lack of representation and freedom. Poverty is a call to action - for the poor and the wealthy alike - a call to change the world so that many more may have enough to eat, adequate shelter, access to education and health, protection from violence, and a voice in what happens in their communities. Poverty is the state of being without, often associated with need, hardship and lack of resources across a wide range of circumstances.

In the developing world, poverty breeds poverty. It goes far beyond simply the lack of income. Poverty in India still remains unabated. The country has hardly been able to establish her identity free from the age old impression 'India is a poor country'. Despite decades long effort most of our population are still struggling below poverty line. The Gandhiji's dream to provide each and every Indian poor an access to basic needs of life is yet to be materialized. Although the planning commission of India has added qualitative parameters to the concept of basic needs, in terms of minimum food, clothing and shelter, our country has failed to provide the same to its citizens.

India has entered the Eleventh Plan period with an impressive record of economic growth. After a lackluster performance in the Ninth Plan period (1997–98 to 2001–02), when gross domestic product (GDP) grew at only 5.5% per annum, the economy accelerated in the Tenth Plan period (2002–03 to 2006–07) to record an average growth of 7.7%, the highest in any Plan period so far. Besides, there was acceleration even within the Tenth Plan period and the growth rate in the last four years of the Plan has averaged 8.7%, making India one of the fastest growing economies in the world. Still poverty is high in India when compared to other developing counties in the world.

The percentage of the population below the official poverty line has come down from 36% in 1993–94 to 28% in 2004–05. However, not only is this still high, the rate of decline in poverty has not accelerated along with the growth in GDP, and the incidence of poverty among certain marginalized groups, for example the STs, has hardly declined at all. Because population has also grown, the absolute number of poor people has declined only marginally from 320 million in 1993–94 to 302 million in 2004–05. This performance is all the more disappointing since the poverty line on which the estimate of the poor is based is the same as it was in 1973–74 when per capita incomes were much lower. Other indicators of deprivation suggest that the proportion of the population deprived of a minimum level of living is much higher. For example, National Family Health Survey-3 (NFHS-3) shows that almost 46% of the children in the 0 to 3 years' age group suffered from malnutrition in 2005–06, and what is even more disturbing is that the estimate shows almost no decline from the level of 47% reported in 1998 by NFHS-2.

Table-1 Poverty Line in India (Rs. per capita per month)

Year	Rural	Urban
1973-1974	49.63	56.76
1983-1984	89.50	115.65
1987-1988	115.20	162.16
1993-1994	205.84	281.35
1999-2000	327.56	454.11
2004-2005	356.30	538.60
2005-2006	365.00	580.00

Source: *www.indiastat.com*

Table-1 shows that, the per capita per month of both rural and urban people is increasing year by year. The per capita per month of rural and urban people in the year 1973-74 is Rs. 49.63 and Rs. 56.76 respectively. In the year the per capita per month of rural and urban people is Rs. 365.00 and Rs. 580.00 respectively.

Table-2 State-wise Projected of Poverty Ratios in India

Major States	1996-97	2001-02	2006-07	2011-12
Andhra Pradesh	17.35	11.13	5.35	2.44
Assam	26.46	10.65	3.82	2.07
Bihar	44.09	27.46	14.08	6.52
Gujarath	17.07	9.05	3.94	1.28
Haryana	18.41	10.16	5	2.58
Himachal Pradesh	22.38	14.02	7.34	3.14
Karnataka	30.72	17.86	8.68	3.45
Kerala	21.22	11.35	4.76	1.38
Madhya Pradesh	33.38	21.97	12.75	6.81
Maharashtra	32.74	20.66	11.41	5.43
Orissa (Odissa)	40.21	22.93	10.76	4.63
Punjab	**8.02**	**2.98**	**0.85**	**0.15**
Rajastan	20.31	10.85	4.7	1.52
Tamil Nadu	30.52	18.11	8.96	3.59
Uttar Pradesh	**32.52**	**21.91**	**12.88**	**6.92**
West Bengal	25.08	13.54	6.26	2.86
India	**29.18**	**17.98**	**9.53**	**4.37**

Source: *www.indiastat.com*

From the above table we conclude that, the projected poverty of India for the year 2011-12 is 4.37 per cent. It was 9.53 per cent in the year 2006-07. Panjab (0.15%) has low projected poverty ratio and Uttar Pradesh (6.92%) has high projected poverty ratio when compared to any other states in India.

Table-3 Projection of National Poverty Ratios in India (1996-97, 2001-02, 2006-07 & 2011-12)

Region	1996-97	2001-02	2006-07	2011-12
Rural	30.55	18.61	9.64	4.31
Urban	25.58	16.46	9.28	4.49
Total	29.18	17.98	9.53	4.37

Source: *www.indiastat.com*

From the table-3 we conclude that, both rural and urban poverty ratios are decreasing gradually. In the year 1996-97 the rural poverty (30.55%) was greater than the urban poverty (25.88%). But, in the case of projected poverty ratio, the urban poverty (4.49%) is greater than the rural poverty (4.31%) and total poverty of India (4.37%).

TYPES OF POVERTY

Poverty may be classified into two types. They are;

1. Rural Poverty; and
2. Urban Poverty

CAUSES OF POVERTY

The main causes of poverty are;

- o Illiteracy and lack of education
- o Unemployment
- o improper utilization of resources
- o Political instability
- o Worthless programmes
- o Corruption in administration

ESTIMATES OF POVERTY

A common method used to measure poverty is based on incomes or consumption levels. A person is considered poor if his or her consumption or income level falls below some minimum level necessary to meet basic needs. This minimum level is usually called the "poverty line". What is necessary to satisfy basic needs varies across time and societies. Therefore, poverty lines vary in time and place, and each country uses lines which are appropriate to its level of development, societal norms and values.

Internationally, the one dollar a day indicator (new $1.25 a day line in 2005 prices) has been fixed as the indicator of poverty; it indicates the purchasing power of the people. This international poverty which takes into account the purchasing power parity (PPP) is required mainly to allow comparisons across countries and to produce estimates of poverty at an aggregate level.

FACTS OF POVERTY ACROSS THE WORLD

The turn of the century was marked by some significant and promising events for world development. The Millennium Declaration—signed by 189 countries in September 2000 led to the adoption of the Millennium Development Goals (MDGs). These goals set clear targets for eradicating poverty and other sources of human deprivation and for promoting sustainable development.

Facts

- Today, across the world, 1.3 billion people live on less than one dollar a day. About 60 percent of the people living on less than $1 a day live in South Asia and Sub-Saharan Africa.
- The number of poor has fallen by 500 million since 1981 (from 52 percent of the developing world's population in 1981 to 26 percent in 2005) and the world is still on track to halve the 1990 poverty rate by 2015. But at this rate of progress, about a billion people will still live below $1.25 a day in 2015. Also, most people who escaped $1.25 a day poverty over 1981-2005 would still be poor by middle-income country standards.
- Thirty-thousand children die every day due to poverty (UNICEF). This includes 11 million children less than five years of age, each year.
- Of the 2.2 billion children in the world, 1 billion are reeling in poverty (every second child). For the 1.9 billion children from the developing world, there are:

- o 640 million without adequate shelter (1 in 3)
- o 400 million with no access to safe water (1 in 5)
- o 270 million with no access to health services (1 in 7)
- o The world's 3 richest people have wealth greater than the combined Gross Domestic Product (the value of all goods and services) of the world's 48 poorest nations.
- o The world's richest 225 people have combined assets equal to the combined annual income of the world's 2.5 billion poorest people.
- o More than 800 million people go hungry every day; of these 300 million are children.
- o Of these 300 million children, only eight percent are victims of famine or other emergency situations. More than 90 percent are suffering long-term malnourishment and micro nutrient deficiency.
- o Every 3.6 seconds a person dies of starvation and a large majority of these are children under the age of five.
- o It has been estimated that 1.1 billion people had consumption levels below $1 a day and 2.7 billion lived on less than $2 a day.

These figures are lower than earlier estimates, indicating that some progress has taken place, but they still remain too high in terms of human suffering, and much more remains to be done.

POVERTY ALLEVIATION

Poverty alleviation is a top priority for governments, along with the international community in their development strategies. The eradication of extreme poverty and hunger was the first Millennium Development Goal, as set by 179 United Nations Member States in 2000. Economists and activists consider epidemic diseases (AIDS, malaria, tuberculosis) as crucial factors in and consequences of extreme poverty.

Poverty reduction or poverty alleviation has been largely as a result of overall economic growth. Extending property rights protection to the poor is one of the most important poverty reduction strategies a nation could take. Securing property rights to land, the largest asset for most societies, is vital to their economic freedom. The World Bank concludes increasing land rights is 'the key to reducing poverty' citing that land rights greatly increase poor people's wealth, in some cases doubling it. In China and India, noted reductions in poverty in recent decades have occurred mostly as a result of the abandonment of collective farming in China and the cutting of government red tape in India.

Poverty alleviation has been on the agenda of the national policy since long before independence. The Indian National Congress constituted a National Planning Committee early 1938 which declared that the social objective should be "to ensure an adequate standard of living for the masses, in other words, to get rid of the appalling poverty of the people". The importance of poverty alleviation and provision of other basic needs has been emphasized in all the successive Plans particularly since the Fifth Five Year Plan. The basic principles of planning in India followed the concept of growth with social justice. It is in this backdrop that poverty alleviation programmes have now been viewed in wider perspective of socio-economic transformation in the country.

Programmes launched to reduce poverty:

- o Integrated rural development programmes that include provision of subsidy and bank credit for productive employment opportunities
- o Training rural youth for self employment (TRYSEM)
- o Development of Women and Children in Rural Areas (DWACRA)
- o Supply of Improved Toolkits to Rural Artisans
- o Drought Prone Area Programme
- o Self employment and Wage employment programmes
- o Creation of Rural Infrastructure (roads, etc.,) for employment generation
- o Employment assurance schemes,
- o Social Security programmes – national social assistance programme – that include old age pension scheme, family and maternity benefit schemes, food and nutrition security, public distribution system etc

- o Land reforms
- o National Rural Employment Guarantee Programme

Poverty reduction in the eleventh plan

The persistence of poverty on the scale at which it still exists is not acceptable. A decisive reduction in poverty and an expansion in economic opportunities for all sections of the population should therefore be a crucial element of the vision for the Eleventh Plan. Rapid growth of the economy is an essential requirement to achieve this outcome since it is an instrument for achieving a steady increase in employment and incomes for large numbers of our people.

Growth in the Eleventh Plan should be better balanced to rapidly create jobs in the industrial and services sectors. This is necessary if a significant portion of the labour force is to shift out of agriculture, where it is currently engaged in low productivity employment, into a non-agricultural activity that can provide higher real incomes per head. This must be accompanied by efforts to improve the income-earning opportunities of those who remain in agriculture by raising land productivity. This process would also lead to higher farm incomes and a rise in real wages of agricultural labour whose bargaining power will improve as surplus labour is shifted out of this sector.

Rapid growth in the economy at large, and especially in the employment generating sectors such as medium and small industry and services, needs to be supplemented by targeted livelihood support programmes aimed at increasing productivity and incomes of the poor in several low income occupations which will continue as important sources of employment for quite some time. Special programmes aimed at target groups such as small and micro enterprises, weavers, artisans, craftsmen, etc. will therefore remain important in the Eleventh Plan period. Considerable experience has been gained over the years in the management of these programmes. This experience must be brought to bear in redesigning the programmes in the Eleventh Plan to make them more effective in achieving their stated objectives.

Poverty alleviation also involves improving the living conditions of people who are already poor. Aid, particularly in medical and scientific areas, is essential in providing better lives, such as the green revolution and the eradication of smallpox. Problems with today's development aid include the high proportion of tied aid, which mandates receiving nations to buy products, often more expensive, originating only from donor countries. Nevertheless, some believe (Peter Singer in his book The Life You Can Save) that small changes in the way each of us in affluent nations lives our lives could solve world poverty.

INCLUSIVE GROWTH

For increasing welfare and wellbeing fueled by economic growth the central theme is that it should be sustainable and inclusive, i.e. incorporate the "People, Planet, Profit-" dimensions:

(1) The People factor: fundamental human rights and social justice are at the core; economic growth should benefit all citizens of the world; to close the extreme poverty-gap recognition must be given to a fundamental human right of "equal access to opportunity";

(2) The Planet (ecosystems/environmental) factor: it recognizes the need for a precautionary approach and "internalizes" the cost to nature into our economic interventions; "from black to green";

(3) The Profit factor: free market, capitalistic approaches are the core drivers for efficient and effective investments & operations, laying the solid foundation for further growth and future initiatives;

What is Inclusive Growth?

- Inclusive Growth focuses on economic growth which is a necessary and crucial condition for poverty reduction.
- Inclusive Growth adopts a long term perspective and is concerned with sustained growth.
  - (a) For growth to be sustained in the long run, it should be broad-based across sectors. Issues of structural transformation for economic diversification therefore take a front stage. Some countries may be an exception and continue to specialize as they develop due to their specific conditions (e.g. small states).
  - (b) It should also be inclusive of the large part of the country's labor force, where inclusiveness refers to equality of

opportunity in terms of access to markets, resources and unbiased regulatory environment for businesses and individuals.

- Inclusive Growth focuses on both the pace and pattern of growth. How growth is generated is critical for accelerating poverty reduction, and any Inclusive Growth strategies must be tailored to country-specific circumstances.
- Inclusive Growth focuses on productive employment rather than income redistribution. Hence the focus is not only on employment growth but also on productivity growth.
- Inclusive Growth has not only the firm, but also the individual as the subject of analysis.
- Inclusive Growth is in line with the absolute definition of pro-poor growth, not the relative one.
- Inclusive Growth is not defined in terms of specific targets such as employment generation or income distribution. These are potential outcomes, not specific goals.
- Inclusive Growth is typically fueled by market-driven sources of growth with the government playing a facilitating role.
- 'Inclusive Growth' is both the title and the overarching goal of the Eleventh Five Year Plan of India. Economic reforms have led, especially over the last five years or so, not only to accelerated growth but to sustained accelerated growth.

Need of Inclusive Growth

However, exclusion continued in terms of low agriculture growth, low quality employment growth, low human development, rural-urban divides, gender and social inequalities and regional disparities etc. There is now recognition that inclusive growth should be achieved in order to reduce poverty and other disparities and raise economic growth. At international level, there is a concern about inequalities and exclusion and now they are also talking about inclusive approach for development.

Elements of Inclusive Growth

Five interrelated elements of inclusive growth

1. Poverty reduction and increase in quantity and quality of employment

2. Agricultural development
3. Social sector development
4. Reduction in regional disparities
5. Protecting the environment

Poverty reduction is the foremost element of inclusive growth.

Inclusive Growth in India

The Common Minimum Programme of the United Progressive Alliance (UPA) Government in India has focused on inclusive growth, on making the benefits of growth and income improvements available to all citizens. Yet, in the last few years, there is the worry that income disparities are increasing, that there is greater well being for a few, much better off. The growth of income disparity is a phenomenon that is being witnessed in all countries, both developed and developing, but in a democracy like India, these disparities are likely to lead to social unrest. There have been two flagship programmes of the Government, the National Rural Employment Guarantee Programme, aimed at providing 100 days of guaranteed employment to all those who seek it, and the Bharat Nirman, focused on developing rural infrastructure. There are some doubts whether these programmes have had the impact that they intended, mostly due to administrative inefficiencies. Both these programmes focus on the rural poor.

The argument is that over 500 million people live in rural areas, and with slow rate of growth in agriculture and increasing dependence on off-farm income generation, poverty alleviation programmes should focus on income generation in the rural areas. The gap in this conceptualization is that it does not address the concern of the urban poor. Nearly 40% of the population lives in urban or urbanizing areas, and the poor in urban areas have concerns that are quite different from those in rural areas. The difference in entitlements stems from the fact that the rural poor have access to shelter, in the form of some land for putting up a house or hut, whether it be own land or public land. They have access to water and to fuel (often firewood or agricultural residues). All these entitlements are free of charge for the rural poor. But as soon as the rural poor migrate to the city in search of employment, all these entitlements become priced goods. Rural farm labour often gets paid in kind for farm work, providing some food security. In urban areas, food is a priced good. Therefore, programmes aimed at the poor need to distinguish between the rural and the urban poor, and need to focus on delivery of food and fuel at prices that are affordable. This would involve a policy of distribution of cooking fuels like kerosene and domestic gas at subsidized prices, as well a food grains at below market prices. Importantly, the difference between the rural poor and the urban poor is that for the latter, employment and wages are not a concern, it is access to reasonably priced food, fuel and shelter. Therefore, programmes like the National Employment Guarantee Programme, cannot make any impact for the poor elsewhere than in rural areas. The urban poor, mostly in informal employment, need to be targeted with subsidies for food and fuel.

If the goal of inclusive growth is to be realized, there is urgent need for programmes that would address the different concerns of the rural poor and the urban poor. Failure to do so would make cities uninhabitable, with pressures on water, transportation, fuel and power. Very little is being planned in this direction.

Finally, for the growth process to be inclusive and sustainable, it is important that skills in demand are matched by skills in supply, to ensure productive employment. In almost every sphere of activity, construction, travel, hotel industry, manufacturing as well as IT, a shortage of skilled personnel drives up labour and wage costs. People with education are not necessarily those with relevant skills. Job mobility increased concurrently with states like Tamil Nadu attracting workers from Orissa or Bihar. It is important that relevant skill development takes place quickly to ensure balanced growth. In the last budget, Government has recognized this problem and set up a large public-private sector initiative that would focus on skill formation. The world at large is concerned about the pace of reforms in India. The focus is on financial and manufacturing sectors, access to markets and labour regulations. But of equal concern are measures that would enable every citizen to participate in India's prosperity.

CONCLUSION

Rapid pace of growth is unquestionably necessary for substantial poverty reduction, but for this growth to be sustainable in the long run, it should be increasingly broad-based across sectors, and inclusive of the large part of the country's labor force. Policies for inclusive growth are an important component of most government strategies for sustainable growth. For instance, a country that has grown rapidly over a decade, but has not seen substantial reduction in poverty rates may need to focus specifically on the inclusiveness of its growth strategy, i.e. on the equality of opportunity for individuals and firms. Inclusive growth is about raising the pace of growth and enlarging the size of the economy, while leveling the playing field for investment and increasing productive employment opportunities. Policies for inclusive growth are an important component of any government strategy for sustainable growth and the frameworks for inclusive growth analytics are eclectic in spirit. The main instrument for a sustainable and inclusive growth is assumed to be productive employment. Employment growth generates new jobs and income for the individual. Through inclusive growth it is easy to remove poverty in our society. Poverty is a main obstacle not only for individual development, but also for national development. Powerful poverty alleviation programmes are necessary to eradicate poverty in our country. We hope poverty will be eliminated at least 2020.

REFERENCES

1. Commission on Growth and Development (2008) *Growth Report: Strategies for Sustained Growth and Inclusive Development*, the World Bank.
2. Deininger, K., and L. Squire (1996) "A New Data Set Measuring Income Inequality." *World Bank Economic Review* 10, pp. 565–91.
3. Li H. and H. Zhou (1998) "Income Inequality is not Harmful for Growth: Theory and Evidence." Review of Development Economics 2(3).
4. NSS 61st round 2004-05, Government of India, New Delhi.
5. Planning Commission of India-2008, Government of India, New Delhi.
6. Poverty Estimates for 2004-05, Government of India, New Delhi.
7. Ravallion, M. (2001) "Growth, Inequality and Poverty: Looking Beyond Averages", *World Development* 29(11), pp 1803-1815.
8. Report of UNDP-2009, UN.
9. The Times of India, 11 September 2008.
10. World Bank Report 2002.
11. World Development Indicators database, April 2002
12. World Development Indicators database, April 2002.

18

Literacy and Employment in India

Literacy in India is key for socio-economic progress, and the Indian literacy rate grew to 66% in 2007 from 12% at the end of British rule in 1947. Although this was a greater than fivefold improvement, the level is well below the world average literacy rate of 84%, and India currently has the largest illiterate population of any nation on earth. Despite government programs, India's literacy rate increased only "sluggishly," and a 1990 study estimated that it would take until 2060 for India to achieve universal literacy at then-current rate of progress. The 2001 census, however, indicated a 1991-2001 decadal literacy growth of 12.63%, which is the fastest-ever on record.

There is a wide gender disparity in the literacy rate in India: adult (15+ years) literacy rates in 2009 were 76.9% for men and 54.5% for women. The low female literacy rate has had a dramatically negative impact on family planning and population stabilization efforts in India. Studies have indicated that female literacy is a strong predictor of the use of contraception among married Indian couples, even when women do not otherwise have economic independence. The 2001 census provided a positive indication that growth in female literacy rates (14.38%) was substantially faster than in male literacy rates (11.13%) in the 1991-2001 decadal period, which means the gender gap appears to be narrowing.

Comparative literacy statistics

About 35% of world's illiterate population is Indian and, based on historic patterns of literacy growth across the world, India may account for a majority of the world's illiterates by 2020.The table below shows the adult and youth literacy rates for India and some neighbouring countries in 2002. Adult literacy rate is based on the 15+ years age group, while Youth literacy rate is for the 15–24 years age group (i.e. youth is a subset of adults).

Country	Adult Literacy Rate	Youth Literacy Rate
China	93.3% (2007)[14]	98.9% (2004)[15]
Sri Lanka	98.8 (2007)	98.0
Burma	89.9% (2007) [16]	94.4% (2004)[17]
Iran	82.4% (2007) [18]	95% (2002)[19]
World Average	84% (1998)[4]	88% (2001)[20]
India	**66.0% (2007)**[3]	**82% (2001)**[3]
Nepal	56.5 (2007)	62.7
Pakistan	54.2 (2007)[21]	53.9
Bangladesh	53.5 (2007)	49.7

Growth of literacy

Literacy in India grew very slowly until independence in 1947. An acceleration in the rate of literacy growth occurred in the 1991-2001 period. During the British period, progress of education was rather tardy. Between 1881-82 and 1946-47, the number of primary schools grew from 82,916 to 134,866 and the number of students grew from 2,061,541 to 10,525,943. Literacy rates in British India rose from 3.2 per cent in 1881 to 7.2 per cent in 1931 and 12.2 per cent in 1947. In 2000-01, there were 60,840 pre-primary and pre-basic schools, and 664,041 primary and junior basic schools. Total enrollment at the primary level has increased from 19,200,000 in 1950-51 to 109,800,000 in 2001-02. The number of high schools in 2000-01 was higher than the number of primary schools at the time of independence.

In 1944, the Government of British India presented a plan, called the Sergeant Scheme for the educational reconstruction of India, with a goal of producing 100% literacy in the country within 40 years, i.e. by 1984. Although the 40 year time-frame was derided at the time by leaders of the Indian independence movement as being too long a period to achieve universal literacy, India had only just crossed the 64% level by the 2001 census.

Post Independence

The provision of universal and compulsory education for all children in the age group of 6-14 was a cherished national ideal and had been given overriding priority by incorporation as a Directive Policy in Article 45 of the Constitution, but it is still to be achieved more than half a century since the Constitution was adopted in 1949. Parliament has passed the Constitution 86th Amendment Act, 2002, to make elementary education a Fundamental Right for children in the age group of 6–14 years. In order to provide more funds for education, an education cess of 2 per cent has been imposed on all direct and indirect central taxes through the Finance (No.2) Act, 2004.

Since independence, the literacy rate grew from 18.33 per cent in 1951, to 28.30 per cent in 1961, 34.45 per cent in 1971, 43.57 per cent in 1981, 52.21 per cent in 1991, and 64.84per cent in 2001. During the same period, the population grew from 361 million to 1,028 million.

Literacy rate variations between states

Kerala is the most literate state in India, with 90.92% literacy,followed closely by Mizoram at 88.80%. Bihar is the least literate state in India with 47% literacy. Several other social indicators of the two states are correlated with these rates, such as life expectancy at birth (71.61 for males and 75 for females in Kerala, 65.66 for males and 64.79 for females in Bihar), infant mortality per 1,000 live births (10 in Kerala, 61 in Bihar), birth rate per 1,000 people (16.9 in Kerala, 30.9 in Bihar) and death rate per 1,000 people (6.4 in Kerala, 7.9 in Bihar). Ernakulam district in Kerala was the first district to reach the 100% literacy level in India.

Every census since 1881 had indicated rising literacy in the country, but the population growth rate had been high enough that the absolute number of illiterates rose with every decade. The 1991-2001 decade is the first census period when the absolute number of Indian illiterates declined (by 32 million), indicating that the literacy growth rate is now outstripping the population growth rate. Bihar, Nagaland and Manipur were the only states in the 1991-2001 period where the absolute number of illiterates rose, although even there the percentage of illiterates fell.

Bihar was the only remaining Indian state in the 2001 census where the majority of the population (53%) was illiterate. It was also the only state where less than 60% of the male population was literate. Six Indian states account for about 70% of all illiterates in India: Uttar Pradesh, Bihar, Madhya Pradesh, Rajasthan, Andhra Pradesh and West Bengal. Slightly less than half of all Indian illiterates (48.12%) are in the six Hindi-speaking states of Uttar Pradesh, Bihar, Rajasthan, Madhya Pradesh, Jharkhand and Chhattisgarh. Large variations in literacy exist even between contiguous states. While there are a few states at the top and bottom, most states are just above or below the national average.

Learnings from state literacy efforts in India

Several states in India have executed successful programs to boost literacy rates. Over time, a set of factors have emerged as being key to success: official will to succeed, deliberate steps to engage the community in administering the program, adequate funding for infrastructure and teachers, and provisioning additional services which are considered valuable by the community (such as free school lunches).

Bihar literacy challenges

Bihar has the lowest literacy rate in India and, in the 2001 census, was the only Indian state where the majority of the population (53%) was illiterate. Even in Bihar, however, the literacy rate is rising: from 39% in 1991 to 47% in 2001. The Government of Bihar has launched several programs to boost literacy, and its Department of Adult Education even won a UNESCO award in 1981.

Extensive impoverishment, entrenched hierarchical social divisions and the lack of correlation between educational attainment and job opportunities are often cited in studies of the hurdles literacy programs face in Bihar. Children from "lower castes" are frequently denied school attendance and harassed when they do attend. In areas where there is no discrimination, poor funding and impoverished families means that children often cannot afford textbooks and stationery. When children do get educated, the general lack of economic progress in the state means that government jobs are the only alternative to farm labor, yet these jobs, in practise, require bribes to secure - which poorer families cannot afford. This leads to educated youths working on the farms, much as uneducated ones do, and leads parents to question the investment of sending children to school in the first place. Bihar's government schools have also faced teacher absenteeism, leading the state government to threaten withholding of salaries of teachers who failed to conduct classes on a regular basis.To incentivize students to attend, the government announced a Rupee 1 per schoolday grant to poor children who show-up to school.

Kerala literacy successes

Kerala undertook a "*campaign for total literacy* in Ernakulam district in the late 1980s," with a "*fusion between the district administration headed by its Collector on one side and, on the other side, voluntary groups, social activists and others.*" On February 4, 1990, Ernakulam was certified as being 100% literate. The Government of Kerala then replicated the initiative on a statewide level, launching the Kerala State Literacy Campaign.First, households were surveyed with door-to-door, multistage survey visits to form an accurate picture of the literacy landscape and areas that needed special focus. Then, *Kala Jathas* (cultural troupes) and *Saksharta Pad Yatras* (Literacy Foot Marches) were organized to generate awareness of the campaign and create a receptive social atmosphere for the program. An integrated management system was created involving state officials, prominent social figures, local officials and senior voluntary workers to oversee the execution of the campaign.

Himachal Pradesh literacy successes

Strong government action and community support made Himachal Pradesh one of India's most literate states by 2001 Himachal Pradesh underwent a "Schooling Revolution" in the 1961-2001 period that has been called "*even more impressive than Kerala's.*" Kerala has led the nation in literacy rates since the 19th century and seen sustained initiatives for over 150 years, whereas Himachal Pradesh's literacy rates in 1961 were below the national average in every age group.[35] In the three decadal 1961-1991 period, female literacy in the 15–19 years age group went from 11% to 86%. School attendance for both boys and girls in the 6-14 year age group stood at over 97% each when measured in the 1998-99 school year. A key factor that has been credited for these advances is Himachal's cultural background. Himachal Pradesh is a Himalayan state with lower social stratification than many other states, which enables social programs to be carried out more smoothly. Once the Government of Himachal Pradesh was able to establish a social norm that "*schooling is an essential part of every child's upbringing,*" literacy as a normal attribute of life was adopted very rapidly. Government efforts in expanding schools and providing teachers were sustained after the 1960s and communities often responded very collaboratively, including with constructing school rooms and providing firewood essential during the Himalayan winters.[35]

Mizoram literacy successes

Mizoram's literacy rate rose rapidly after independence: from 31.14% in 1951 to 88.80% in 2001. As in Himachal Pradesh, Mizoram has a social structure that is relatively free of hierarchy and strong official intent to produce total literacy. The government identified illiterates and organized an administrative structure that engaged officials and community leaders, and manned by "animators" who were responsible for teaching five illiterates each. Mizoram established 360 continuing education centers to handle continued education beyond the initial literacy teaching and to provide an educational safety net for school dropouts.

Tamil Nadu literacy successes

Tamil Nadu is the most literate state of India according to the HRD ministry of India's 2003 statistics. Starting in 1982, Tamil Nadu took an approach to promoting literacy based on free lunches for schoolchildren, "*ignoring cynics who said it was an electoral gimmick and economists who said it made little fiscal sense.*" The then chief minister of Tamil Nadu, M G Ramachandran launched the program, which resembled a similar initiative in 19th century Japan, because "*he had experienced as a child what it was like to go hungry to school with the family having no money to buy food*". Eventually, the program covered all children under the age of 15, as well as pregnant women for the first four months of their pregnancy. Tamil Nadu's literacy rate rose from 54.4% in 1981 to 73.4% in 2001. In 2001, the Supreme Court of India instructed all state governments to implement free school lunches in all government-funded schools, but implementation has been patchy due to corruption and social issues. Despite these hurdles, 120 million receive free lunches in Indian schools every day, making it the largest school meal program in the world.

Rajasthan literacy successes

Rajasthan had the biggest percentage decadal (1991-2001) increase in literacy of all Indian states, from about 38% to about 61%, a leapfrog that has been termed "spectacular" by some observers. Aggressive state government action, in the form of the District Primary Education Programme, the Shiksha Karmi initiative and the Lok Jumbish programme, are credited with the rapid improvement. Virtually every village in Rajasthan now has primary school coverage. When statehood was granted to Rajasthan in 1956, it was the least literate state in India with a literacy rate of 18%.

Social commentary

In his essay on *Social Infrastructure As Important As Physical Infrastructure* published in *India Development Report 2002*, Kirit S. Parikh had pointed out, "With a literacy rate of 65, we have 296 million illiterates, age seven years and above, as per the 2001 census. The number of illiterates today exceeds the population of the country of around 270 million at Independence, age seven and above."

In his book *The Argumentative Indian*, Amartya Sen notes, on the basis of investigations by Pratichi Trust, set up with the proceeds of his Nobel award, carried out in West Bengal and Jharkhand, that absenteeism of comparatively well-paid teachers, particularly where bulk of the students come from scheduled castes and tribes, poses a major problem. Students are circumstantially forced to go in for private tuitions. He concludes, "Sometimes the very institutions that were created to overcome disparities and barriers have tended to act as reactionary influences in reinforcing inequality... The teachers' unions, which have a very positive role to play in protecting the interests of teachers and have played that part well in the past, are often are turning into an influence that reinforces the neglect of the interests of children from desperately underprivileged families. There is evidence of hardening of class barriers that separate the newly affluent teachers from the impoverished rural poor."

Literacy efforts

The right to education is a fundamental human right, and UNESCO aims at education for all by 2015. India, along with the Arab states and sub-Saharan Africa, has a literacy level below the threshold level of 75%, but efforts are on to achieve that level. The campaign to achieve at least the threshold literacy level represents the largest ever civil and military mobilization in the country. *International Literacy Day* is celebrated each year on 8 September with the aim to highlight the importance of literacy to individuals, communities and societies.

National Literacy Mission

The *National Literacy Mission*, launched in 1988, aimed at attaining a literacy rate of 75 per cent by 2007. It imparts functional literacy to non-literates in the age group of 15–35 years. The *Total Literacy Campaign* is the principal strategy of the NLM for eradication of illiteracy. The *Continuing Education Scheme* provides a learning continuum to the efforts of the Total Literacy and Post literacy programmes.

Sarva Siksha Abhiyan

The *Sarva Siksha Abhiyan* (Hindi for *Total Literacy Campaign*) was launched in 2001 to ensure that all children in the 6–14 year age-group attend school and complete eight years of schooling by 2010. An important component of the scheme is the *Education Guarantee Scheme and Alternative and Innovative Education*, meant primarily for children in areas with no formal school within a one kilometre radius. The centrally sponsored *District Primary Education Programme*, launched in 1994, had opened more than 160,000 new schools by 2005, including almost 84,000 alternative schools.

Mid-day Meal Scheme

Of the estimated 205 million child population in the age group 6–14 years on March 1, 2002, nearly 82.5% were enrolled in schools. However, the drop-out rate in 2002-03 was 34.9% at the primary level and 52.8% at the upper primary level. The high drop-out rate has been a matter of major concern. One of the most popular schemes adopted to attract children to schools is the *Mid-day Meal Scheme*, launched in 1995. Several other special programmes have also been launched with varying degrees of success.

Non-governmental efforts

The bulk of Indian illiterates live in the country's rural areas, where social and economic barriers play an important role in keeping the lowest strata of society illiterate. Government programmes alone, however well intentioned, may not be able to dismantle barriers built over centuries. Major social reformation efforts are sometimes required to bring about a change in the rural scenario.

Asha for Education

Sandeep Pandey won a Ramon Magsaysay Award in 2002 in recognition of "*the empowering example of his commitment to the transformation of India's marginalized poor.*" While pursuing a Ph.D. at the University of California, Berkeley, he co-founded *Asha for Education* to support education for poor children in India by tapping the resources of Overseas Indians, raising ten thousand dollars in the first year. The organization has since expanded to 36 North-American chapters and disbursed nearly one million dollars for programs in India.

Pandey has returned to India and works full-time towards Asha's stated mission of bringing about socio-economic change in India through education. Asha's teachers are unpaid volunteers and support themselves with side-occupations, such as making candles and greeting cards from handmade paper. While working with impoverished low caste families and dalits in Ballia district of Uttar Pradesh, Pandey discovered that few children went to school and those that did remained unemployed. With local volunteers, Pandey established schools in the villages of Reoti and Bhainsaha focused on instilling self-reliance and the value of social justice among students. He has also established an *Asha Ashram* in the predominantly Dalit village of Lalpur, outside Lucknow, where students live and study among traditional artisans, and learn the crafts of bee-keeping, vegetable gardening and cottage industries.

Mamidipudi Venkatarangaiya Foundation

Shantha Sinha won a Magsaysay Award in 2003 in recognition of "*her guiding the people of Andhra Pradesh to end the scourge of child labour and send all of their children to school.*" As head of an extension program at the University of Hyderabad in 1987, she organized a three-month-long camp to prepare children rescued from bonded labour to attend school. Later, in 1991, she guided her family's *Mamidipudi Venkatarangaiya Foundation* to take up this idea as part of its overriding mission in Andhra Pradesh. Her original transition camps grew into full-fledged residential "bridge schools." The foundation's aim is to create a social climate hostile to child labour, child marriage and other practices that deny children the right to a normal childhood. Today the MV Foundation's bridge schools and programs extend to 4,300 villages.

Definition of literacy

The United Nations Educational, Scientific and Cultural Organization (UNESCO) has drafted a definition of literacy as the "ability to identify, understand, interpret, create, communicate, compute and use printed and written materials associated with varying contexts. Literacy involves a continuum of learning in enabling individuals to achieve their goals, to develop their knowledge and potential, and to participate fully in their community and wider society."

The National Literacy Mission defines literacy as acquiring the skills of reading, writing and arithmetic and the ability to apply them to one's day-to-day life. The achievement of functional literacy implies

(i) self-reliance in 3 R's, (ii) awareness of the causes of deprivation and the ability to move towards amelioration of their condition by participating in the process of development, (iii) acquiring skills to improve economic status and general well being, and (iv) imbibing values such as national integration, conservation of environment, women's equality, observance of small family norms.

The working definition of literacy in the Indian census since 1991 is as follows:

- o *Literacy rate*: The total percentage of the population of an area at a particular time aged seven years or above who can read and write with understanding. Here the denominator is the population aged seven years or more.
- o *Crude literacy rate*: The total percentage of the people of an area at a particular time aged seven years or above who can read and write with understanding, taking the total population of the area (including below seven years of age) as the denominator.

The History of HIV/AIDS in India

At the beginning of 1986, despite over 20,000 reported AIDS cases worldwide, India had no reported cases of HIV or AIDS. There was recognition, though, that this would not be the case for long, and concerns were raised about how India would cope once HIV and AIDS cases started to emerge. One report, published in a medical journal in January 1986, stated: "Unlike developed countries, India lacks the scientific laboratories, research facilities, equipment, and medical personnel to deal with an AIDS epidemic. In addition, factors such as cultural taboos against discussion of sexual practices, poor coordination between local health authorities and their communities, widespread poverty and malnutrition, and a lack of capacity to test and store blood would severely hinder the ability of the Government to control AIDS if the disease did become widespread."

Later in the year, India's first cases of HIV were diagnosed among sex workers in Chennai, Tamil Nadu. It was noted that contact with foreign visitors had played a role in initial infections among sex workers, and as HIV screening centres were set up across the country there were calls for visitors to be screened for HIV. Gradually, these calls subsided as more attention was paid to ensuring that HIV screening was carried out in blood banks.

In 1987 a National AIDS Control Programme was launched to co-ordinate national responses. Its activities covered surveillance, blood screening, and health education. By the end of 1987, out of 52,907 who had been tested, around 135 people were found to be HIV positive and 14 had AIDS. Most of these initial cases had occurred through heterosexual sex, but at the end of the 1980s a rapid spread of HIV was observed among injecting drug users (IDUs) in Manipur, Mizoram and Nagaland - three north-eastern states of India bordering Myanmar (Burma).

At the beginning of the 1990s, as infection rates continued to rise, responses were strengthened. In 1992 the government set up NACO (the National AIDS Control Organisation), to oversee the formulation of policies, prevention work and control programmes relating to HIV and AIDS. In the same year, the government launched a Strategic Plan for HIV prevention. This plan established the administrative and technical basis for programme management and also set up State AIDS bodies in 25 states and 7 union territories. It was able to make a number of important improvements in HIV prevention such as improving blood safety.

By this stage, cases of HIV infection had been reported in every state of the country. Throughout the 1990s, it was clear that although individual states and cities had separate epidemics, HIV had spread to the general population. Increasingly, cases of infection were observed among people that had previously been seen as *'low-risk'*, such as housewives and richer members of society. In 1998, one author wrote: "HIV infection is now common in India; exactly what the prevalence is, is not really known, but it can be stated without any fear of being wrong that infection is widespread... it is spreading rapidly into those segments that society in India does not recognise as being at risk. AIDS is coming out of the closet."

In 2001, the government adopted the National AIDS Prevention and Control Policy. During that year, former Prime Minister Atal Bihari Vajpayee addressed parliament and referred to HIV/AIDS as one of the most serious health challenges facing the country. Vajpayee also met the chief ministers of the six high-prevalence states to plan the implementation of strategies for HIV/AIDS prevention.HIV had now spread extensively throughout the country. In 1990 there had been tens of thousands of people living with HIV in India; by 2000 this had risen to millions.

Current estimates

In 2006 UNAIDS estimated that there were 5.6 million people living with HIV in India, which indicated that there were more people with HIV in India than in any other country in the world. In 2007, following the first survey of HIV among the general population, UNAIDS and NACO agreed on a new estimate – between 2 million and 3.1 million people living with HIV.

In 2008 the figure was confirmed to be 2.31 million,[19] which equates to a prevalence of 0.3%. While this may seem a low rate, because India's population is so large, it is third in the world in terms of greatest number of people living with HIV. With a population of around a billion, a mere 0.1% increase in HIV prevalence would increase the estimated number of people living with HIV by over half a million.

The national HIV prevalence rose dramatically in the early years of the epidemic, but a study released at the beginning of 2006 suggests that the HIV infection rate has recently fallen in southern India, the region that has been hit hardest by AIDS. In addition, NACO released figures in 2008 suggesting that the number of people living with HIV has declined from 2.73 million in 2002 to 2.31 million 2007.

Some AIDS activists are doubtful that the situation is improving:

"It is the reverse. All the NGOs I know have recorded increases in the number of people accepting help because of HIV. I am really worried that we are just burying our head in the sand over this." *Anjali Gopalan, the Naz Foundation, Delhi* "the statement that India has the AIDS problem under control is not true. There is a decline in prevalence in some of the Southern states... In the rest of the county, there are no arguments to demonstrate that AIDS is under control"

The HIV/AIDS situation in different states

Map of India showing the worst affected states.

The vast size of India makes it difficult to examine the effects of HIV on the country as a whole. The majority of states within India have a higher population than most African countries, so a more detailed picture of the crisis can be gained by looking at each state individually.

The HIV prevalence data for most states is established through testing pregnant women at antenatal clinics. While this means that the data are only directly relevant to sexually active women, they still provide a reasonable indication as to the overall HIV prevalence of each area.

The following states have recorded the highest levels of HIV prevalence at antenatal and sexually transmitted disease (STD) clinics over recent years.

Andhra Pradesh

Andhra Pradesh in the southeast of the country has a total population of around 76 million, of whom 6 million live in or around the city of Hyderabad. The HIV prevalence at antenatal clinics was 1% in 2007. This figure is smaller than the reported 1.26% in 2006, but is still highest out of all states. HIV prevalence at STD clinics was very high at 17% in 2007. Among high-risk groups, HIV prevalence was highest among men who have sex with men (MSM) (17%), followed by female sex workers (9.7%) and IDUs (3.7%).

Goa

Goa, a popular tourist destination, is a very small state in the southwest of India (population 1.4 million). In 2007 HIV prevalence among antenatal and STD clinic attendees was 0.18% and 5.6% respectively. The Goa State AIDS Control Society reported that in 2008, a record number of 26,737 people were tested for HIV, of which 1018 (3.81%) tested positive.

Karnataka

Karnataka, a diverse state in the southwest of India, has a population of around 53 million. HIV prevalence among antenatal clinic attendees exceeded 1% from 2003 to 2006, and dropped to 0.5% in 2007. Districts with the highest prevalence tend to be located in and around Bangalore in the southern part of the state, or in northern Karnataka's "devadasi belt". Devadasi women are a group of women who have historically been dedicated to the service of gods. These days, this has evolved into sanctioned prostitution, and as a result many women from this part of the country are supplied to the sex trade in big cities such as Mumbai. The average HIV prevalence among female sex workers in Karnataka was just over 5% in 2007, and 17.6% of men who have sex with men were found to be infected.

Maharashtra

Maharashtra is a very large state of three hundred thousand square kilometres, with a total population of around 97 million. The capital city of Maharashtra - Mumbai (Bombay) - is the most populous city in India, with around 14 million inhabitants. The HIV prevalence at antenatal clinics in Maharashtra was 0.5% in 2007. At 18%, the state has the highest reported rates of HIV prevalence among female sex workers. Similarly high rates were found among injecting drug users (24%) and men who have sex with men (12%).

Tamil Nadu

With a population of over 66 million, Tamil Nadu is the seventh most populous state in India. Between 1995 and 1997 HIV prevalence among pregnant women tripled to around 1.25%. The State Government subsequently set up an AIDS society, which aimed to focus on HIV prevention initiatives. A safe-sex campaign was launched, encouraging condom use and attacking the stigma and ignorance associated with HIV. Between 1996 and 1998 a survey showed that the number of men reporting high-risk sexual behaviour had decreased.

In 2007 HIV prevalence among antenatal clinic attendees was 0.25%. HIV prevalence among injecting drug users was 16.8%, third highest out of all reporting states. HIV prevalence among men who have sex with men and female sex workers was 6.6% and 4.68% respectively.

Manipur

Manipur is a small state of some 2.4 million people in northeast India. Manipur borders Myanmar (Burma), one of the world's largest producers of illicit opium. In the early 1980s drug use became popular in northeast India and it wasn't long before HIV was reported among injecting drug users in the region. Although NACO report a state-wise HIV prevalence of 17.9% among IDUs, studies from different areas of the state find prevalence to be as high as 32%.

HIV is no longer confined to IDUs, but has spread further to the general population. HIV prevalence at antenatal clinics in Manipur exceeded 1% in recent years, but then declined to 0.75% in 2007. Estimated adult HIV prevalence is the highest out of all states, at 1.57%.

Mizoram

The small northeastern state of Mizoram has fewer than a million inhabitants. In 1998, an HIV epidemic took off quickly among the state's male injecting drug users, with some drug clinics registering HIV rates of more than 70% among their patients. In recent years the average prevalence among this group has been much lower, at around 3-7%. HIV prevalence at antenatal clinics was 0.75% in 2007.

Nagaland

Nagaland is another small northeastern state where injecting drug use has again been the driving force behind the spread of HIV. In 2003 HIV prevalence among IDUs was 8.43%, but has since declined to 1.91% in 2007. HIV prevalence at antenatal clinics and STD clinics was 0.60% and 3.42% respectively in 2007.

The Punjab

The Punjab, a state in northern mainland India, has shown an increase in prevalence among injecting drug users (13.8% in 2007) in recent years. One of the richest cities in the Punjab, Ludhiana, has an HIV prevalence of 21% among IDUs. Denis Broun, head of UNAIDS in India has stated..."the problem of IDUs has been underestimated in mainland India, as most of the problem was thought to be in the northeast."

Who is affected by HIV and AIDS in India?

People living with HIV in India come from incredibly diverse cultures and backgrounds. The vast majority of infections occur through heterosexual sex (80%), and most of those who become infected would not fall into the category of 'high-risk groups' - although members of such groups, including sex workers, men who have sex with men, truck drivers and migrant workers, do face a disproportionately higher risk of infection. See our page on affected groups in India for more information.

HIV prevention

Educating people about HIV/AIDS and how it can be prevented is complicated in India, as a number of major languages and hundreds of different dialects are spoken within its population. This means that, although some HIV/AIDS prevention and education can be done at the national level, many of the efforts are best carried out at the state and local level.

Each state has its own AIDS Prevention and Control Society, which carries out local initiatives with guidance from NACO. Under the second stage of the government's National AIDS Control Programme (NACP-II), which finished in March 2006, state AIDS control societies were granted funding for youth campaigns, blood safety checks, and HIV testing, among other things. Various public platforms were used to raise awareness of the epidemic - concerts, radio dramas, a voluntary blood donation day and TV spots with a popular Indian film-star. Messages were also conveyed to young people through schools. Teachers and peer educators were trained to teach about the subject, and students were educated through active learning sessions, including debates and role-play.

The third stage of the National AIDS Control Programme (NACP-III), was launched in July 2007 and runs until 2012. The programme has a budget of around $2.6 billion, two thirds of which is for prevention and one sixth for treatment. Aside from the government, this money will come from non-governmental organisations, companies, and international agencies, such as the World Bank and the Bill and Melinda Gates Foundation.

The government has announced that this campaign will place a strong focus on condom promotion. It has already supported the installation of over 11,000 condom vending machines in colleges, road-side restaurants, stations, gas stations and hospitals. With support from the United States Agency for International Development (USAID), the government has also initiated a campaign called 'Condom Bindas Bol!' (Condom-Just say it!), which involves advertising, public events and celebrity endorsements. It aims to break the taboo that currently surrounds condom use in India, and to persuade people that they should not be embarrassed to buy them.

In one unique scheme, health activists in West Bengal are attempting to promote condom use through kite flying, which is popular before the state's biggest festival, Durga Puja: "The colourful kites carry the message that using a condom is a simple and instinctive act... they can fly high in the sky and land at distant places where we cannot reach."

This initiative is an example of how HIV prevention campaigns in India can be tailored to the situations of different states and areas. In doing so, they can make an important impact, particularly in rural areas where information is often lacking. Small-scale campaigns like this are often run or supported by non-governmental organisations, which play a vital role in preventing infections throughout India, particularly among high-risk groups. In some cases, members of these risk groups have formed their own organisations to respond to the epidemic.

The government has however funded a small number of national campaigns to spread awareness about HIV/AIDS to complement the local level initiatives. On World AIDS Day 2007 India flagged off its largest national campaign to date, in the form of a seven-coach train called the 'Red Ribbon Express.' A year later the train journey was completed, having travelled to 180 stations in 24 states and reaching around 6.2 million people with HIV/AIDS education and awareness.

PMTCT

In 2004 only 5% of pregnant women living with HIV received antiretrovirals to prevent mother-to-child transmission. By 2007 this had risen to 14% but with such low coverage 21,000 children below the age of 15 are still infected every year through mother-to-child transmission in India.

Testing

The general consensus among those fighting AIDS worldwide is that HIV testing should be carried out voluntarily, with the consent of the individual concerned. This view has been supported by the Indian government and NACO, who have helped to establish hundreds of integrated counselling and testing centres (ICTCs) in India. By the end of 2008 there were 4817 ICTCs in India, compared to just 62 in 1997. In 2007 these centres tested 5.9 million people for HIV, an increase from 0.14 million in 2001.

Although voluntary testing is officially supported in India, some states have tried to implement policies that would force people to be tested for HIV against their will. In Goa and Andhra Pradesh the state governments proposed a bill in 2006 to make HIV tests compulsory before marriage, and in Punjab it has been proposed that all people wishing to obtain or retain a driver's license should be tested for HIV. Neither of these plans have come to pass, but they have concerned activists, who argue that HIV testing should never be imposed on people against their wishes.

Unfortunately, cases of people being tested without their consent or knowledge are common in Indian hospitals. In one 2002 study, it was suggested that over 95% of patients listed for surgical procedures are tested against their will, often resulting in their surgery being cancelled. Hospital staff and health professionals, much like the rest of the Indian population, are often unaware of the facts about HIV. This leads to unnecessary fears and, in some cases, causes them to stigmatise HIV positive people and discriminate against them, including testing them without consent.

India has certainly made progress in expanding HIV testing to its large population. However, considering only 50% of those currently infected with HIV are aware of their status there is still significant work to be done in this area.

Treatment for people living with HIV

Antiretroviral drugs (ARVs), which can significantly delay the progression from HIV to AIDS – have been available in developed countries since 1996. Unfortunately, as in many resource-poor areas, access to this treatment is limited in India; an estimated 285,000 people were receiving ARVs by November 2009 through government health centres and another 35,000 through private health facilities. This represents less than half of those estimated to be in need of antiretroviral treatment in India.

While the coverage of treatment remains unacceptably low, improvements are being made. The government has started to expand access to ARVs in a number of areas; by November 2009 there were 266 reported sites providing antiretroviral therapy.

Increasing access to ARVs also means that an increasing number of people living with HIV in India are developing drug resistance. When HIV becomes resistant to the ARVs the treatment regimen needs to be changed to 'second-line' ARVs. As with many other parts of the world, second-line treatment in India is far more expensive than first-line treatment.

In 2008, NACO began to roll out government funded second-line antiretroviral treatment in two centres in Mumbai and Chennai. By 2009 second-line therapy was available in a total of eight states but treatment remains very limited. Of the 3,000 who need to be on second line treatment, about 750 were receiving it as of December 2009. One reason for this is expense; second line ARV drugs, unlike first line ARVs, are not produced on a large scale in India due to patent issues that control drug pricing and can be more than 10 times more expensive than first line ARVs. Another reason why coverage is so limited is the eligibility requirements imposed on second line ARVs; only those 'living below the poverty line, widows and children' and those who have received first-line ARVs from a government centre for at least two years are eligible.

Ironically, India is a major provider of cheap generic copies of ARVs to countries all over the world. However, the large scale of India's epidemic, the diversity of its spread, and the country's lack of finances and resources continue to present barriers to India's antitretroviral treatment programme. "It is a sad irony that India is one of the biggest producers of the drugs that have transformed the lives of people with AIDS in wealthy countries. But for millions of

Indians, access to these medicines is a distant dream" *Joanne Csete, Director of the HIV/AIDS programme at Human Rights Watch.*

Stigma and discrimination in India

In India, as elsewhere, AIDS is often seen as *"someone else's problem"* – as something that affects people living on the margins of society, whose lifestyles are considered immoral. Even as it moves into the general population, the HIV epidemic is still misunderstood among the Indian public. People living with HIV have faced violent attacks, been rejected by families, spouses and communities, been refused medical treatment, and even, in some reported cases, denied the last rites before they die.

As well as adding to the suffering of people living with HIV, this discrimination is hindering efforts to prevent new infections. While such strong reactions to HIV and AIDS exist, it is difficult to educate people about how they can avoid infection. AIDS outreach workers and peer-educators have reported harassment, and in schools, teachers sometimes face negative reactions from the parents of children that they teach about AIDS: "When I discussed with my mother about having an AIDS education program, she said, 'you learn and come home and talk about it in the neighbourhood, they will kick you'. She feels that we should not talk about it."

Discrimination is also alarmingly common in the health care sector. Negative attitudes from health care staff have generated anxiety and fear among many people living with HIV and AIDS. As a result, many keep their status secret. It is not surprising that for many HIV positive people, AIDS-related fear and anxiety, and at times denial of their HIV status, can be traced to traumatic experiences in health care settings. "There is an almost hysterical kind of fear ... at all levels, starting from the humblest, the sweeper or the ward boy, up to the heads of departments, which make them pathologically scared of having to deal with an HIV positive patient. Wherever they have an HIV patient, the responses are shameful."

A 2006 study found that 25% of people living with HIV in India had been refused medical treatment on the basis of their HIV-positive status. It also found strong evidence of stigma in the workplace, with 74% of employees not disclosing their status to their employees for fear of discrimination. Of the 26% who did disclose their status, 10% reported having faced prejudice as a result. People in marginalized groups - female sex workers, hijras (transgender) and gay men - are often stigmatised not only because of their HIV status, but also because they belong to socially excluded groups.

Stigma is made worse by a lack of knowledge about AIDS. Although a high percentage of people have heard about HIV and AIDS in urban areas (94% of men and 83% of women) this is much lower in rural areas where only 77% of men and 50% of women have heard of HIV and AIDS. However, the real challenge lies with ignorance about how HIV is transmitted - for example the majority of men and women in rural areas believe that AIDS can be transmitted by mosquito bites. In 2009, NACO carried a population based survey in Nagaland, which showed that 72.8% of people believed HIV could be transmitted by sharing food with someone.

The future of HIV and AIDS in India

Various groups have made predictions about the effect that AIDS will have on India and the rest of Asia in the future, and there has been a lot of dispute about the accuracy of these estimates. For instance, a 2002 report by the CIA's National Intelligence Council predicted 20 million to 25 million AIDS cases in India by 2010 - more than any other country in the world. India's government responded by calling these figures completely inaccurate, and accused those who cited them of spreading panic. The government has also disputed predictions that India's epidemic is on an African trajectory, although it claims to acknowledge the seriousness of the crisis.

Indeed, recent surveys do suggest that national HIV prevalence has probably fallen slightly in recent years. This trend is mainly due to a drop in infections in southern states; in other areas there has been no significant decline. "In the north-east, the dual HIV epidemic driven by unsafe sex and injecting drug use is highly concerning. Moreover, there are many areas in the northern states where HIV is increasing, particularly among injecting drug users." *Sujatha Rao, Director General of NACO*

HIV spending has been steadily increasing in India in recent years. In 2006-2007 $171 million was spent to contain and prevent the growth of HIV, which represented an increase of 28% from the previous year. Currently, India spends about 5% of its health budget on HIV and AIDS. However, the World Bank has warned that India will have to scale up prevention efforts in order to avoid spending more of its health budget in the future. According to the World Bank's report, by 2020 India will have to spend 7% of its health budget on AIDS if the rising tide of the AIDS epidemic in New Delhi, Mumbai, the north and the north east is not halted. This would put further strain on a struggling health sector which, on top of HIV and AIDS, faces a growing multitude of health challenges including malaria, diabetes, heart disease and cancer.

Even if the country's epidemic does not match the severity of those in southern Africa, it is clear that HIV and AIDS will have a devastating effect on the lives of millions of Indians for many years to come. It is essential that effective action is taken to minimise this impact.

Specimen Data Tables: Demographics

Statewise Population in India
(Census 2001)

State	Total	Male	%	Female	%
INDIA	1027015247	531277078	51.7	495738169	48.3
Jammu & Kashmir	10069917	5300574	52.6	4769343	47.4
Himachal Pradesh	6077248	3085256	50.8	2991992	49.2
Punjab	24289296	12963362	53.4	11325934	46.6
Chandigarh	900914	508224	56.4	392690	43.6
Uttaranchal	8479562	4316401	50.9	4163161	49.1
Haryana	21082989	11327658	53.7	9755331	46.3
Delhi	13782976	7570890	54.9	6212086	45.1
Rajasthan	56473122	29381657	52	27091465	48
Uttar Pradesh	166052859	87466301	52.7	78586558	47.3
Bihar	82878796	43153964	52.1	39724832	47.9
Sikkim	540493	288217	53.3	252276	46.7
Arunachal Pradesh	1091117	573951	52.6	517166	47.4
Nagaland	1988636	1041686	52.4	946950	47.6
Manipur	2388634	1207338	50.5	1181296	49.5
Mizoram	891058	459783	51.6	431275	48.4
Tripura	3191168	1636138	51.3	1555030	48.7
Meghalaya	2306069	1167840	50.6	1138229	49.4
Assam	26638407	13787799	51.8	12850608	48.2
West Bengal	80221171	41487694	51.7	38733477	48.3

Jharkhand	26909428	13861277	51.5	13048151	48.5
Orissa	36706920	18612340	50.7	18094580	49.3
Chhatisgarh	20795956	10452426	50.3	10343530	49.7
Madhya Pradesh	60385118	31456873	52.1	28928245	47.9
Gujarat	50596992	26344053	52.1	24252939	47.9
Daman & Diu	158059	92478	58.5	65581	41.5
Dadra & Nagar Haveli	220451	121731	55.2	98720	44.8
Maharashtra	96752247	50334270	52	46417977	48
Andhra Pradesh	75727541	38286811	50.6	37440730	49.4
Karnataka	52733958	26856343	50.9	25877615	49.1
Goa	1343998	685617	51	658381	49
Lakshadweep	60595	31118	51.4	29477	48.6
Kerala	31838619	15468664	48.6	16369955	51.4
Tamil Nadu	62110839	31268654	50.3	30842185	49.7
Pondicherry	973829	486705	50	487124	50
Andaman & Nicobar Islands	356265	192985	54.2	163280	45.8

Percent Distribution of Estimated Population byAge-Group, Sex and Residence in India (1999)

Age-Group	Total			Rural			Urban		
	Total	Male	Female	Total	Male	Female	Total	Male	Female
0-4	11.6	11.8	11.5	12.2	12.4	12.0	10.0	10.1	9.9
5-9	11.2	11.3	11.1	11.7	11.8	11.6	9.9	9.9	9.8
10-14	12.0	12.2	11.8	12.3	12.5	12.0	11.0	11.1	10.9
15-19	10.3	10.6	9.9	10.2	10.6	9.8	10.3	10.4	10.2
20-24	9.2	9.1	9.3	8.8	8.8	8.9	10.1	9.9	10.4
25-29	8.1	8.0	8.2	7.9	7.7	8.0	8.9	8.9	8.9
30-34	7.5	7.3	7.8	7.3	7.0	7.6	8.2	8.1	8.2
35-39	6.3	6.3	6.4	6.1	6.1	6.2	6.9	6.9	6.9
40-44	5.7	5.7	5.7	5.5	5.5	5.5	6.3	6.3	6.3
45-49	4.4	4.5	4.3	4.2	4.3	4.2	4.9	5.2	4.6
50-54	3.8	3.8	3.8	3.7	3.7	3.8	4.0	4.1	3.9
55-59	2.9	2.9	2.9	2.8	2.8	2.9	2.9	3.0	2.8
60-64	2.5	2.4	2.7	2.6	2.4	2.7	2.3	2.2	2.4
65-69	2.0	1.9	2.1	2.0	1.9	2.1	1.8	1.7	1.9
70-74	1.3	1.2	1.4	1.3	1.2	1.4	1.2	1.1	1.3
75-79	0.7	0.7	0.8	0.7	0.7	0.8	0.7	0.6	0.7
80-84	0.3	0.3	0.4	0.3	0.3	0.4	0.3	0.3	0.3
85+	0.2	0.2	0.2	0.2	0.2	0.2	0.2	0.2	0.2
Total	100.0	100.0	100.0	100.0	100.0	100.0	100.0	100.0	100.0

Growth of Indian Population by Sex(1901-11 to 1991-2001)

Year	Average Annual ExponentialGrowth rate Percent Female	Male	Total
1901-1911	0.53	0.61	0.56
1911-1921	-0.08	0.01	-0.03
1921-1931	1.01	1.06	1.04
1931-1941	1.30	1.36	1.33
1941-1951	1.27	1.25	1.25
1951-1961	1.93	1.99	1.96
1961-1971	2.15	2.27	2.22
1971-1981*	2.23	2.18	2.20
1981-1991**	2.10	2.17	2.14
1991-2001	1.97	1.90	1.94

Note : * : The 1981 Census could not be held in Assam. The Populationfigures for 1981 for Assam worked out by interpolation have been included. ** : The 1991 Census was not held in Jammu & Kashmir. The population figures include projected population of Jammu & Kashmir as projected by the Standing Committee of Experts on population projections (Oct 1989).

Data table headings are shown Year-wise in descending order)

Summary-Training and Employment Opportunities

Several organizations in three countries, including NYC in the Philippines, DoVE and DSD in Thailand, and MARD in Viet Nam, have undertaken measures to provide training for the rural youth. However, there was limited access to formal training in all the survey sites. This was either because such training programmes did not exist, or the respondents were unaware of them. While a few respondents in each surveyed sites had informal training from their parents, almost all respondents expressed an interest in receiving formal training.

In terms of employment, an evident trend is the influx of rural youth into the urban areas in search of employment. This is against the backdrop of the concentration of employment opportunities in urban areas, especially those created due to trade and technology advancements in the anufacturing and service sectors. Meanwhile, the field studies suggested potential for community-based employment opportunities. The areas of employment common to the three countries are tourism, handicraft making (such as bamboo, rattan crafts and embroidery), and service related work (such as motorcycle delivery, security guard and domestic work), in addition to fishing (in the case of the Philippines), and agribusiness and construction (in the case of Thailand), and brick making and infrastructure projects, and public sector works, including teaching and commune office work (in the case of Viet Nam).

Recommendations

Policy coordination

The findings from the country studies demonstrated that there are four, interrelated areas of major challenges with regard to employment and training of the rural youth. These areas are education, training, employment and income generation, and labour market information. While the governments of the Philippines, Thailand and Viet Nam have all sought to address concerns in these areas, local level impacts have been limited. This is due to the limited human (both in number and quality) and financial resources particularly in terms of reaching the local and community levels. *Recommendation 1: There is a need for better policy coordination, both among national level government agencies and between the national and local level government agencies, as a means to address the challenges relating to resource limitations including their use and effective policy implementation. In addition, decentralization of implementation may also be pursued, on the condition that appropriate monitoring and evaluation are provided by the respective central and/ or decentralized governments. It is also essential to ensure broad-based ownership in improving the employment and training prospects of the rural youth, through capacity building of the staff involved, as well as collaboration with other stakeholders, such as labour market institutions (i.e. employers' and workers' organizations, and representatives of interest groups, such as youth associations).*

This section summarizes the opportunities and challenges concerning the promotion of training and employment among the rural youth, and presents recommendations.

Employment and Income Generation

Rather than a lack of employment opportunities per se, a major issue is a lack of decent work opportunities. While large numbers of rural youth migrate to urban areas, they are often disappointed by a lack of such opportunities. The youth may prefer to stay in rural areas provided that employment and income generation opportunities are improved. *Recommendation 2 a): Given the important role of agriculture in rural communities, priority must be directed towards improving productivity in the agricultural sector, which can contribute to economic development and poverty reduction in rural areas. Livelihood diversification, along with the application of improved agri-business and technology application, can be explored. Recommendation 2 b): It is critical to create options for the rural youth to seek employment in rural areas through creating and improving the quality of employment in the on, off and non-farm sectors. In this undertaking, it is important to take local contexts into account to ensure that knowledge and skills attained are in line with rural labour markets and employment needs. Recommendation 2 c): There is a need to promote an entrepreneurial culture and enabling environment for youth in wage- and/or self-employment sectors. Entrepreneurship provides greater opportunities for employment, skills development, as well as innovation in products and services. Consideration needs to be taken that entrepreneurship does not come at the expense of education. Recommendation 2 d): It is important to place greater emphasis on improving access to micro-credit schemes, financial/business training, business development services and market information, as a means to encourage youth entrepreneurial activity/self employment.*

Training

In addition to the availability and affordability of training, a major issue facing the rural youth is the lack of information and resultant awareness among the youth, their families and communities on the available training, particularly the ones meeting labour market demands. In addition, the youth or their families do not deem the time spent in training as a desirable trade-off to earning immediate income which may come from a low-paying and low-productivity job.

- *Recommendation 3 a): In order to ensure the quality and relevance of training, efforts must be made to first assess the labour market needs in the given local context, and then to create opportunities for skills training to meet these needs, as well as the preferences of the rural youth.*

- Recommendation 3 b): It is important to encourage families and the rural youth to recognize the benefits of training, while disseminating information on available training opportunities, scholarships, youth programmes, and job fairs through the use of appropriate media, such as newspapers, television and radio. The promotion of training should not come at the expense of higher level education, but can be promoted in such a way as to supplement formal education.
- Recommendation 3 c): It is important to secure funding for training programmes to benefit the current and future youth, and make training affordable and accessible to women and disadvantaged groups.

Formal Education

The main barriers to formal education identified from the case studies are access, affordability, quality and relevance, particularly in rural areas where physical access to secondary schools is difficult and the incidence of poverty is high. An added problem is a lack of teachers, appropriate learning equipment and infrastructure.

- Recommendation 4 a): Countries should continue to strive for free, quality education and training up until the minimum working age. For those countries still striving to achieve free basic education, lowering the direct (e.g. school fees) and indirect costs (e.g. text books, uniforms, transport) of education can help prevent early school drop-out among poor families and ensure that young people have a smooth transition from school to work in the rural and remote areas.
- Recommendation 4 b): There is a need for continuous efforts to ensure gender parity and raise overall equality in education for migrant, minority, working children, and otherwise marginalized, disadvantaged groups in order for inclusive and easily accessible education.
- *Recommendation 4 c): In order to improve the quality of education available for rural youth, greater investment is needed to ensure adequate classroom materials, safe and well-maintained school environments, quality of teachers through training, along with better remuneration.* **Labour Market**

Information There is a scarcity of labour market information in general, particularly in rural areas. This is an obstacle for governments to devise informed policies and also for the youth to make informed decisions on employment and training. It is also a challenge in matching the supply and needs of rural youth with the demands of the labour market.

- Recommendation 5 a): It is essential to strengthen the promotion and dissemination of information on the opportunities and services that are available to rural youth, as well as the risks and benefits associated with migration to urban areas or abroad. Appropriate media needs to be used, such as radio, newspapers, television, internet and leaflets, in addition to schools and training institutions, as well as call centres and private companies. Recommendation 5 b): It is important to enhance employment assistance and career guidance for rural youths by creating and improving facilities in rural areas with trained professionals and access to technologies such as Internet-based information databases.

Country specific observations and recommendations

The following country specific observations are highlighted as possible areas for country specific recommendations and follow up action:

Philippines

- "Ladderized education", (i.e. the breaking-up of the four-year curricular programme into several associate programmes that can be completed in one or two years) can be explored. Upon the completion of one associate programme, students can either seek employment or pursue the next level associate programme until a Baccalaureate degree is obtained.
- Emphasis should be placed on creating jobs in the areas of business and entrepreneurship, ICTs, tourism related services and environment and sustainable development related occupations. There is also the need to focus more on ICT employment opportunities in rural areas, such as call centres, business procurement outsourcing, and internet cafes. The youth are generally knowledgeable about ICT, and are well

placed to take advantage of such job opportunities. ICTs are also a source for labour market information.

- Institutions such as the National Youth Commission and the Technical Education and Skills Development Authority, as well as local NGOs are well placed to disseminate information regarding grants, and scholarships available to youth, and the labour market.

Thailand

- His Majesty the King's philosophy of a "sufficiency economy", which stresses balanced development and highlights the importance of development of each a region relevant to their resource conditions, is considered essential to the development and integration of the principles of the sufficiency economy into the school curriculum. This concept should be further encouraged and strengthened. The principles and farm-level diversification should be further explored to reduce unemployment among the rural poor. Educational opportunities for youth in remote and poor areas should be broader, more diverse and more flexible to meet diver se backgrounds, needs and abilities. In addition, strategies should be developed to promote cooperative enterprises and social services, as well as an entrepreneurial culture. These initiatives are an important means of enhancing job opportunities for the rural youth.

Viet Nam

- It is particularly important in Viet Nam to create community-based employment opportunities, since the country study indicated that many youths would prefer to stay in rural areas provided that better training, employment and income generation opportunities are available. In this regard, areas of off-farm employment to be explored include bamboo and rattan product and handicraft making. These can supply marketable and environmentally friendly products while providing income generation opportunities for the youth.
- The export of labour to other countries is a priority in Viet Nam's employment strategy. This may be pursued as a means

to develop the technical skills of the rural youth who, upon returning to their country, could contribute to a raised human resource capacity. This programme needs to be balanced with appropriate and sustained investment in enhancing coordinated education, training and decent work opportunities in rural communities.

KEY PUBLICATIONS

- World Youth Reports 2003, 2005 and 2007
- Guide to the Implementation of the World Programme of Action for Youth
- Making commitments matter: a toolkit for young people to evaluate national youth policy
- A brief guide to youth delegates to the United Nations General Assembly
- Various Reports of the Secretary-General related to youth issues

Index

O

P

Q

R

S